Maida Heatter's Pies & Tarts

Maida Heatter's
Pies & Tarts

Illustrations by
Melanie Marder Parks

CADER BOOKS • NEW YORK

Andrews McMeel
Publishing

Kansas City

Thank you for buying this Cader Book—we hope you enjoy it. And thanks as well to the store that sold you this, and the hardworking sales rep who sold it to them. It takes a lot of people to make a book. Here are some of the many who were instrumental:

Editorial: Verity Liljedahl, Jake Morrissey, Nora Donaghy, Dorothy O'Brien
Design: Charles Kreloff
Copy Editing/Proofing: Libby Kessman
Production: Polly Blair, Carol Coe
Legal: Renee Schwartz, Esq.

If you would like to share any thoughts about this book, or are interested in other books by us, please write to:
Cader Books, 38 E. 29 Street, New York, New York 10016
Or visit our web site: http://www.caderbooks.com

Printed in the United States of America.

Library of Congress Cataloging-in-Publication Data

Heatter, Maida.
    Maida Heatter's pies & tarts / illustrations by Melanie Marder Parks. —1st ed.
        p.   cm.
    ISBN 0-8362-5075-3
    1. Pies.   I. Title.
TX773.H352 1997
641.8'652—dc21   97-31254
                                                                                          CIP

October 1997

First Edition

10 9 8 7 6 5 4 3 2 1

ATTENTION: SCHOOLS AND BUSINESSES
Andrews McMeel Publishing books are available at quantity discounts with bulk purchase for educational, business, or sales promotional use. For information, please write to: Special Sales Department, Andrews McMeel Publishing, 4520 Main Street, Kansas City, MO 64111.

Contents

Foreword ix
Introduction xi

Pie and Tart Basics

Ingredients 2
Equipment 9
Techniques 12
Pie Crust 17
Crumb Crust 22

Pies and Turnovers

Mom's Apple Pie 24
Apple Pie, U.S.A. 26
Fresh Apricot Pie 29
Blueberry Pie #1 32
Blueberry Pie #2 33
Blackberry Pie 35
Kirsch Strawberry Pie 37
Individual Deep-Dish Strawberry-
    Rhubarb Pies 38
Strawberry Chiffon Pie 40
Lemon Meringue Pie 43
Mrs. Foster's Lime Pie 44
Key Lime Pie 46
Frozen Key Lime Pie 48
Orange Angel Pie 48
Colorado High Pie 51
Savannah Banana Pie 53
Old-Fashioned Butterscotch Pie 55
Coconut Cream Pie 56
Coffee and Cognac Cream Pie 57
Frozen Peanut Butter Pie 60
Marbleized Chiffon Pie 61
Salted Almond Chocolate Pie 63

Chocolate Mousse Pie 65
Florida Cream Cheese Pie 67
Creamy Coconut
    Cream Cheese Pie 68
Apple Cream Cheese Pie 70
Blueberry Cream Cheese Pie 71
Peach Cream Cheese Pie 72
Lemon Cream Cheese Pic 74
Date Pecan Pie 75
Pumpkin Pie 77
Honey Yam Pie 78
Shoofly Pie 80
Prune and Apricot Turnovers 82

Tarts

French Tart Pastry 88
Tart Tatin 89
Apricot Tart 91
Sour Cream Apple Tart 96
Orange Tart 99
Strawberry Tart 101
Strawberry and Blueberry Tart 103
Blueberry Custard Tart 105
Pear and Almond Tart 107
Purple Plum and Almond Tart 110
Peach and Almond Tart 112
Lemon and Almond Tart 114

Lemon Tartlets 117
Rancho Santa Fe Lemon Tart 119
Grape Tart 122
Individual Maple Pecan Tarts 124
Cottage Cheese and Jelly Tart 127

Shortcakes, Cobblers, and More

Strawberry Shortcake 130
Washington State Cherry Cobbler . 132
New York State Apple Cobbler . . . 135
Down Home Apple Casserole 136
Apple and Orange Cobbler 138
Georgia Peach Cobbler 140
Peach Pandowdy 142
Pennsylvania Dutch Peach
        Cobbler 143
Peach Crisp 145
Peach Kuchen 146
Blueberry and Peach Buckle 148
Blueberry Crumble 150
Colonial Blueberries 151
Rhubarb Crumble 153
Cranberry Grunt 154

Fruit Desserts

Fresh Strawberries with
        Sour Cream 158
Strawberries De Luxe 159
Brandied Strawberries with Cream . 160
Southampton Strawberries 161
Fresh Strawberries in Honeyed
        Raspberry Sauce 162
Fresh Strawberries with Raspberry
        Sauce 163
Rhubarb Strawberries 164

Saidie Heatter's Apple Fritters 165
Banana Fritters 166
Vermont Baked Apples 167
American Beauty Apples 168
Brandied Apples 169
Ginger-Honey Baked Apples 170
Apple Bread Pudding 172
Almond-Apple Pudding 174
Connecticut Apple Betty 175
Sugarbush Mountain Peaches 177
Stewed Peaches 178
Stewed Peaches with Brandy 179
Brandied Fresh Peaches 180
Stewed Apricots with Brandy 180
Cassis Raspberries 181
Cassis Grapefruit 181
Raspberry Pears 182
Broiled Peppered Pears 183
Ginger Pears 184
Ginger-Pear Crisp 185
Blueberries and Cream 187
Oranges à la Grecque 188
Raspberry Oranges 189
Broiled Grapefruit 190
Honeyed Grapes 191
Brandied Prunes 191
California Fresh Figs 192
Mangoes, Key West Style 193
Island Pineapple 194
Portuguese Pineapple 195

Mousses, Puddings, Custards, etc.

French Baked Custard 198
Grape-Nut Custard 199
Orange Custard 200
Crème Renversée 201
Lemon Mousse 203
Tangerine Mousse 204

Orange Mousse with Blueberries . . 206
Grapefruit Mousse 208
Sour Lime Mousse with
        Strawberries 209
Zabaglione Freddo 211
Raspberry Bavarian 212
Cold Orange Soufflé 214
Hot Lemon Soufflé 217
Ginger-Marmalade Yogurt 219
Yogurt Cheese 220
Apricot Bread Pudding 221
Fried Bread Pudding 223
Bread Pudding with Peaches 224
Mother's Spanish Cream 226
Banana Pudding 228
Cream Cheese Flan
        (Flan de Queso Crema) 229
California Lemon Pudding 231
Raspberry Pâté 233
Strawberry Yogurt Cream 235
Grand Marnier Strawberry Soufflé . 237
Apple-Cranberry Pudding 239
Grapefruit Ice 240
Orange Ice 240
Lemon Ice 241
Strawberry Sorbet 242
Plum Sorbet 243
Sorbet Cassis 244

Frozen Grand Marnier Mousse 245
Joan's Frozen Lemon Mousse 246
Frozen Lemon-Rum Soufflé 248

Sauces and Extras

Top Secret 252
Ricotta Cream 253
Honey Ricotta Cream 253
White Custard Cream 254
Sweet Sour Cream 255
Crème Fraîche 255
The Governor's Crème Fraîche . . . 256
Gingered Crème Fraîche 256
Brandied Butterscotch Sauce 257
Butterscotch Custard Sauce 258
Raisin Blueberry Sauce 258
Cranberry Topping 259
Strawberry-Strawberry Sauce 260
California Cream 261
Fantastic Vanilla Ice Cream 262
Devil's Food Chocolate Sauce 263

Index 265
Metric Conversion Chart 275

Foreword

*M*aida Heatter's desserts make you smile. She has prepared cakes, pies, turnovers, ice cream, and cookies for U.S. presidents as well as run a restaurant, where her thorough knowledge of production enabled her to supply the requisite tray of desserts day after day.

There are extraordinary pies and tarts in this book, from the Key Lime Pie and the Chocolate Mousse Pie to the Peach and Almond Tart and the easy Tart Tatin. But this book is not only about pies and tarts; add turnovers, shortcakes, pandowdy, mousse, custards, and all kinds of fruit desserts. The choice, versatility, and range of these desserts is more than you will need throughout your lifetime, but even though they are quite different from one another, they have one thing in common: They are all sinfully good.

Maida is never miserly with her ingredients or her knowledge. In her recipes, she shares her invaluable cooking techniques and cooking secrets, explaining her procedures so carefully and so precisely that her desserts are easily prepared by the neophyte as well as the expert. She truly represents the best of what America has to offer, and her inimitable style and prose make this book not only a joy to cook from but also a joy to read.

Pies & Tarts will become the dessert book you will use again and again, and just as it does for me, it will bring a big smile to your face.

JACQUES PÉPIN

The recipes in this book
were originally published in
Maida Heatter's New Book of Great Desserts (1982)
and
Maida Heatter's Book of Great American Desserts (1985).

Introduction

Talking about pies — did you hear the story about the Key lime pies I made for the 1983 Economic Summit for President Reagan and seven other heads of state? The White House had asked Craig Claiborne to plan all the food for the three-day event, which was held in Colonial Williamsburg, Virginia. Craig asked Wolfgang Puck and Paul Prudhomme each to prepare a dinner. Wolf made quail and Paul made blackened redfish. Zarella Martinez did a lunch. Leo Steiner, who owned the Carnegie Deli in New York City, did a lunch. I don't remember who else, but Craig asked me to make Key lime pies for the State dinner. Craig said he thought that Key lime pie was one of the most authentic and traditional American desserts. He told me to plan for about eighty people.

Key limes are almost impossible to buy because there is no commercial crop. There used to be, but many years ago when a hurricane wiped out all of the Key lime trees that was the end. Since then, no one has grown them commercially. But some people do have them in their backyards here in Florida where I live. I spent days telephoning many people I knew and many more I didn't know, and I finally contacted several people who said they would give me some Key limes.

My husband and I then spent days driving around Florida to collect them. No one had more than a few. (I swapped brownies for the limes.) We had stopped at a Miami fruit stand to ask if they had any. We said it was for the President. The young man said we should come back the next day. When we did he gave us five limes. He had driven 25 miles just to get five Key limes. He was from the Middle East, and he said this country had done so much for him and his family that he wanted to help any way he could. When he handed us the little bag of five limes he said he was very proud to be doing something for America.

I squeezed all the juice and froze it.

I made about fifteen graham cracker crusts and froze those also. When the time came we were ready. We packed the car and drove to Williamsburg.

The government had arranged luxurious accommodations for all of us in a gorgeous townhouse alongside a golf course. We each had a plush apartment. Craig was directly above us and Wolfgang and Barbara were next door.

Williamsburg is important historically and architecturally, and due to the intense security all around the town at that time it was especially dramatic and exciting.

The food was prepared in a large commissary that I think was a city block square. The day before the pies were to be served I spent several hours in the commissary. And then, again, shortly before they were to be served I whipped cream and decorated the pies.

The dining room was in an adjoining building.

Before anything was actually served the Secret Service men had to taste it to be sure it wasn't poisoned, and then they carried the food from the commissary to the dining room.

When my work was done we went back to our apartment. Craig and Wolf and Barbara came along. We had some wine and were ready to relax when the phone rang. I answered it, and I heard a man introduce himself as a reporter for the Associated Press. He asked,

"*What did you think when the Secret Service men dropped all the pies?*"

"*WHAT?*"

I put my husband on the phone.

The next day's papers flashed the following headlines: "Keystone Kops Pitch Pies," "Serving the Pies Not a Cakewalk at the Summit," and "Damned Fools Dropped the Pies." (That last one was a quote from my husband.) The Miami Herald quoted me as saying, "Anybody who does much cooking and baking has learned to be prepared for calamities and disasters all the time. It didn't upset me one bit."

Don't believe everything you read.

Maida Heatter

Pie and Tart Basics

Ingredients

Eggs

SIZE
Use eggs graded "large."

TO OPEN EGGS
If directions call for adding whole eggs one at a time, they may all be opened ahead of time into one container and then poured into the other ingredients, approximately one at a time. Do not open eggs directly into the ingredients—you would not know if a piece of shell had been included.

TO SEPARATE EGGS
Eggs separate more safely—there is less chance of the yolk breaking—when they are cold. Therefore, if a recipe calls for separated eggs, it is usually the first thing I do when organizing the ingredients so that they are cold from the refrigerator.

The safest way to separate eggs is as follows: Place three small glass custard cups or shallow drinking glasses or bowls in front of you. One container is for the whites and one is for the yolks. The third might not be needed, but if you should break the yolk when opening an egg, just drop the whole thing in the third container and save it for some other use.

Tap the side of the egg firmly (but not too hard or you might break the yolk) on the edge of the cup or glass or bowl to crack the shell, with luck, in a rather straight, even line. Then, holding the egg upright and with both hands (so that the halves each make a cup), separate the halves of the shell, letting some of the white run into the cup or glass or bowl. Pour the yolk back and forth from one half of the egg shell to the other, letting all of the white run out. Drop the yolk into the second cup or glass or bowl.

Many professional cooks simply open the egg into the palm of one hand, then hold their fingers, slightly separated, over a bowl. They let the white run through their open fingers, and then slide the left-behind yolk into a second bowl.

As each egg is separated the white should be transferred to another container (that is, in addition to the three—it could be another bowl or glass or it might be the mixing bowl you will beat the whites in), because if you place all of the whites in one container there is a chance that the last egg white might have some yolk in it, which could spoil all of the whites.

Generally, a tiny bit of yolk or shell can be removed from the whites with an empty half shell. Or try a piece of paper towel dipped in cold water.

To Beat Egg Whites

The success of many recipes depends on properly beaten egg whites. After you have learned how, it becomes second nature.

First, the bowl and the beaters must be absolutely clean. A little bit of fat (egg yolks are fat) will prevent the whites from incorporating air as they should and from rising properly.

Second, do not overbeat or the whites will become dry and you will not be able to fold them into other ingredients without losing the air you have beaten in.

Third, do not beat them ahead of time. They must be folded in immediately after they are beaten; if they have to wait they separate. (Incidentally, if the whites are being folded into a cake batter, the cake must then be placed in the oven right away.)

You can use an electric mixer, a rotary beater, or a wire whisk (although a wire whisk and a copper bowl are said to give the best results).

If you use an electric mixer or a rotary beater, be careful not to use a bowl that is too large or the whites will be too shallow to get the full benefits of the beaters' action. If the bowl and beaters do not revolve by themselves (as they do in electric mixers on a stand), move the mixer or beater around the bowl to beat all the whites evenly. If you use a mixer on a stand, use a rubber spatula frequently to push the whites from the side of the bowl into the center.

If you use a wire whisk, it should be a large, thin-wired balloon type, at least 4 inches wide at the top. The bowl should be very large, the larger the better, to give you plenty of room for making large circular motions with the whisk. An unlined copper bowl is the best, or you may use glass, china, or stainless steel—but do not beat egg whites in aluminum, which might discolor the whites, or plastic, which is frequently porous and might be greasy from some other use.

A copper bowl should be treated each time before using as follows: Put 1 or 2 teaspoons of salt in the bowl and rub thoroughly with half a lemon, squeezing a bit of the juice and mixing it with the salt. Then rinse with hot water (no soap) and dry. After using a copper bowl, wash it as you would any other, but be sure to treat it before beating egg whites again.

When I beat egg whites with an electric mixer, if they do not have sugar added (sugar makes them more creamy and slightly lessens the chance of overbeating), I always—and I recommend this to everyone—finish the beating with a wire whisk. There is less chance of overbeating, and the wire whisk seems to give the whites a slightly creamy consistency. At this stage you can use a smaller whisk than the one mentioned above—use any one that seems right for the bowl the whites are in.

People often ask me if I bring whites to room temperature before beating them. If I do, it is a rare occasion and not planned. They are usually cold when I beat them (because I do not plan ahead and do not have the patience to wait and because I have had equally good results whether cold or at room temperature).

To Freeze Egg Whites or Yolks

Some of the recipes in this book call for yolks and no whites, and some call for only whites. (If you have just a few extra of either left over and do not want to save them for something else, add them to scrambled eggs.)

Leftover egg whites may be kept covered in the refrigerator for a few days or they may be frozen. I freeze them individually (or occasionally two to four together) in ovenproof glass custard cups. When they are frozen, hold one cup upside down under hot running water until the frozen egg white can be removed (but not until it melts). Quickly wrap each frozen egg white individually in plastic wrap and return to the freezer. To use, remove the number you want, unwrap, place them in a cup or bowl, and let stand at room temperature to thaw. Or place them, in a cup or bowl, in a slightly warm oven or in a pan of shallow warm water.

To freeze egg yolks, stir them lightly just to mix, and for each yolk stir in ⅓ teaspoon of granulated sugar or ½ teaspoon of honey. Freeze them in a covered jar, labeling so you will know how many yolks and how much sugar or honey. When thawed, stir to mix well—they will not look exactly the same as before they were frozen (not as smooth), but they will work in recipes.

Flour

Many of these recipes call for sifted flour. That means that even if the package is labeled "presifted," you should sift the flour before measuring. If not, since flour packs down while standing, 1 cup of unsifted flour is liable to be a few spoonfuls more than 1 cup of just-sifted flour.

Sift the flour onto a piece of wax paper. Make sure there is no flour left in the sifter. Then transfer the sifter to another piece of wax paper. Use a metal measuring cup (from a set of graded cups) and lightly spoon the sifted flour into the cup or lift it on a dough scraper and transfer it to the cup—do not pack or press the flour down— and scrape the excess off the top with a dough scraper or any flat-sided implement. If the sifted flour is to be sifted with other ingredients, return it to the sifter, then add the ingredients to be sifted with it, and sift onto the second piece of wax paper. Again, make sure there is nothing left in the sifter.

It is not necessary ever to wash a flour sifter; just shake it out firmly and store it in a plastic bag.

Bleached or unbleached flour can be used in those recipes that call for all-purpose flour.

Fresh Ginger

Do not buy any that is soft and wrinkled—it should be firm and hard (like potatoes). To store: For a few days—or even weeks, if it is firm and fresh—it can just stand at room temperature (like potatoes). For a longer time, it can be stored in the vegetable crisper in the refrigerator—wrapped or unwrapped does not seem to make any difference. Or it can be frozen, wrapped airtight in plastic or foil.

(A chef at a famous San Francisco restaurant told me that he keeps fresh ginger for weeks at room temperature, lying on its side in a shallow dish with about half an inch of water in the dish, and he adds water occasionally as it evaporates. About a month ago, when I had just bought some nice, fresh ginger, I put one piece in water, and another alongside it but not in water. Now, a month later, the piece that is not in water looks healthier. The piece that is in water looks barely wrinkled—or is it my imagination? This experiment proves that if it is in good condition when you buy it, ginger is strong and hardy and lasts well almost in spite of what you do to it.)

It is not necessary to peel ginger. It may be grated on a standing metal grater on the side that has small round openings (rather than diamond-shaped openings). It may be grated if it is at room temperature, or refrigerated, or frozen. Either way, it is slow work to grate much. But it is quick and easy—it is a breeze—to grate it in a food processor. First slice it crossways into very thin slices, or about ⅛ inch thick. (Although the processor will grate the ginger very well, it will leave fibers in the mixture; slicing it thin before processing reduces the length of fibers. Incidentally, older ginger is more fibrous than young ginger; it is also more gingerly and favorable. But either is wonderful.) Fit the processor with the metal chopping blade. With the motor going, add the slices of ginger one or two at a time through the feed tube, pausing briefly between additions. Stop the machine once or twice to scrape the sides of the bowl with a rubber spatula and then process again for a few seconds.

If you plan to freeze the ginger and then grate it, frozen, in a food processor, it is best to slice it thin before you freeze it. But it is possible, if necessary, to cut up (slice) frozen ginger with a heavy Chinese cleaver, a strong arm, and patience.

It is also possible to grate the ginger (easiest in a processor), wrap it in measured amounts, and freeze it; thaw before using. Or coarsely chop the block of frozen, grated ginger with a heavy cleaver, and drop the pieces through the feed tube of a processor (fitted with the metal chopping blade) with the motor going, and process until it returns to the grated texture. It will be wetter than ginger that has been grated but not frozen, but that does not noticeably affect its use in baking (although sometimes I think that ginger that has been frozen is not as sharp and gingery as it was before it was frozen, but that is hard to judge).

Incidentally, fresh-produce people tell me that Hawaiian ginger is the best.

Nuts

Nuts can turn rancid rather quickly—walnuts and pecans more so than almonds. Always store all nuts airtight in the freezer or refrigerator. In the refrigerator nuts last well for 9 months; in the freezer at zero degrees they will last for 2 years. Bring them to room temperature before using; smell and taste them before you use them (preferably when you buy them)—you will know quickly if they are rancid. If you even suspect that they might be, do not use them; they would ruin a recipe.

TO TOAST PECANS

Pecans occasionally become limp after they are frozen, so I toast them. Toasted pecans are so great that now I toast all pecans (those that have been frozen and those that have not) before using them, as follows: Place them in a shallow pan in the middle of a preheated 350° oven for 15 to 20 minutes, stirring them occasionally, until they are very hot but not until they become darker in color.

TO BLANCH (OR SKIN) ALMONDS

Cover the almonds with boiling water. The skin will loosen almost immediately. Spoon out a few nuts at a time and, one by one, hold them under cold running water and squeeze them between your thumb and forefinger. The nuts will pop out and the skin will remain. Placed the peeled almonds on a towel to dry. Then spread them in a shallow baking pan and bake in a preheated 200° oven for 30 minutes or so until they are completely dry. Do not let them brown.

If the almonds are to be split, sliced, or slivered, they should remain in the hot water longer to soften; let them stand until the water cools enough for you to touch it comfortably. Then, one at a time, remove the skin from each nut and immediately, while the nut is still soft, place it on a cutting board and cut with a small, sharp paring knife. Then bake to dry them as above. Sliced almonds are those that have been cut into very thin slices; slivered almonds are the fatter, oblong, "julienne"-shaped pieces. Don't expect sliced or slivered almonds that you have cut up yourself to be as even as store-bought ones. (Sometimes I think I like the uneven look better.)

PISTACHIO NUTS

A light sprinkling of chopped green pistachio nuts is a nice touch. Don't overdo it; less is better than more. Chop the pistachios coarse or fine on a board using a long, heavy knife. Don't worry about the little pieces of skin that flake off; you can leave them with the nuts (or pick out the large pieces of skin, if you wish).

Sugar

All sugars should be graded in the graded measuring cups made for measuring dry ingredients.

BROWN SUGAR

Most brown sugars are made of white granulated sugar to which a dark syrup has been added. Dark brown sugar has a mild molasses, and light brown sugar has a milder, lighter syrup (which may also be molasses). Dark brown has a slightly stronger flavor, but dark and light may be used interchangeably. The label on Grandma's Molasses says, "You can easily make your own brown sugar as you need it by blending together ½ cup of granulated sugar with 2 tablespoons of unsulphured molasses. The yield is equivalent to ½ cup of brown sugar."

Brown sugar is moist; if it dries out it will harden, so it should be stored airtight. If it has small lumps, they should be strained out. With your fingertips press the sugar through a large, wide strainer set over a large bowl. The Savannah Sugar Refinery is now printing the following directions on its boxes of brown sugar: "If your brown sugar has been left open and becomes hard, placed a dampened (not wet) paper towel inside the resealable poly bag and close the package tightly for 12 hours or more. A slice of apple can be used in place of the dampened towel."

CONFECTIONERS SUGAR

Confectioners sugar and powdered sugar are exactly the same. They are both granulated sugar that has been pulverized and had about 3 percent cornstarch added to keep it powdery. Of the confectioners sugars, 4-x is the least fine and 10-x is the finest. They may be used interchangeably. Confectioners sugar should be strained; you can do several pounds at a time, if you wish. It does not have to be done immediately before using, as flour does. Store it airtight.

If directions say to sprinkle with confectioners sugar, place the sugar in a fine strainer, hold it over the top of the pie or tart, and tap the strainer lightly with your hand or shake it to shake out the sugar.

VANILLA CONFECTIONERS SUGAR

This is flavored confectioners sugar that is used to sprinkle over pies and tarts. It adds a nice mild flavor and a delicious aroma. To make it, fill a jar that has a tight cover with confectioners sugar. Split one or two vanilla beans the long way and bury them in the sugar. Cover tightly and let stand for at least a few days before using. As the sugar is used it may be replaced. The vanilla beans will continue to flavor and perfume the sugar for at least a month or two.

When you make this, don't bother to strain the sugar beforehand. The vanilla beans give off a small amount of moisture that the sugar absorbs, causing it to become lumpy and making it necessary to strain it just before using.

CRYSTAL SUGAR

Crystal sugar, also called pearl sugar, or *Hagelzucker* in German, is generally used to sprinkle over certain pies and tarts before baking. It is coarser than granulated sugar. It is available from Sweet Celebrations in Minneapolis, MN, (800) 480-2505. I use "Medium Grain."

Strawberries

First of all, there seems to be much confusion about how much to buy and how much you get when you buy a 1-pint box. Actually, if you measure the berries in a glass measuring cup, the little box or basket of berries that is called 1 pint will measure 1 quart. And it will weigh 1 pound. To be sure we understand each other, every time I call for a 1-pint box, I also say "1 pound." And if you measure it, it will be 1 quart. Okay?

It has recently become popular to grind a little black pepper over strawberries, either in recipes where the berries are mixed with other ingredients, or when they are eaten just by themselves. And some people sprinkle a tiny bit of mild vinegar (for instance, raspberry vinegar) over the berries. Me, I like both—pepper and vinegar.

Whipping Cream

Plain old-fashioned whipping cream is scarce nowadays unless you have your own cow. Too bad, because the super- or ultra-pasteurized (known as UHT—ultra-high-temperature pasteurized) is not as good, at least I don't think so. The reason dairies make it is that it has a 6- to 8-week shelf life. (They call it a "pull date"; the stores have to pull it off their shelves if it is not sold by the date stamped on the container.) This product is called either "heavy whipping cream" or "heavy cream," depending on the manufacturer. Either one can be used in recipes calling for "whipping cream."

The process of making ultra-pasteurized cream involves heating the cream to 250° for 1 second. It gives the cream a slight caramel flavor (so mild you might not notice it) and makes it more difficult to whip (it will take longer). It is advisable to chill the bowl and beaters in the freezer for about half an hour before whipping. And keep the cream in the refrigerator until you are ready to whip; do not let it stand around in the kitchen—it should be as cold as possible.

It seems to me that baked custards take longer to set if they are made with UHT cream, and ice cream takes longer to churn.

How to Whip Cream

The best way to whip either plain old-fashioned or UHT cream is to place it in a large bowl, set the bowl in a larger bowl of ice and water, and whip with a large, thin-wired, balloon-type whisk. You get more volume that way, and it tastes better.

If that seems like more than you want to fuss with, use an electric mixer or an eggbeater, and chill the bowl and beaters before using them. If the bowl does not revolve by itself, then move the beaters around the bowl to whip all the cream evenly at the same time.

When I whip cream with an electric mixer, I always (and I recommend this to everyone) finish the whipping by hand with a wire whisk; there is less chance of overwhipping. At this stage you can use a smaller whisk than if you are doing it all by hand.

Whipped cream, which can be heavenly, is not quite so delicious if it is whipped until it is really stiff—softer is better.

Equipment

Double Boilers

Many of the recipes in this book call for a double boiler. You can buy them kitchen supply stores. The thing to look for is one in which the upper section is not too deep and is smooth (no ridges). I like the Revere Ware double boilers; they come in two sizes, and I use both.

If necessary, you can create your own by placing a heatproof bowl over a saucepan of shallow hot water. The bowl should be wide enough at the top to rest on the rim of the saucepan, keeping the bowl suspended over (not touching) the water.

Electric Mixers

I use an electric mixer on a stand that comes with two different-size bowls and a pair of beaters (rather than one, as some mixers have). Mine is a Sunbeam Mixmaster.

I think it is important, or at least extremely helpful, for many dessert recipes to use a mixer that:

a. is on a stand;

b. comes with a small and large bowl; and

c. has space to scrape the sides of the bowl with a rubber spatula while the mixer is going.

I especially recommend that you buy an extra set of bowls and extra beaters—they are generally available at the service center for your mixer.

Incidentally, although I have a hand-held electric mixer, I could live without it. (But if I did not have any other, I'm sure I would learn to love it.) If you are using a hand-held mixer or an eggbeater, when I say "small bowl of an electric mixer" that means one with a 7-cup capacity, and "large bowl of an electric mixer" means a 16-cup capacity.

Pastry Bags

The best pastry bags for many years have been those that are made of canvas and are coated on one side only with plastic. Use them with the plastic coating inside. The small opening just has to be cut a bit larger to allow the metal tubes (tips) to fit.

They should be washed in hot soapy water, then just set aside to dry. (I usually stand them upright or over a glass to dry.)

When filling a pastry bag, always fold down a deep cuff on the outside of the bag.

Unless there is someone else to hold it for you, it is generally easiest if you support the bag by placing it in a tall, wide glass, or jar. After the bag is filled, unfold the cuff and twist the top closed.

Quiche Pans and Flan Rings

Some recipes call for a variety of sizes of shallow, loose-bottomed metal quiche pans or narrow flan rings (not china one-piece quiche pans). I use them interchangeably, but if I have a choice I recommend the quiche pans, because occasionally the butter in the pastry runs out under the flan ring. And if the ring itself and the cookie sheet it is on are not absolutely flat, the pastry itself runs out. However, even that can be coped with. Just cut it away with a small sharp knife as soon as the pastry is removed from the oven.

If you have never used either the quiche pans or flan rings for making dessert tarts, please do. It is a wonderful baking experience, and the results are especially gorgeous. (And many people have told me that they find these recipes easier than regular pies.)

Look for black steel quiche pans; they will make the bottom crust brown better than shiny metal pans.

The pans and rings are more and more popular lately and are generally available at kitchen supply stores. As with nearly all of the pans and related equipment mentioned in this book, they can be ordered from Williams-Sonoma, (800) 541-2233, or Bridge Kitchenware, (800) 274-3435, in New York.

Rolling Pins

If you have many occasions to use a rolling pin (and I hope that you will), you really should have different sizes and different shapes. Sometimes, a very long, thick, and heavy pin will be best; for other doughs you will want a smaller, lighter one. The French style, which is extra long (actually 20 inches long), narrow, and tapered at both ends, is especially good for rolling dough into a large, round shape, as for a pie crust, while the straight-sided pin is better for an oblong shape.

In the absence of any rolling pin at all, other things will do a fair job. Try a straight-sided bottle, tall jar, or drinking glass.

Small, Narrow Metal Spatula

Many of these recipes call for this tool for smoothing the icing around the sides of a cake. Mine is 8 inches long; it has a 4-inch blade and a 4-inch wooden handle. The blade is ⅝ inch wide and has a rounded top. Although it can bend, it is more firm than flexible. A table knife can sometimes be used in place of this small spatula. Metal spatulas are available in a variety of sizes and shapes at kitchen supply stores.

Thermometers

OVEN TEMPERATURE

One of the most important and most overlooked requirements for good results in baking is correct oven temperature. No matter how new or how good your oven is, *please* double-check the temperature every time you bake. Use a small portable oven thermometer from the kitchen supply store. Buy the mercury kind—it is best. Heat your oven at least 20 minutes ahead of time and place the thermometer on a rack close to the middle of the oven. Give the oven plenty of time to heat and cycle and reheat before you read the thermometer. If it does not register the heat you want, adjust the thermostat up or down until the mercury thermometer registers the correct heat—no matter what the oven setting says. If you check the temperature on a portable oven thermometer during the first 10 minutes of baking, don't think that your oven suddenly got sick; give it time to reheat.

OTHER THERMOMETERS

A friend told me she did not know her refrigerator was too warm until she served a large chocolate icebox cake at a dinner party and, at the table—with everyone watching—she found that the middle was soft and runny instead of firm as it should have been. And once I didn't know that my freezer wasn't right until the very last minute, when a photographer was here to take pictures of a chocolate dessert; I had waited until he was ready to shoot before I took out of the freezer the big, gorgeous chocolate curls that I had made so carefully and found they had melted and flattened and were no longer curls.

Keep a frozen thermometer in your freezer and a refrigerator thermometer in your refrigerator—and look at them often.

And for many of the recipes in this book you will need a thermometer labeled a "candy-jelly-frosting thermometer," even if you never use it for candy or jelly; it is important to have for making many dessert sauces.

Always bend down and read the thermometer at eye level in order to get a correct reading.

Techniques

Adding Dry Ingredients Alternately with Liquid

Begin and end with dry. The procedure is generally to add about one third of the dry, then half of the liquid, a second third of the dry, the rest of the liquid, and then the rest of the dry.

Use the lowest speed on an electric mixer (or it may be done by hand stirring with a rubber spatula or wooden spoon). After each addition mix only until smooth. If your mixer is the type that allows you to scrape the sides with a rubber spatula while the mixer is going, do so to help the mixture along. If the mixer does not allow room, or if it is a hand-held mixer, stop it frequently and scrape the bowl with a rubber spatula; do not beat any more than necessary.

Folding Ingredients Together

Many of the recipes in this book call for folding beaten egg whites and/or whipped cream into another mixture. The whites and/or cream have had air beaten into them, and folding rather than mixing is done in order to retain the air.

This is a very important step and should be done with care. The knack of doing it well comes with practice and concentration. Remember that you want to incorporate the mixtures without losing any air. That means handle as little as possible.

It is important not to beat the whites or whip the cream until they are actually stiff. If you do, you will have to stir and mix rather than fold, thereby losing the air.

Other don'ts: Do not let beaten whites stand around or they will become dry and will separate. Do not fold whipped cream into a warm mixture or the heat will deflate the cream. Generally it is best actually to *stir* a bit of the beaten whites or whipped cream into the heavier mixture (to lighten it a bit) before you start to fold in. Then, as a rule, it is best not to add all of the remaining light mixture at once; do the folding in a few additions. The first additions should not be folded thoroughly.

Although many professional chefs use their bare hands for folding, most home cooks are more comfortable using a rubber spatula. Rubber is better than plastic because it is more flexible. Spatulas come in three sizes. The smallest is called a bottle scraper. For most folding the medium size is the one to use. But for folding large amounts in a large bowl, the largest size can be very helpful. The one I mean might measure about 13 to 16 inches from the end of the blade to the end of the handle; the blade will be about 2¾ inches wide and about 4½ inches long.

To fold ingredients together it is best to use a bowl with a rounded bottom, and it is better if the bowl is too large rather than too small.

Hold the rubber spatula, rounded side toward the bottom and over the middle of the bowl, and cut through to the bottom of the bowl. Bring the spatula toward you against the bottom, then up the side and out, over the top, turning your wrist and the blade as you do this so the blade is upside down as it comes out over the top. Return the spatula to its original position, then cut through the middle of the mixture again. After each fold, rotate the bowl slightly in order to incorporate the ingredients as much as possible. Continue only until both mixtures are barely combined.

Occasionally a bit of beaten egg white will rise to the top. If just one or two small pieces rise, instead of folding more, simply smooth over the top gently with the spatula.

If the base mixture has gelatin in it, it should be chilled until it just starts to thicken before beaten egg whites or whipped cream are folded in, or the heavier mixture will sink.

When folding, it is ideal to have the gelatin mixture, the whipped cream, and/or the egg whites all the same consistency (although in some cases it is not possible).

Measuring

Meticulously precise measurements are essential for good results in baking.

Glass or plastic measuring cups with the measurements marked on the side and the 1-cup line below the top are only for measuring liquids. Do not use them for flour or sugar. With the cup at eye level, fill carefully to exactly the line indicated.

Measuring cups that come in graded sets of four (¼ cup, ⅓ cup, ½ cup, and 1 cup—as well as a new 2-cup size that is pretty handy) are for measuring, flour, sugar, and other dry ingredients—and for thick sour cream and peanut butter. Fill the cup to overflowing and then scrape or cut off the excess with a dough scraper, a metal spatula, or the flat side of a knife.

Standard measuring spoons must be used for correct measurements. They come in sets of four (¼ teaspoon, ½ teaspoon, 1 teaspoon, and 1 tablespoon). For dry ingredients, fill the spoon to overflowing and then scrape off the excess with a metal spatula or the flat side of a knife.

Homemade Bread Crumbs

Use sliced white bread, with or without the crusts. Place the slices in a single layer on cookie sheets in a 225° oven and bake until the bread is completely dry and crisp (although if the bread is so stale that it is completely dry, it is not necessary to bake it). Break up the slices coarsely and grind them in a food processor or blender until the crumbs are rather fine, but not as fine as a powder.

To Grind Nuts in a Food Processor

Add about one-quarter (or more) of the sugar or flour called for in the recipe; that will prevent the nuts from becoming oily. And process for 50 to 60 seconds even though you will think it is done sooner—the finer the nuts are, the better.

To Wash Blueberries

They should be washed ahead of time to allow them to dry. Fill a large bowl with cold water. Place the berries in a wide strainer or a colander and dip it into the water; then let the rim of the strainer rest on the rim of the bowl. Pick out any loose stems or leaves or green berries. Raise the strainer or colander from the water to drain, and repeat as necessary with clean water until the water remains clean (no sand) after the berries are removed. Spread the berries in a single layer on paper towels and let stand, uncovered, to drain and dry.

To Wash Strawberries

Remove them from their boxes as soon as possible. Place them in a single layer on a tray lined with paper towels and refrigerate until you are ready to wash them. They can be washed many hours before serving or just shortly before.

Fill a large bowl with cool water. Place a wide strainer in the bowl, so that the rim of the strainer rests on the rim of the bowl. Place the berries in the strainer, and raise and lower it into the water a few times to rinse the berries. Then lift the strainer and pour the water out of the bowl, and replace the strainer on the rim of the bowl. If you are going to remove the green hulls do it now, and then place the berries in a single layer on a tray covered with paper towels and refrigerate uncovered.

To Prepare Oranges, Grapefruits, and Lemons

I use the juice of fresh lemons or oranges in all recipes calling for their juice. In recipes that call for the grated rind of oranges or lemons, the grated rind of fresh fruit has a better flavor than bought dried grated rind.

To Grate the Rind

It is best to use firm, deep-colored, thick-skinned fruit. And it is best if the fruit is cold; the rind is firmer and it grates better. Use a standing metal grater—usually they have four sides, although some are round. Hold the grater up to the light and look at the shapes of the opening from the back or the inside. You should use the small holes that are round, not diamond-shaped. Place the grater on a piece of wax paper on the work surface. Hold the grater firmly in place with your left hand. With your right hand hold the fruit cupped in your palm at the top of the grater. Move your fingers back a bit so the tips don't get scraped. Now, press the fruit down toward the bottom of the grater. Press firmly, but do not overdo it—all you want is the zest (the thin, colored outside part), so do not work over the same part on the fruit or you will be grating the white underneath; rotate the fruit in your hand as you press against the grater. It is easy.

Remove the gratings that stick to the inside of the grater with a rubber spatula.

There is no reason ever to hurt yourself grating lemon or orange rind. (Be sure you hold the fruit as described.)

TO PARE THE RIND

Use a vegetable peeler with a swivel blade to remove the thin, colored outer rind.

TO PEEL AN ORANGE, LEMON, OR GRAPEFRUIT

Place the fruit on a cutting board on its side. With a sharp thin knife cut off the top and bottom. Turn the fruit right side up resting on either end. Hold the fruit with your left hand as you cut down toward the board with a sharp knife in your right hand, curving around the fruit and cutting away a strip of peel—cut right to the fruit itself in order not to leave any of the white underskin. Rotate the fruit a bit and cut away the next strip of peel. Continue all the way around. Then hold the fruit in the palm of your left hand and carefully trim away any remaining white parts.

TO SECTION AN ORANGE, LEMON, OR GRAPEFRUIT

Work over a bowl to catch the juice. With a small, thin, sharp knife cut down against the inside of the membrane of one section on both sides, releasing the section and leaving the membrane. After removing one or two sections, continue as follows: Cut against the membrane on the left side of a section and then, without removing the knife, turn the blade up against the membrane on the right side of the section. The section will fall out clean. After removing all the sections, squeeze the leftover membrane in your hand to extract any juice. Carefully remove any seeds.

Adding Vanilla Extract

I have read reviews that question the fact that I add vanilla (and other extracts) to the soft butter instead of waiting and adding it last. Since no one has ever said a recipe did not work because of this, I wonder why it matters to some people. However, if you care, here's why I do it.

Many years ago I read an article about cooking by someone who seemed much smarter than I am about food chemistry. The article said that adding the vanilla extract to the butter at the beginning seals in the flavor—something about adding it to the fat before liquid has been added. I have no idea if this is true or not. I just do it that way in case it is. The results seem to be okay.

To Wash a Pastry Brush

If you have used the brush for a sugar glaze or preserves, just rinse it under hot running water, separating the bristles a bit with your fingers so the water reaches all of them. If you have used it to butter a pan, it is important to remove every bit of butter or it will become rancid on the brush and I don't know any way ever to get rid of that. First, rinse the brush briefly under hot running water. Then rub it well on a cake of soap, rubbing first one side of the bristles and then the other. Rinse well under hot running water, then repeat the soaping or rinsing once or twice more to be sure. To dry, just let it stand bristles up in a dish drainer or a glass.

About Cutting Pies and Tarts

I can do a better job if I stand rather than sit.

Pies and tarts should be cut carefully and neatly with a very sharp knife that is long enough. You might not use the whole blade but it gives leverage. If it is a round pie or tart, always start cutting each pie-shaped wedge from the exact center. Mark the center with the tip of a knife. Or, to find the center, lightly score the pie or tart in half first in one direction, then in the opposite direction. Then, if you don't trust yourself to cut freehand, mark each quarter lightly with the tip of the knife, marking the outside edge into 2 to 6 portions, depending on the size of the pie or tart and the size of the portions. But always keep your eye on the center so that the slices all radiate out from there.

Talking about size of portions, unless it is for a restaurant—and sometimes even if it is—small portions are better than large.

Sometimes it is best to wipe the blade after each cut.

Mainly, take your time. And if it isn't going well, remember all the options—try a different knife, or a wet blade, or simply wipe the blade.

Pie Crust

Although pies may not have been created in America, they became an American specialty.

However, many good American cooks have never baked a pie. I am so sorry about all the people who cook and bake and are not intimidated by lengthy or demanding recipes but are afraid to make a pie. Or, for whatever reason, they just never do. They are missing one of the greatest eating experiences of all.

A plain American pie is a work of art. Every time you make one it is a challenge and when it turns out right you have accomplished something major of which you and your family and friends should be extremely proud. And I would like to add my compliments to the chef.

This recipe is for a 9-inch crust. I recommend using an ovenproof glass pie plate.

Pie Pastry

(For a 10-inch crust, increase the amounts to 1¼ cups of flour, generous ½ teaspoon of salt, 3¾ tablespoons of vegetable shortening, 3¾ tablespoons of butter, and 3¾ tablespoons of ice water.)

1 cup sifted all-purpose flour
Scant ½ teaspoon salt
3 tablespoons vegetable shortening (e.g., Crisco), cold and firm
3 tablespoons unsalted butter, cold and firm, cut into very small squares
About 3 tablespoons ice water

*I*f the room is warm, it is a good idea to chill the mixing bowl and even the flour beforehand. Some pie pros store their flour in the freezer or refrigerator so it will be cold and ready.

Place the flour and salt in a large, wide mixing bowl. Add the shortening and butter. With a pastry blender cut them in until the mixture resembles coarse crumbs. It is all right to leave a few pieces about the size of tiny peas.

Sprinkle 1 tablespoon of the ice water by small drops all over the surface. Stir, mix, or toss with a fork. Continue adding the water only until the flour is barely moistened. (Too much water makes the pastry sticky, soggy, or tough. Too little makes it hard to roll out without cracks and breaks in the dough.) Do not ever dump a lot of water in any one spot. (I know one cook who uses a laundry-sprinkling container and another who uses a salt shaker to add the water; that way they distribute it in a fine spray all over.) If you add the water too quickly—if you don't stir, mix, or toss enough while you are adding it—you might be convinced that you need more water. But maybe you don't; maybe you just need to add the water more slowly and stir or mix more. When adequate water has been added, the mixture will still be lumpy and will not hold together, but with practice you will know by the look of it that it will form a ball when pressed together. I have occasionally had to add a little more water, but very little—1 to 2 teaspoons at the most.

The shortening and butter must not melt (they should remain in little flour-coated flakes), so do not handle now any more than necessary. Turn the mixture out onto a large work surface and, with your hands, just push the mixture together to form a ball. (My mother never touched the dough with her hands at this stage—she turned it out onto a piece of plastic wrap, brought up the sides and corners of the plastic, and squeezed them firmly together at the top, letting the mixture form a ball without actually touching it. Then she flattened it slightly. Now I do it this way too.)

If the dough is too dry to hold together, do not knead it (don't even think about kneading it) but replace it in the bowl, cut it into small pieces with a knife, add a few more drops of water, and then stir again.

However you do it, form it into a ball quickly, flatten it slightly, smooth the edges, wrap it in plastic wrap, and refrigerate for at least an hour but preferably overnight. Chilling the dough not only makes it firmer, less sticky, and easier to handle, but also allows time for the water to moisten the flour more evenly. If it has been refrigerated overnight let it stand at room temperature 10 to 15 minutes before rolling it out.

Baked Pie Shell

Rolling out the dough is easiest if you work on a pastry cloth. Flour the cloth by rubbing in as much flour as the cloth will absorb, then lightly wipe off any loose excess flour. Rub flour on the rolling pin. (I use a French-style rolling pin that is long and narrow and tapered at both ends. It is too long and too narrow for the stockinette cover that is sold with the pastry cloth; I just reflour it frequently while I use it.)

Place the flattened ball of dough on the cloth. If the dough is very firm, pound or whack it sharply, but not too sharply, in all directions with the rolling pin to flatten it into a circle about 7 inches in diameter. (Don't pound the dough so hard that it forms deep cracks on the rim.) With your fingers, smooth and pinch together any small cracks at the edges.

Now start to roll, preferably from the center out rather than back and forth, and do not turn the dough upside down (it absorbs too much flour and becomes tough). Roll first in one direction and then another, trying to keep the shape round. If the edges crack slightly, pinch them together before the cracks become deep. If the dough cracks anywhere other than on the edges, or if the circle is terribly uneven, do not reroll the dough; simply cut off uneven edges and use the scraps as patches. Moisten the edges of the patch with water, turn the patch upside down, and press it firmly into place.

Reflour the rolling pin as necessary. It should not be necessary to reflour the cloth, but if there is any hint that the dough might stick, reflour it lightly.

Roll the dough into a circle 12 or 13 inches in diameter according to the recipe. It is important that the rolled-out dough be exactly the same thickness all over (a scant ⅛ inch thick) so it will bake evenly.

To transfer the dough to the pie plate, drape it over the rolling pin as follows:

Hold the pin over the left side of the dough, raise the left side of the pastry cloth to turn the dough over the rolling pin, roll it up loosely, then move it to the right side of the pie plate and unroll it, centering it evenly. Or fold it in half and lift it over the plate. With your fingers, ease the sides down into the plate. Do not stretch the dough or it will shrink during baking.

If you have a cake-decorating turntable place the pie plate on it.

Press the dough into place all over. If your fingernails are in the way, cut a small portion of the dough from an uneven edge, form it into a small ball, flour it lightly, and use it as a tamping tool to press the dough.

With scissors cut the edge of the crust, leaving an even ½- to ¾-inch overhang beyond the outside edge of the pie plate.

Now, to form a hem. I had always believed it was correct to turn the edge of the dough toward the outside and under—back onto itself. Recently I have been turning it toward the inside, and back onto itself. I like it better. So, with floured fingertips, fold the edge to make a hem that extends about ½ inch higher than the rim. Press the hem lightly together between your floured fingertips, pressing it a bit thinner, and making it stand upright.

FLUTING THE SHELL

There are many ways of forming a decorative edge. Here's one: Flour your fingertips. You will be working clockwise around the rim, starting at three o'clock. Place your left forefinger at a right angle across the rim of the dough. (Your left hand will be over the inside of the plate with your finger sticking over to the outside.) With your right hand grip the dough rim, using the thumb and bent-under forefinger. Grip slightly ahead (clockwise) of your left finger, and twist the dough edge toward the center of the plate. Remove both hands and then replace your left forefinger just ahead (clockwise again) of the twist you have just formed. This will be at about four o'clock on the rim. Repeat the twists all around. Check and reshape any uneven spots.

Prick fork holes in the bottom of the pastry ¼ inch apart when baking an empty pie shell.

Place the shell in the freezer for 15 minutes or more until it is frozen firm (this helps prevent shrinking). Wrapped airtight (after it is firm), it may be frozen for months, if you wish.

About 15 or 20 minutes before baking, adjust a rack one-third up from the bottom of the oven and preheat the oven to 450°.

In order to keep the pastry shell in place during baking, cut a 12-inch square of aluminum foil and place it shiny side down in the frozen shell. Press it into place all over. Do not fold the corners of the foil over the rim; let them stand up. Fill the foil at least three-quarters full with dried beans or with pie weights. (I use about 5 cups of a combination of black beans and black-eyed peas that I have been using for the same purpose for about 25 years.)

Bake the frozen shell at 450° for 12 to 13 minutes until it is set and slightly colored on the edges. Remove the pie plate from the oven. Reduce the heat to 400°.

Gently, slowly, remove the foil and beans by lifting the four corners of the foil.

Replace the plate in the oven and continue to bake for about 7 or 8 minutes, or longer if necessary. Watch the pie shell almost constantly; if it starts to puff up anywhere, reach into the oven and pierce the puff carefully with a cake tester to release trapped air. Bake until the edges are golden. Do not underbake. A too-pale crust is not as attractive as one with a good color. The bottom will remain paler than the edges. (During baking, if the crust is not browning evenly, reverse the position of the pan.)

Place on a rack and let cool.

NOTES: The ingredients for the crust may easily be doubled for two shells or for a pie with both a bottom and a top crust.

It is a great luxury to have an unbaked pie shell in the freezer. I try to keep one, frozen in the pie plate, all ready for the oven. When it is frozen I wrap it in plastic wrap or in a freezer bag. Then I have only to line it with foil and fill it with beans or pie weights when I am ready to bake. (I think a pie shell freezes better unbaked than when already baked.)

To Form an Extra-Deep Pie Shell

Follow the above directions (rolling the dough ½ inch wider—or 13½ inches) up to folding the hem of the pastry. Fold the hem toward the inside and fold a ¾-inch (rather than a ½-inch) hem. You should have a raised ¾-inch hem standing straight up all around the inner edge of the rim. Form it into a straight, even wall all around. To flute it (keeping it high), leave it upright, lightly flour the thumb and the tip of the index finger of your right hand, and pinch from the outside so the outer edge of the raised wall of pastry forms a horizontal V (or a V that has the point facing the outside). It seems easiest to me to start at the right side (three o'clock) of the plate. Use the index finger of your left hand to support the inside of the crust while you pinch it.

Pinch again 1 inch away from the first. Continue to pinch and form V's all around the outside of the rim 1 inch apart. Then do the same thing on the inside of the rim, this time starting at the left side (nine o'clock) of the plate, pinching between two out-pointing V's on the outside and forming a nice, neat zigzag pattern all around, standing ¾ inch straight up.

Patching the Pastry

I was making a recipe in which the pastry is baked empty and then a juicy filling is poured in and the pastry is baked again. But while the crust baked empty, it formed a 3- or 4-inch crack right down the middle. If I had poured the filling in, it would have run through the crack, stuck to the pan, and been a disaster. I stood there looking at it, feeling totally helpless.

My husband walked into the room and I didn't think he even saw what had happened, but he did, and without a moment's pause he said, "Patch it with almond paste." It took a few seconds for his brilliant comment to sink in—it was genius. I still cannot understand how he knew so quickly what was probably the only solution possible, and one I have never heard of before.

Since then I have used this trick many times; just a few minutes ago I used it for Date Pecan Pie (see page 75). Whatever would I have done if I had not known about this?

I have used both marzipan and almond paste. The brand I buy is Odense, which is made in Denmark and is generally available at fine food stores all over America. It seems to last forever (either at room temperature or refrigerated), but do not allow it to dry out. After you open it, be sure to wrap it airtight. I use both plastic wrap and aluminum foil.

Cut off a thin slice or break off a small chunk of the marzipan or almond paste, and press it between your fingers to make a thin patch slightly larger than the damaged area. Beat a bit of egg white lightly (only until foamy), then use it as a paste. With your fingertip, brush the white onto one side of the patch and place it, egg white down, over the damage. (I have also used just a bit of water as paste and it worked, but if you have egg white, I think it might be safer than water.) Flour your fingertips and press gently around the rim of the patch.

Then pour in the filling and no one will ever know, and you will say thank you to Ralph every time you patch pastry this way.

An Aluminum Foil Frame

To prevent overbrowning of the edge of a pie crust, make an aluminum foil frame as follows: Cut a 12-inch length of regular aluminum foil (not heavy-duty foil). Fold in half and then in the opposite direction in half again, making a square. Fold once more, making a triangle, the point of which is the middle of the piece of foil. To make a 7-inch hole in the middle, measure 3½ inches from the point of the triangle and cut out a shallow arc from the long side of the triangle to one short side. Open the folded foil frame and lay it over the top of the pie so the edges are covered and the center is exposed to get brown.

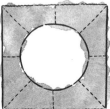

(You might want to make two frames and use them both at the same time, placing one over the other so that the points of the second frame are between the points of the first frame.)

After using the frame, reserve it to use over and over again.

Crumb Crust

*A*djust a rack to the center of the oven and preheat oven to 375°. In a bowl, mix the crumbs with the sugar and nutmeg. Then add the butter and stir with a rubber spatula until the butter is evenly distributed; the mixture will not hold together. Although the crumb mixture can be pressed into place directly in the pie plate, I line the plate with foil first, and then remove the foil before filling the crust. This guarantees easy serving—the crust *cannot* stick to the plate. It is a bit more work (or play) but I think well worth it.

1¼ cups graham cracker crumbs
¼ cup granulated sugar
Scant ¼ teaspoon nutmeg
2 ounces (½ stick) unsalted butter, melted

For a 9-inch pie plate (I use a glass one), use a 12-inch square of foil. Turn the plate over on a work surface. Place the foil shiny side down over the outside of the plate and, with your hands, press it firmly against the plate all around. Remove the foil. Turn the plate over again and place the shaped foil in the plate. Press the foil firmly into place in the plate with a potholder or a folded towel. Fold the edges of the foil down over the rim of the plate.

Turn the crumb crust mixture into the foil-lined plate. Using your fingertips, distribute the mixture evenly and loosely over the sides first and then the bottom. Then press the crust firmly and evenly on the sides, pushing it up from the bottom a bit to form a rim slightly (barely) higher than the edge of the pie plate. Be careful that the top of the crust is not too thin. To shape a firm edge, use the fingertips of your right hand against the inside and press down against it with the thumb of your left hand. After pressing the sides and the top edge firmly, press the remaining crumbs evenly and firmly over the bottom. There should be no loose crumbs.

Bake for 8 minutes. Then cool to room temperature.

Freeze for at least 1 hour, overnight if possible. It must be frozen solid.

Remove from the freezer. Raise the edges of the foil and carefully lift the foil (with the crust) from the plate. Gently peel away the foil as follows: Support the bottom of the crust on your left hand and peel away the foil, a bit at a time (do not tear the foil) with your right hand. As you do so, rotate the crust gently on your left hand.

Supporting the bottom of the crust with a small metal spatula or a table knife, ease it back into the plate very gently in order not to crack it. It will not crack or crumble if it has been frozen long enough.

Pies and Turnovers

Mom's Apple Pie

This is my mother's Florida version of the classic apple pie. It has both top and bottom crusts with a thick filling of apple slices poached before they are put into the pie, and held together with a delicious cinnamon-nutmeg-orange syrup that is not so thin that it runs and not too thick so it still oozes slightly as it should and is perfectly delicious.

Pie Crust

Prepare a double amount of pie pastry for a 9-inch pie (see page 17). Divide the pastry in half, gently shape each half into a ball, flour the balls lightly and flatten them slightly, wrap in plastic wrap, and refrigerate while you prepare the filling.

Have ready 2 tablespoons fine, dry bread crumbs.

Filling

Peel the apples and cut them into quarters. Remove the cores, then cut each quarter into four or five lengthwise slices, each about ½ inch thick at the outside edge. There should be about 12 cups.

You will need a large, preferably shallow, pan (a frying pan or a sauté pan) that has a tight cover. Place ½ cup of the orange juice (reserve the remaining ¼ cup) in the pan. Add the water and sugar. Place over moderate heat, stirring occasionally until the syrup comes to a low boil. Add the orange rind and the apples, cover the pan, and cook gently, stirring the apples occasionally, until they are barely tender but still hold their shape. As the apples finish cooking, remove them from the pan (a slotted spoon is easiest) and place them in a large colander or strainer set over a large plate.

Measure the remaining syrup—you need 1 cup. If there is more, boil it down; if there is less, add water.

Place the reserved ¼ cup orange juice in a small mixing bowl with the flour, salt, cinnamon, and nutmeg. Beat with a small wire whisk until smooth. Add the 1 cup of syrup, transfer to a small saucepan over moderate heat, and cook,

8 apples (3¼ pounds; see Note)
¾ cup orange juice (grate the rind to use below before squeezing the juice)
½ cup water
1 cup granulated sugar
Finely grated rind of 2 oranges
2 tablespoons plus 1 teaspoon unsifted all-purpose flour
Pinch of salt
1 teaspoon cinnamon
1 teaspoon nutmeg
1 teaspoon vanilla extract
1½ tablespoons unsalted butter

6 GENEROUS PORTIONS

stirring constantly with a rubber spatula or wooden spoon, until the mixture thickens. It should be about as thick as a thick cream sauce. Then reduce the heat to lowest and cook, stirring occasionally, for 2 minutes more. Remove from the heat, stir in the vanilla and the butter, and set aside. Stir occasionally until the syrup cools.

To Make the Pie

Adjust an oven rack one-third up from the bottom of the oven and preheat oven to 425°.

If the pastry was refrigerated overnight let it stand at room temperature for 10 to 15 minutes before rolling it out. Use one piece of the pastry as follows to line a 9-inch glass pie plate (which should not be buttered).

Flour a pastry cloth and a rolling pin. Place the pastry on the cloth. Press down on it gently with the rolling pin to flatten it without rolling until it is a circle 6 to 7 inches wide. Then, rolling gently from the center out toward the rim, in all directions, roll the pastry out to a 12-inch circle. (If the edge begins to crack while you are rolling it, pinch the cracks together before they become large.)

Either fold the rolled-out pastry in half and lift it, or drape it over the rolling pin and lift it—whichever feels best to you—and place it evenly in the plate. Press the sides into the plate without stretching the dough. With scissors, cut the rim even with the outside edge of the plate. Sprinkle the bread crumbs on the bottom and set aside.

Roll out the other half of the dough, rolling it out to a 12-inch circle (the same as the first half).

Fold it in half. Then, for steam to escape, use the tip of a teaspoon to make a half-moon-shaped cut about ½ inch in from the fold and an equal distance from both top and bottom of the semicircle of dough. Cut through both layers. Then make two more cuts, one an inch above the first and another an inch below. Let stand.

Place the cooked, cooled, drained apple slices in the bottom crust. Pour the cooled syrup evenly over the apples.

Then, wet the top rim of the bottom crust; either use a small, soft brush dipped into water, or use your fingertips dipped into water.

Place the folded pastry over the apples, carefully centering the fold; then unfold it to cover the whole pie.

Now cut the edge of the top pastry with scissors, leaving an overhang ½ inch wider than the bottom crust. Then, with your fingers, fold that extra ½ inch over and under the rim of the bottom crust (not the plate). Flour your fingertips and press the rim together to seal the top and bottom crusts, and also to make the edge a little thinner and standing upright. Then, with floured fingers, flute the crust into an attractive design (see page 19). It should be a high, standing-up rim.

Glaze

Mix the yolk and water and brush the mixture on the crust, including the fluted rim.

1 egg yolk
1 teaspoon water

Bake for 30 to 35 minutes until the pie is richly colored—do not underbake.

Place on a rack.

Serve while warm or at room temperature.

NOTE: Use any apples that are firm, crisp, tart, and delicious. The better the apples are, the better the pie will be. My favorites are Granny Smith. But apple pie experts also recommended Cortland (tart and snowy), Rhode Island Greening (for sour apple pie), Green Newton Pippin (sharp), and Golden Delicious (dry and sweet).

Apple Pie, U.S.A.

This is the traditional, old-fashioned, "American as apple pie" apple pie. Once you have made it, you will glory in the spotlight, be thrilled with pride, and be in apple-pie-in-the-sky heaven.

It is best to put together the pie dough at least an hour before using it, or the day before. (It will be easier to handle cold, and waiting before you use the dough allows for the water to be absorbed more equally.)

Choose the apples carefully. Some are too watery (McIntosh), some are too dry, some have more flavor than others. But there are many varieties that are just right. Granny Smith, Jonathan, Winesap, and Cortland are among the best. (There are others—ask your produce seller.)

Pie Crust

Prepare a double amount of pie pastry for a 9-inch pie (see page 17). Divide the pastry in half, gently shape each half into a ball, flour the balls lightly and flatten them slightly, wrap in plastic wrap, and refrigerate for from an hour up to overnight.

1 teaspoon unsifted *all-purpose flour*

If the pastry was refrigerated overnight let it stand at room temperature for 10 to 15 minutes before rolling it out. Place one ball of dough on a lightly floured pastry cloth. Pound it lightly with a floured rolling pin. With a rolling pin roll out the dough, keeping the pin, the cloth, and the top of the dough very lightly floured. Roll from the center of the dough out toward the edges. As you start to roll out the dough, watch the rim; if cracks form, pinch them together before they become deep. Keep the shape round and the thickness even. Roll out until you have a circle about 12 inches in diameter.

There are two ways to transfer the circle of dough to the pie plate. One is to fold it in half and place it in the plate. Then unfold it and ease it gently into place in the pan. The other is to roll it up loosely around the rolling pin and unroll it over the plate and then ease it gently into place in the pan. (I think the choice of methods depends on the fingernails; if they are long you will probably prefer rolling the dough on the pin to transfer it.)

If you have a cake-decorating turntable place the pie on it. Trim the edges of the dough with scissors, leaving enough for the dough to lie down flat on the rim of the plate and extend only a scant ¼ inch beyond the outside of the rim.

Place the flour in the crust and, with a dry pastry brush, spread it over the bottom. Refrigerate the pie plate with the bottom crust in place.

Lightly reflour the pastry cloth and roll out the second piece of dough until it is about 12 inches wide (the same as the bottom crust). Slide a flat-rimmed cookie sheet (or anything else that will work) under the pastry cloth and transfer the cloth and dough to the refrigerator.

Adjust a rack one-third up from the bottom of the oven. Preheat oven to 450°.

Filling

The amount of flour in the filling depends on how juicy the apples are and on how juicy you like your pie. Many people—especially country and farm people, who have probably eaten more pies than most of us—think that any thickening at all is un-American; to those people a good pie has to be eaten from a soup bowl with a spoon.

In a small bowl mix together the flour with the sugar, cinnamon, nutmeg, and salt, and set aside.

With a vegetable parer peel the apples and place in a large bowl. Add the sugar and flour mixture and toss with your hands to mix thoroughly.

Turn the mixture into the floured bottom crust. Use your fingers to move things around and make an even mound, but do not press down on the apples or you will punch a hole in the crust. Scatter the pieces of butter over the top.

Place a little cup of cold water next to you. With a soft brush or your fingers wet the top of the rim of the bottom crust.

Transfer the top crust (using the same procedure you used for the bottom crust) over the apples, centering it carefully.

Flour your fingertips and press the rim of the top crust against the wet top rim of the bottom crust. Then, with scissors, trim the top crust, allowing it to extend about ¼ to ½ inch beyond the bottom crust. With your fingertips and a bit of cold water, wet the bottom (the underside) of the rim. Fold the edge of the top crust over and then under the rim of the bottom crust (like tucking in a sheet around a mattress). Press together firmly. Now raise the rim so it stands upright and with your fingers flute a simple zigzag design on the rim (see To Form an Extra-Deep Pie Shell, page 20). Be very careful that the crust does not extend out over the rim of the pan, or it might droop and sag and fall off when the pie is baked.

With a small sharp knife cut eight 1-inch slits in the top, starting 1 inch from the center of the pie and radiating outwards, to allow steam and/or juices to escape.

With a pastry brush, brush milk over the top of the crust (except the rim), being careful not to use so much that it runs down in puddles against the rim; if it does, sponge it up with a small piece of paper towel. Sprinkle generously with sugar.

Be prepared to slide a cookie sheet or foil on a rack below to catch juices that might bubble over. If you do not have a rack below you might want to put foil on the floor of the oven, but wait until the pie is almost baked and until it might start to bubble over (which depends on how juicy the apples are) because the cookie sheet or foil might interfere with the baking.

Bake at 450° for 15 minutes. Then open the oven and quickly reach in to cover the rim with an aluminum foil frame (see page 21), folding the points down as quickly as possible.

Lower the oven temperature to 425° and bake for about 45 minutes more (total time is about 1 hour), until the crust is nicely browned and the apples are tender (you can test them with a toothpick through the slits on top).

Cool on a rack. Serve when barely cooled or at room temperature.

3 tablespoons unsifted *all-purpose flour*
¾ cup granulated sugar
1 teaspoon cinnamon
¼ teaspoon nutmeg
¼ teaspoon salt
About 3 pounds apples (to make 8 to 9 cups, sliced)
1 ounce (¼ stick) unsalted butter, cut into small pieces (it is best to cut the butter ahead of time and refrigerate it)
Milk
Additional granulated sugar

6 PORTIONS

Fresh Apricot Pie

This is an old favorite in northern California, but down here in Florida it is exciting and unusual. Fresh apricots are a great luxury, mainly because they are available for only a short time (although the season seems to get longer each year). When and if you can get them remember this divine pie. It is extravagantly high and gorgeous, loaded with a generous amount of fruit; juicy and slightly runny, sweet/slightly sour, it is pure, plain, simple—the classic American two-crust pie. It has become the specialty of the house at our house and it will remain so as long as fresh apricots are available.

Make the pastry ahead (an hour is passable but a day ahead it best), make the pie early in the day for that night (it should have at least 6 hours to cool and chill a bit), and invite someone special.

You will need a 9-inch Pyrex pie plate.

Pie Crust

Prepare a double amount of pie pastry for a 9-inch pie (see page 17) with this one addition: Add 2 teaspoons of granulated sugar along with the salt. Divide the pastry in half, gently shape each half into a ball, flour the balls lightly and flatten them slightly, wrap in plastic wrap, and refrigerate for from an hour up to overnight.

Filling

Adjust a rack one-third up from the bottom of the oven and preheat oven to 500°.

Cut the apricots in half, remove the pits, and place the halves in a wide mixing bowl.

In a small cup combine the Amaretto and almond extract, drizzle it all over the prepared apricots, toss gently with a rubber spatula until completely mixed, and set aside.

In a bowl stir the granulated and brown sugars together until they are thoroughly mixed. Add the tapioca and mix with a rubber spatula, pressing against the ingredients until thoroughly mixed again (this mixing is extremely important; otherwise the pie will have unpleasant lumps of tapioca). Or do this step with your fingers.

Now, this next step must be done slowly and carefully (again, to avoid lumps of tapioca). Very gradually add the sugar mixture to the apricots, adding only a rounded tablespoonful at a time and stirring or folding thoroughly and gently with a rubber spatula after each addition to mix the ingredients without breaking or mashing the fruit. After all of the sugar mixture has been added, let the apricot mixture stand for about 15 minutes, stirring and folding frequently with the rubber spatula. (During this time, the sugars will melt and juices will form and a dark syrup will appear, which will begin to soften the tapioca.)

Meanwhile, roll out one piece of the pastry as follows. (If it has been refrigerated overnight let it stand at room temperature for about 10 minutes before being unwrapped.) Flour a pastry cloth and a rolling pin. Place the flattened ball of pastry on the cloth. Press down on the pastry with the rolling pin to flatten it into a circle about 6 inches in diameter. (If cracks form on the edges pinch them together and smooth over them with your fingertips before they become deep.)

Roll the pastry into a 12-inch circle.

If you have a cake-decorating turntable place the pie plate on it.

Either fold the pastry in half and lift it or drape it over the rolling pin and lift it (whichever feels better to you), and center it carefully over a 9-inch Pyrex pie plate.

Press the sides of the pastry against the plate. With scissors cut the rim, allowing a scant ¼-inch overhang. Place the lined plate in the refrigerator.

Roll out the other half of the dough to the same size as the first half (a 12-inch circle). Then slide a flat cookie sheet under the pastry cloth with the rolled-out dough and transfer the whole thing to the refrigerator.

You will place the apricot halves in the crust to form two rows of fruit, one row toward the rim of the plate and the other row inside—toward the center of the plate.

Important: The bottom layer of fruit should be placed cut side up (rounded side down). The pieces of fruit should overlap. Drizzle or spoon on some of the sugar and tapioca syrup that has formed.

After making the two rows (which are the bottom layer of fruit and should fill the crust), make two more rows on top of the bottom rows (this will make a second layer of fruit).

Important: The second, or top layer of fruit should be placed cut side down (rounded side up)—the opposite of the first layer. And the pieces should overlap one another again. Drizzle or spoon on some more of the sugar and tapioca syrup.

Any remaining apricot halves should be placed evenly in the center (making three rows deep), cut side down—curved side up.

(The reason for all of this "cut side/curved side up or down," et cetera, is that the cut side should always face away from the pastry. I once had the experience that the cut edges of the fruit formed cuts in the bottom of the pastry and allowed juices and syrup to run out.)

With a rubber spatula scrape the bowl clean and distribute every bit of sugar and tapioca syrup evenly over and among the pieces of fruit.

2½ pounds (22 to 24 medium-size) fresh apricots, just barely ripe (to make 8 to 10 cups pitted halves)
1 tablespoon Amaretto or any other liquor or liqueur, or orange juice
½ teaspoon almond extract
¾ cup granulated sugar
½ cup dark brown sugar, firmly packed
3 tablespoons plus 1 teaspoon "Minute" tapioca

6 TO 8 PORTIONS

If you have a cake-decorating turntable place the pie plate on it.

Wet the top rim of the crust with a bit of cold water, using a soft brush or your fingertips.

Remove the top crust from the refrigerator and either fold it in half or drape it over the rolling pin, and lift it and place it over the fruit, centering it carefully.

With your fingers press down on the edges of the crusts to seal them together. Then, with scissors, cut the top crust, allowing it to extend a scant ½ inch beyond the bottom crust.

With your fingertips, and a bit of cold water, wet the bottom (the underside) of the rim of the crust.

Dry your hands, flour your fingertips, and fold the edge of the bottom crust. Make it an even hem. And with your fingertips press the rim to seal the top and bottom crusts together and also to make the edge a little thinner. Shape the rim (the hem) so it stands upright.

Then flute the edge into a neat design (preferably the technique described for an extra-deep pie shell—see page 20). See Note.

Topping

Brush all over the top—not the rim—with milk. Sprinkle it all generously with granulated sugar.

Milk
Granulated sugar

With a small sharp knife cut six or eight slits in the crust, each about 1 inch long, starting 1 inch from the center of the pie and radiating outwards.

If some of the milk has made a puddle in the trench just inside the rim, soak it up with a soft brush or with an edge of paper towel or paper napkin.

Place the pie in the oven and immediately reduce the temperature to 450°. After 10 minutes reduce the temperature again to 375° and continue to bake for 35 or 40 minutes more (total baking time is 45 to 50 minutes) until the crust is nicely colored and the filling just starts to bubble up through the slits in the crust.

During the last few minutes of baking, the juices might bubble over the plate; watch for it and be prepared ahead of time either to slide a cookie sheet on a rack below or place aluminum foil on the floor of the oven. (Do not place the cookie sheet or foil in the oven at the beginning of the baking because it might interfere with the bottom crust baking properly.)

Cool completely on a rack. Then refrigerate.

Serve the pie cold, plain or with ice cream.

NOTE: Be careful—if the rim is too heavy (if you have allowed too much overhang when you trimmed the crusts) or if you have shaped it too close to the outside edge of the plate, when it is placed in the oven and softens from the heat it might fall toward the outside of, or even off, the plate.

Blueberry Pie #1 (single crust)

This can have either a baked pie crust or a crumb crust. Either way, the crust is baked empty, and part of the filling is cooked in a saucepan on top of the stove. Then, when both the crust and the filling have cooled, the filling is mixed with more whole, uncooked berries, poured into the crust, and refrigerated until serving time. The pie needs at least 3 hours in the refrigerator before it is served, but it can wait for most of the day if you wish.

Place the berries in a large bowl of cold water. Let the water run off between your fingers as you scoop up the berries and place them on paper towels to drain. As you do so, pick over them carefully to remove any unripe berries, loose stems, etc.

In a small bowl stir the cornstarch in the cold water until it dissolves. Then add the boiling water and stir until smooth. Place in a 1-quart saucepan. Add the sugar, salt, and ½ cup (reserve the remaining 5½ cups) of the berries. Place over medium-low heat and stir constantly. While cooking and stirring, press the berries against the sides of the pan to crush them. Cook until the mixture comes to a low boil, then thickens and becomes somewhat clear. It should take about 10 minutes. Then reduce the heat to low and cook very gently for about 3 or 4 minutes more.

Stir in the juice and butter. Then, in a large bowl, gently mix the reserved berries with the warm sauce. Stir occasionally until cool.

Pour the cooled mixture into the prepared crust.
Refrigerate for at least 3 hours.

1 9-inch baked *pie shell (see page 17) or crumb crust (see page 22)*
2 small boxes (2 pounds) blueberries (each box will measure about 3 cups, even though it is generally called 1 pint)
¼ cup cornstarch
¼ cup cold tap water
¾ cup boiling water
1 cup granulated sugar
¼ teaspoon salt
1½ tablespoons fresh lemon juice
1 tablespoon unsalted butter

6 GENEROUS PORTIONS

Whipped Cream

Whipped cream and this pie go wonderfully well together. Be prepared with plenty of it.

Place all of the ingredients in a chilled bowl and beat with chilled beaters only until the cream holds a soft shape. It should not be stiff. (If you whip the cream more than an hour or so ahead of

time, refrigerate it. It will probably separate slightly while it stands. Just beat it a bit with a small wire whisk right before using.) Serve the cream separately, ladling a generous amount over the side of each portion.

2 cups heavy cream
3 tablespoons granulated or confectioners sugar
3 tablespoons kirsch or cassis, or ¾ teaspoon vanilla extract

Blueberry Pie #2 (double crust)

This is the classic, traditional blueberry pie than which there is none more delicious or delectable, none to be prouder of, none to serve with more fanfare, and none to enjoy more.

The crust can be prepared ahead and it can be ready to roll out. The berries can be washed and drained and ready to use. Then the actual "making the pie" is not too much work.

Pie Crust

Prepare a double amount of pie pastry for a 9-inch pie (see page 17). Divide the pastry in half, gently shape each half into a ball, flour the balls lightly and flatten them slightly, wrap in plastic wrap, and refrigerate for from an hour up to overnight.

Filling

Fill a large bowl with cold water. Place the berries in the bowl and, with your hands, fingers slightly spread, transfer the berries to a towel to drain and dry.

Sift together the flour, sugar, salt, and mace, and set aside.

When you are ready to bake, adjust a rack one-quarter or one-third up from the bottom of the oven (according to how many rack settings your oven has—lower is better). Preheat oven to 450°. You will need a 9-inch Pyrex pie plate.

Flour a pastry cloth and a rolling pin. Work with one piece of the dough at a time. Place the dough on the cloth, press down on it with the rolling pin (flattening it without rolling) until it is a circle 6 to 7 inches wide. Then, rolling gently from the center out toward the rim, roll the pastry out to a 12-inch circle.

Either fold the rolled-out pastry in half and lift it, or drape it over the rolling pin and lift it, placing it evenly in the plate. Press the sides into the pan without stretching the dough. With scissors, cut the edge even with the outside rim of the plate. Sprinkle 3 tablespoons of the sifted flour mixture evenly over the bottom of the pastry. Refrigerate.

Roll the remaining half of the pastry out to another 12-inch circle. Let it stand briefly on the pastry cloth.

Place the berries in a large bowl. Add the grated rind and toss gently with a rubber spatula. Add about half of the remaining sifted dry ingredients and toss gently, just a bit, with the rubber spatula.

Place half of the berries in the crust. Sprinkle with half of the now-remaining sifted dry ingredients. Cover with the remaining berries, mounding them high in the middle, and then sprinkle with the last of the dry ingredients. With your fingers, press down gently to flatten the mound slightly without spreading any berries toward the rim.

Have a small dish of cold water handy. Wet your three middle fingers and, with your fingers, generously wet the rim of the lower crust.

Fold the rolled-out pastry in half. Carefully lift it and place it with the fold across the middle, over the berries. Unfold and carefully arrange the top crust to touch the bottom crust around the sides. With scissors, cut the top crust, leaving a ½-inch border beyond the bottom crust.

Starting at a spot on the edge of the crust away from you, use your left hand to raise the rim of the bottom crust, and use your right hand to fold the border of the upper crust over, around, and then under the bottom crust—not the plate. Flour your fingertips as necessary. Continue all around the plate. As you do this you can at the same time press against the two edges to seal the top and bottom crusts together well.

To finish the edge, stand it all upright around the rim, forming a little wall to control any juices that bubble out. Then, with your fingertips, flute the edge (see page 19).

2 small boxes (2 pounds) fresh blueberries
6 tablespoons unsifted all-purpose flour
1 cup granulated sugar
¼ teaspoon salt
¼ teaspoon mace
Finely grated rind of 1 lemon

6 TO 8 PORTIONS

Egg Wash

Beat the egg just to mix and brush it gently with a soft brush all over the top of the crust, including the rim. You will use only a small amount of the egg wash to brush on the pie. (I have made it a rule never to write a recipe that is different from the way I make it. And I never have—until now. But I will explain and then leave it up to you. I use only the yolk and 1 teaspoon of water mixed together. That makes a much darker glaze. However, I am afraid that if you see how dark the crust becomes after only 20 minutes of baking you will get worried and possibly take the pie out of the oven before it has baked enough.)

1 egg

Now, one last thing before this beauty goes into the oven. You must cut air vents for steam to escape. Use a small sharp paring knife. Cut six or seven sunburst or fan lines radiating out from the center directly on top, leaving a 1- to 2-inch space in the middle (the cuts should not get too close to the outside edge or too much juice will bubble out). Each cut should be about 1½ inches long. Cut each one twice to open the cut a little. That's it.

Bake at 450° for 20 minutes. Then reduce the temperature to 375° and bake for 40 minutes longer. (Total baking time is 1 hour.)

Cool on a rack. Refrigerate until cold and serve cold. (The filling might be too runny until it is chilled.) This is even better with vanilla ice cream.

Blackberry Pie

We drove through the spectacular redwood forest called the Avenue of the Giants in northern California where the trees are so tremendous that in two locations the road goes right through the middle of tree trunks. Just on the outskirts of the forest we saw a billboard that read **Prize-Winning Homemade Blackberry Pie**. *The sign was for a small restaurant in a private home. I'd never had blackberry pie before. The thick layer of deep magenta filling was somewhat soft and juicy and just the merest bit runny, slightly and wonderfully tart with a flavor reminiscent of raspberries—but different. They had used wild blackberries that grow profusely in that area. The topping was a buttery, brown sugar, spicy, crumbly crumb mixture. I'll never forget it.*

The prebaked crust and the crumb topping can be prepared ahead of time and refrigerated or frozen, if you wish. Putting the filling together takes only minutes. It is best to bake the pie only a few hours before serving.

Pie Crust

Since this filling becomes very juicy as it bakes and since the juices would run out of any places they could get through (which would make the bottom crust stick to the plate), please hold the empty crust (in the glass plate) up to

1 9-inch baked extra-deep pie shell (see page 17)

the light and examine it carefully for any little holes or even any too-thin spots. If there are any and if you have a bit of almond paste or marzipan, please cover the holes or thin spots (see Patching the Pastry, page 20). Or, since the pastry is going to be baked again, you can make patches with any little leftover scraps that were cut off the sides of the unbaked crust while you trimmed and shaped it. They can be pasted on with a bit of lightly beaten egg white or with a bit of water.

Crumb Topping

In a wide bowl stir the flour, brown sugar, cinnamon, and nutmeg to mix thoroughly. Cut in the butter with a pastry blender until the mixture makes coarse crumbs. There may be some small pieces of butter still visible; that's fine. If necessary, rub the ingredients. Refrigerate, freeze, or use right away.

Adjust a rack one-third up from the bottom of the oven and preheat oven to 350°.

½ cup unsifted *all-purpose flour*
½ cup *dark brown sugar, firmly packed*
1 teaspoon *cinnamon*
¼ teaspoon *nutmeg*
3 ounces (¾ stick) *unsalted butter, cold and firm, cut into small pieces*

Filling

In a wide bowl combine the granulated sugar and tapioca, add the frozen berries, stir gently with a rubber spatula, and let stand for 15 minutes, stirring occasionally. Meanwhile, peel, quarter, and core the apple and cut it into ¼- to ⅓-inch cubes. Stir it into the berry mixture. Sprinkle the lemon juice over the fruit and gently stir together.

Spread the berry mixture in a smooth layer in the crust. Slowly and carefully, sprinkle the crumb topping evenly over the berry mixture.

To prevent the rim of the pie from overbrowning, cover it with an aluminum foil frame (see page 21) and fold down the corners of the foil loosely over the crust.

Bake at 350° for 1 hour. Then remove the foil frame, raise the heat to 450°, and continue to bake for 8 to 10 minutes more—only until the filling begins to bubble up around the edges. (Watch it frequently and do not let it bubble over.)

Remove from the oven. At this point the filling will be thin and soupy, but when it cools it will become firm and will slice nicely. Serve at room temperature, plain or with vanilla ice cream, or slightly sweetened vanilla-flavored whipped cream.

⅔ cup *granulated sugar*
2 tablespoons *"Minute" tapioca*
1 1-pound box (4 cups) *frozen dry-packed blackberries (individually frozen)*
1 tart cooking apple (to make 1 cup, dried)
2 tablespoons *lemon juice*

6 TO 8 PORTIONS

NOTE: It is especially important that the crust be high and not have any low spots or the filling will bubble over.

Kirsch Strawberry Pie

Kirsch and strawberries are sensational, especially topped with whipped cream. This pie is beautiful, easy, and unusual. It is a gelatin pie, must be refrigerated until served, and is best the day it is made.

Wash the berries quickly, remove the hulls, and let drain on paper towels. Slice the berries, cutting each one into three or four lengthwise slices. In a processor or a blender purée enough of the berries to make 1 cup. (Or you can mash them to a pulp with a fork.) Chill the remaining sliced berries in the refrigerator.

In a small cup sprinkle the gelatin over the cold water and let stand.

Place the 1 cup of berry pulp in a 6- to 8-cup saucepan. Add the ¾ cup warm water. Stir occasionally over moderate heat until the mixture comes to a boil. Add the sugar and stir to dissolve. Remove from the heat.

Add the softened gelatin and stir to dissolve.

Add enough red food coloring to give the mixture a nice rich color. Strain through a large but rather fine-meshed strainer to remove the seeds.

Place the bowl of the gelatin mixture in a larger bowl partly filled with ice and water and stir occasionally until the mixture thickens and becomes syrupy (this might take longer than you expect).

When the mixture thickens, stir in the kirsch and Grand Marnier, and then the refrigerated berries. Mix well but gently and turn into the prepared pie shell or crumb crust.

Refrigerate from 4 to about 10 hours.

1 9-inch baked *pie shell* (see page 17) or baked crumb crust (see page 22)
2 pint boxes (2 pounds) fresh strawberries
1 envelope plus 1½ teaspoons unflavored gelatin
¼ cup cold water
¾ cup warm water
1 cup granulated sugar
Red food coloring
¼ cup kirsch
1 tablespoon Grand Marnier, Cointreau, or brandy

6 TO 8 PORTIONS

Whipped Cream Topping

The whipped cream may be put on the pie an hour or two before serving; it is best if it does not stand longer.

In a chilled bowl with chilled beaters whip the cream with the sugar and vanilla until the cream holds a definite shape. Either spread it over the firm filling or, with a pastry bag fitted with a star-shaped tube, form a border of swirls around the outside edge; let the red show in the middle.

Sprinkle the cream lightly with the optional almonds.

NOTE: If you wish, you can also add a few fresh blueberries when you fold in the refrigerated sliced strawberries.

1 cup heavy cream
2 tablespoons granulated or
  confectioners sugar
½ teaspoon vanilla extract
Optional: a few toasted
  slivered almonds

Individual Deep-Dish Strawberry-Rhubarb Pies

Strawberries and rhubarb are a fantastic combination and they make a wonderful pie. However, since they are both extremely juicy, it is best not to use a bottom crust, which would get wet. And since serving this is something like serving soup, I make it in individual bowls; that solves all the problems and it is attractive!

You will need six ovenproof bowls, each with a 10-ounce capacity. Pyrex makes bowls that measure 4½ inches across the top and are called "10-ounce deep pie cups." Or use onion soup bowls.

Prepare a double amount of pie pastry for a 9-inch pie (see page 17). Divide the pastry in half, gently shape each half into a ball, flour the balls lightly and flatten them slightly, wrap in plastic wrap, and refrigerate for from an hour up to overnight.

Adjust a rack to the center of the oven and preheat oven to 400°. Lightly butter the bottoms of six 10-ounce individual ovenproof bowls. Wash, hull, and drain the berries. If they are very large, cut them in half. The rhubarb should be washed, not peeled, and cut into pieces. Place the berries and rhubarb in a large bowl. Mix the rind and juice and sprinkle it over the fruit. Toss gently to mix.

In a bowl mix together the sugar, flour, and salt. Then sift the mixture over the fruits and stir gently with a rubber spatula. Set aside.

Now the pie crust. Lightly flour a pastry cloth and rolling pin, work with half of the dough at a time, and roll it until it is ⅛ inch thick (thin). Do not worry too much about the shape, but make it an even thickness.

To cut rounds of the dough: You will need a plate or something to use as a pattern that measures 1 to 1¼ inches more in diameter than the tops of the bowls. Set the plate, or the pattern, on the rolled-out dough, placing it against an edge. With a pizza cutter, a pastry cutter, or a small sharp knife, cut around the plate or pattern. Cut two more rounds (three from each half of the dough). Then, with a wide metal spatula, carefully transfer the rounds to a piece of wax paper until you are ready to use them. (See Note about left-over scraps of dough.) Roll out the other half of the dough and cut three more rounds. Let the rounds wait a moment.

With a large spoon divide the floured and sugared fruits evenly among the six buttered bowls, mounding them slightly, and letting most of the dry ingredients remain in the mixing bowl. Then spoon the dry ingredients remaining in the bowl evenly over the fruit.

Wet your fingertips with water and wet the rim of one of the bowls. Pick up a round of pastry and place it over the fruit but do not press it onto the wet rim. To form a thick edge on the pastry, flour your fingertips and fold a hem, folding under a scant ½ inch of the pastry. The hem should be wide enough—or narrow enough—so the pastry extends about ¼ inch beyond the rim of the bowl.

Now, with your fingertips, press down on the doubled rim to seal it to the bowl. To be sure it is well sealed, press all around with the back of the tines of a fork, flouring the tines as necessary.

Repeat to prepare all six pies.

With a pastry brush, brush some milk over the tops, and then sprinkle with granulated sugar.

Place all the pies on a jelly-roll pan (the pan must have sides).

With a small sharp knife cut a slit about ¾ inch long in the very center of each pie crust. It is important to make sure that the slits are open and that they do not close; flour the knife blade and recut the slits, pushing the sides slightly apart. (The slits serve two purposes: One, they allow steam to escape; and two, they serve as receptacles for "pastry handles"—see Note.)

Bake for 30 minutes until the tops are nicely colored. Do not underbake; these should not be pale (dark is better). If the baking time is almost up and the tops are still pale, raise the rack (the top of

1 pint box (1 pound) fresh
  strawberries
3 generous cups (about 1
  pound) fresh rhubarb, cut
  into ½-inch pieces
Finely grated rind of 1 large,
  deep-colored orange
1½ tablespoons orange juice
1½ cups granulated sugar
4½ tablespoons unsifted all-
  purpose flour
⅛ teaspoon salt
Milk (to brush on the crusts)
Additional granulated sugar
  (to sprinkle over the tops)

6 INDIVIDUAL PIES

the oven is hotter). And if the pies in the back of the oven are darker, reverse the pan front to back.

The filling should bubble and it may bubble over—okay.

Cool to room temperature. (If you have baked these in glass, as they cool you will see that the filling sinks about an inch below the crust—okay.)

Refrigerate for at least 4 hours, or up to 10 or 12 hours, before serving.

Serve a spoon with each pie.

NOTE: To decorate these pies, cut the dough that remains after the rounds are cut, cutting six handle-shaped pieces. They can be cut freehand; they do not all have to be exactly the same. Or, if you are more comfortable with a pattern, cut one out of paper. What you want is an elongated teardrop shape, about 4 inches long, 1¼ inches wide at the top, and ½ inch wide at the bottom (the bottom does not come to a point like a real teardrop). Cut the "handles" with a pizza cutter, a pastry cutter, or a small sharp knife. Then you will need something to cut a small round hole out of the wide part of each handle—use a ½- to ¾-inch cookie cutter, pastry-bag tube, or a thimble. Place the handles on an unbuttered cookie sheet, brush them lightly with milk, sprinkle with sugar, and bake at 400° until they are nicely colored and extra crisp.

Let the handles wait until serving time. Immediately before serving, place a handle, narrow end down, into the slit of each pie.

While making these handles recently, I discovered something. I still had some scraps of dough after the handles were all cut. Very carefully, I placed the scraps on top of each other in layers. Then, without straightening or smoothing the edges, I rolled the dough with a rolling pin until it was about ⅛ inch thick. I used a small, round scalloped cookie cutter and cut out the rounds, placed them on a cookie sheet, brushed with milk and sprinkled with sugar, and baked them. They were marvelous, puffed-up, light, flaky, crisp, delicious cookies.

Strawberry Chiffon Pie

This has a light, delicate, creamy, dreamy filling made with mashed berries and gelatin, and a topping of whipped cream and more berries. It is as pretty as a picture and as delicious as it looks. It is best if the filling is made the same day the pie is served, but it must chill for at least 3 hours.

ash the berries quickly, remove the stems and hulls, and drain them well on paper towels. Then cut the berries into very small dice or mash them coarsely with a potato masher or with a large fork, or process them briefly in a food processor. (If the berries are large they should be halved or quartered, and then processed only 2 cups at a time—process with three or four on and off pulses, but not so long that they liquefy.) There should be 2 generous cups of diced or mashed berries. Set the berries aside.

Sprinkle the gelatin over the water in a small cup and let stand.

In the small bowl of an electric mixer beat the yolks until they are pale colored. Then beat in the lemon juice and ¼ cup of the sugar (reserve the remaining ½ cup).

Transfer the mixture to the top of a large double boiler over hot water on moderate heat. Stir constantly with a rubber spatula, scraping the bottom and the sides, until the sugar dissolves and the mixture thickens to the consistency of a medium cream sauce.

Then add the softened gelatin and stir to dissolve. Add the prepared berries and stir to mix well.

Remove the top of the double boiler and transfer the mixture to a large bowl. Place the large bowl into a larger bowl partly filled with ice and water. Stir frequently with a rubber spatula until the mixture barely (only barely) starts to thicken. Remove it from the ice temporarily.

In the small bowl of an electric mixer beat the egg whites with the salt and cream of tartar until the whites thicken and hold a definite shape but not until they are stiff and dry. Reduce the speed to moderate and gradually add the reserved ½ cup of sugar. Increase the speed to high again and continue to beat until the whites are glossy and resemble a thick marshmallow cream.

Replace the bowl of strawberry mixture over the ice again for a few moments. Stir constantly with a rubber spatula until the mixture thickens enough to form a slight mound when some of it is dropped back onto itself off the spatula. (If possible, it should be the same thickness as the beaten whites.)

Gradually fold about half of the strawberry mixture into the beaten egg whites. Then fold the whites into the remaining strawberry mixture.

Pour the mixture into the baked pie shell. If you have made a 9-inch crust you might have more filling than the crust will hold. That's okay. Pour in as much filling as the shell holds—up to the rim—then place the filled crust in the freezer for about 10 minutes until the filling sets a bit. Meanwhile, reserve the excess filling at room temperature. Then add a bit of the remaining filling to the top of the pie, place it in the freezer again very briefly, and then add the rest of the filling.

Refrigerate.

1 9- or 10-inch baked *extra-deep pie shell (see page 17)*
1 pint box (1 pound) fresh strawberries
1 envelope unflavored gelatin
¼ cup cold water
3 eggs, separated
1 tablespoon fresh lemon juice
¾ cup granulated sugar
Scant ¼ teaspoon salt
½ teaspoon cream of tartar

6 TO 8 PORTIONS

There are many ways you can decorate and present this. Whipped cream can be spread over the top, or it can be applied with a pastry bag fitted with a star-shaped tube. If you would like to take care of the whipped cream early in the day and not worry about the cream standing too long, here's the way to do it.

Whipped Cream Topping

Sprinkle the gelatin over the water in a small heatproof custard cup. Let stand for 5 minutes to soften.

Place all but about 2 tablespoons of the cream in a small chilled bowl of the electric mixer. Add the sugar and vanilla. With chilled beaters, beat until the cream holds a very soft shape. Let stand briefly while you melt the gelatin.

Place the cup of gelatin in a little hot water in a small pan over low heat and let stand until the gelatin dissolves.

½ teaspoon unflavored gelatin
1 tablespoon cold water
1 cup heavy cream
1 tablespoon granulated or confectioners sugar
½ teaspoon vanilla extract

Remove the dissolved gelatin from the hot water. Start the mixer again, quickly stir the reserved 2 tablespoons of cream into the warm gelatin, and immediately, while beating, add it to the whipped cream and continue to beat until the cream is stiff enough. Do not overbeat. (This small amount of gelatin will only keep the cream from separating or running; it is not enough to actually set the cream.)

Place the cream over the top of the filling and either smooth it or form it into swirls and peaks. Or fit a pastry bag with a large star-shaped tube, fill the bag with the cream, and form a wreath of whipped cream (by making a series of small, touching, S-shaped turns) or form six or eight large rosettes around the outer edge.

Strawberry Topping (optional)

You will need about 2 cups of berries, washed, hulled, drained, and cut into halves or quarters if they are the very large ones. Mound them in the space left inside the whipped cream. Or, if you have covered the top with whipped cream, do not cut the berries; place them whole, standing point up, all over the top.

A few sprigs of fresh mint in the center look lovely.

Lemon Meringue Pie

This is heaven—pie-in-the-sky heaven. The crust is crisp, bland, flaky; the filling is slightly runny but not too runny and not wet, with a sharp, sour flavor to make you squeal; and the meringue is a sweet cloud on your plate.

It should be baked the day it is served.

Adjust a rack to the center of the oven and preheat oven to 400°. Mix the rind and juice, and set aside. Place the yolks in the small mixing bowl and set aside.

Place the cornstarch, sugar, and salt in a heavy 2-quart saucepan and stir to mix. Gradually add the water, stirring with a rubber spatula until smooth. Place over medium heat and stir gently and constantly until the mixture comes to a low boil. Boil gently, stirring with the rubber spatula, for 1½ minutes.

Add the butter and stir briefly to melt.

Remove from the heat. Add a few large spoonfuls of the hot cornstarch mixture to the yolks, stirring well to mix thoroughly. Then pour the yolk mixture into the cornstarch mixture, stirring gently. Also stir in the lemon rind and juice.

Return to moderate heat and stir gently until the mixture comes to a boil again. Boil, stirring gently, for 1 minute.

Immediately pour the hot mixture into the pie crust and begin to make the meringue (the filling should not be completely cool when you cover it with the meringue).

1 9-inch baked *pie shell (see page 17)*
Finely grated rind of 3 lemons
⅓ *cup fresh lemon juice*
4 egg yolks (you will use the whites for the meringue)
⅓ *cup cornstarch (it is not necessary to sift the cornstarch)*
1½ *cups granulated sugar*
¼ *teaspoon salt*
1½ *cups warm tap water*
2 tablespoons unsalted butter, cut into pieces, at room temperature

6 TO 8 PORTIONS

Meringue

Place the whites, salt, and cream of tartar in the small bowl of an electric mixer and beat at high speed until the whites hold a soft point when the beaters are raised. Reduce the speed to moderate and gradually add the sugar, adding 2 tablespoons at a time and beating about 20 seconds between additions. Then increase the speed to high again and beat only until the mixture holds a firm point when the beaters are raised—it should be stiff but do not overbeat.

It is essential that the meringue touch the crust all around the plate or the meringue will shrink away from the crust when it is baked. The filling should still be quite warm when you put the meringue on. Place the meringue by teaspoonfuls (use

4 egg whites (left from the filling)
Pinch of salt
½ *teaspoon cream of tartar*
½ *cup granulated sugar*

two spoons, one to pick up the meringue and one to push it off) all around the edge, sealing the meringue to the crust. Then gradually place the remaining meringue over the center. First spread it smooth and then, with the back of a teaspoon, pull up the meringue, forming peaks and swirls. It is more attractive if the peaks are few and large rather than many and small.

Bake the pie immediately but only until the meringue is lightly colored on the peaks; it will take 7 to 9 minutes.

Have a draft-free spot ready to cool the pie—a draft could make the meringue fall or weep. (I clear a spot in a dish cabinet.) Place the pie on a rack and let it cool completely.

Serve immediately or refrigerate. The filling becomes firmer when refrigerated; delicious both ways, but I like it best refrigerated.

Mrs. Foster's Lime Pie

For years I had heard raves about a certain pie that was served at a lovely, small, family-style restaurant in New York City. The restaurant was Mr. and Mrs. Foster's Place, but unfortunately it is no longer in business. The pie is a frozen chiffon dream. It tastes somewhat like an extra-sour, fluffy ice cream. I was thrilled when I met Mrs. Foster and she gave me the recipe. It is one that she created years ago—as good as can be, and easy. It can be frozen up to 2 or 3 weeks, and is served directly from the freezer.

Crumb Crust

Prepare a crumb crust (see page 22) with this one exception: Do not use the scant ¼ teaspoon of nutmeg.

Filling

Adjust a rack one-third up and preheat oven to 350°.

In the small bowl of an electric mixer beat the yolks with ½ cup of the sugar (reserving remaining ¼ cup of sugar) at high speed for 5 minutes until the mixture is very pale and thick.

On low speed gradually add the lime juice, scraping the bowl with a rubber spatula and beating only until mixed.

Remove from the mixer and stir in the grated rind.

Turn the mixture into the top of a large double boiler over shallow hot water on moderate heat (the water should simmer gently). Cook, scraping the sides and bottom constantly for 6 or 7 minutes or until the mixture thickens enough to coat a wooden spoon. When it is just done, a candy thermometer will register 175° to 180°.

Remove the top of the double boiler immediately and pour the mixture into a large mixing bowl. Stir occasionally until it cools.

In the large bowl of an electric mixer add the salt to the egg whites and beat until they hold a soft shape. Reduce the speed to moderate and gradually add the reserved ¼ cup of sugar. Increase the speed again and continue to beat until the mixture holds a definite point but not until it is actually stiff or dry.

Gradually, in three additions, fold the yolk mixture into the whites, handling very little and very carefully. It is not necessary to fold the first and second additions thoroughly.

Turn the mixture into the crust. It will look like there is too much filling, but it is all right, just mound it high. (It will be about 4 inches high in the middle.)

Bake for 15 minutes until the top is lightly browned.

Cool on a rack to room temperature. (The pie will shrink slightly as it cools— okay.) Then freeze the pie. When it is frozen, cover it with plastic wrap. The pie may be kept frozen for up to 3 weeks. Serve it frozen.

5 eggs, separated
¾ cup granulated sugar
⅔ cup fresh lime juice (grate the rind of 2 limes before squeezing, to use below; see Notes)
Finely grated rind of 2 limes
⅛ teaspoon salt

8 PORTIONS

Whipped Cream Topping

In a chilled bowl with chilled beaters whip the ingredients until the cream holds a soft shape. (It is better if it is not too stiff.)

The whipped cream may be spread over the top of the pie just before serving. Or, if you do not plan to serve the entire pie at once, the cream may be spooned over each portion individually.

Use a very firm and heavy sharp knife for serving.

1½ cups heavy cream
3 tablespoons granulated sugar
1 teaspoon vanilla extract

NOTES: This is indeed sour. Wonderfully sour! For a sweeter pie, Mrs. Foster suggests cutting down the lime juice to ½ cup. But Mrs. Foster and I both love the full amount.

This is very nice with fresh strawberries put on top just before serving.

Key Lime Pie

People who don't live in South Florida often ask if I have a recipe for Key Lime Pie. They are surprised when I tell them that you need a certain kind of lime called a Key lime (Citrus auranti-folia). They are small, round, and yellow, with a different taste from green Persian limes. These limes grow in the Florida Keys and in the Miami area—and Mexico and the West Indies. They are seldom sold commercially. They were originally planted by the Spaniards for seamen because citrus wards off scurvy.

The original Key Lime Pie was made with a baked crust because it was created before graham crackers were manufactured. And it was topped with baked meringue, never ever with whipped cream, since the recipe, made with canned milk, came about because of a lack of both refrigeration and grazing land for milk cows in the Florida Keys.

But there are endless variations now: crumb crust or baked crust; 2, 3, 4, or 5 eggs; egg whites folded into the filling, or as meringue on top, or not at all; whole eggs used in the filling; whipped cream on top or not; baked or unbaked filling; frozen or unfrozen pie, etc., etc., etc.

Nellie and Joe have been bottling local lime juice for over 20 years now. It is sold all over the country. There is a question about whether or not it is actually Key lime juice, although it is the juice of limes from South Florida and the West Indies. The juice is not reconstituted, and it is indeed the very same juice that is used by most if not all of the South Florida restaurants for what they call Key Lime Pie. (And it is great for limeade or seviche.)

This is the most popular version of all the Key lime pies. It is so easy you will think something is missing. If you are not going to bake it, it must be made the day before serving or it will be too runny.

This recipe can be made with green limes or with lemons, but then it is not a Key Lime Pie. Although it is close. The grated rind of Key limes is bitter and should not be used in the pie. However, if you make this recipe with green limes or with lemons, it will be better if you include the grated rind of 1 or 2 limes or lemons.

Crumb Crust

Mix together the ingredients and follow the directions for a crumb crust (see page 22).

1½ cups graham cracker crumbs
3 tablespoons granulated sugar
½ teaspoon cinnamon
¼ teaspoon nutmeg
3 ounces (¾ stick) unsalted butter, melted

Filling

You can use an electric mixer, an eggbeater, or a wire whisk. Beat the yolks lightly to mix. Add the condensed milk and mix. Gradually add the lime juice, beating or whisking only until mixed.

4 egg yolks
1 14-ounce can sweetened condensed milk
½ cup Key lime juice

Pour into the crumb crust. It will make a thin layer; the color will be pale lemon—not green. It will be fluid now, but as it stands a chemical reaction takes place and the filling will become about as firm as a baked custard.

6 TO 8 PORTIONS

Refrigerate overnight.

Or, if you wish, bake the filled pie for 10 minutes in a 350° oven, then cool and chill.

Whipped cream is optional on this, natives do not use it—restaurants do. (I do.)

Whipped Cream Topping

In a chilled bowl with chilled beaters whip the ingredients until the cream holds a shape and is firm enough to spread over the pie. If you whip the cream ahead of time, refrigerate it. It will separate slightly as it stands; just whisk it a bit with a wire whisk when you are ready to use it.

2 cups heavy cream
¼ cup granulated or confectioners sugar
1 teaspoon vanilla extract

Spread the whipped cream over the cooled filling.

OPTIONAL: Fresh strawberries and Key Lime Pie are a divine combination. Either form a border of them standing up around the rim, or serve them separately.

Frozen Key Lime Pie

A variation of Key Lime Pie. This does not freeze too hard and is delicious served right from the freezer. It will resemble sherbet. I have frozen this pie for weeks and even months and then when I served it, it was perfect.

Follow the preceding recipe with these changes. Use 2 whole eggs, separated (instead of 4 yolks).

*I*n a small bowl beat the yolks until they are pale. Gradually add the condensed milk, beating only to mix.

6 TO 8 PORTIONS

Then on low speed beat in the lime juice. Set aside.

Beat the egg whites with a pinch of salt until they hold a point when the beaters are raised but not until they are stiff or dry.

Fold about one-third of the whites into the lime juice mixture and then, in a large bowl, fold together the lime juice mixture and the remaining beaten whites. Do not handle any more than necessary.

Turn into the prepared crumb crust and smooth the top.

Freeze for about an hour and then wrap airtight with plastic wrap. Continue to freeze the pie.

Orange Angel Pie

This is a famous Florida recipe. Many years ago it won first prize and best-in-show in a Florida cooking contest. Famous Southern hostesses have since made it their own specialty. It has a meringue shell, an orange custard and cream filling, and a whipped cream and fresh orange topping. Luscious!

The meringue shell and the filling should both be made a day before serving (the meringue is too sticky to serve when it is fresh). The topping should be put on shortly before serving.

You will need a 10-inch ovenproof glass pie plate.

Meringue Shell

Adjust a rack one-third up from the bottom of the oven and preheat oven to 275°. Butter a 10-inch ovenproof glass pie plate and set it aside.

In the small bowl of an electric mixer at moderate speed beat the egg whites for a few seconds until they are foamy. Add the salt and cream of tartar, and beat until the whites hold a soft shape but not until they are stiff. Continue to beat at moderate speed and start to add the sugar, adding 1 rounded tablespoonful at a time. Beat for about half a minute between additions. When about half of the sugar has been added, add the vanilla and then continue to add the remaining sugar as before. When all of the sugar has been added, increase the speed to high and beat for 7 to 8 minutes more until the sugar is dissolved—test it by rubbing a bit between your fingers. If it feels grainy, beat some more. The meringue will be very stiff and beautifully shiny. (Total beating time from start to finish is 15 to 18 minutes.)

4 egg whites (you will use the yolks for the filling)
¼ teaspoon salt
¼ teaspoon cream of tartar
1 cup granulated sugar
1 teaspoon vanilla extract

The meringue will be sticky and hard to handle. Use a tablespoon to pick it up with and a rubber spatula to push it off. Place well-rounded tablespoonfuls of the meringue, touching one another, around the side of the plate. (While placing each spoonful around the sides, try to make it form a high peak as you scrape it off the spoon; and remember—the less you fool with it the better it will look.) Then place the remaining meringue over the bottom of the plate. Spread it to form a shell about 1 inch thick, and extending about 1 inch above the sides of the plate. Be careful not to spread the meringue over the edge of the plate; the meringue rises and spreads out during baking and if it has been spread over the edge it might run over the sides and be difficult to serve. (I use the back of a teaspoon along the inside of the rim to bring the meringue up in high peaks, forming a high shell without letting it spread over the rim.)

Bake for 1¼ to 1½ hours until the meringue is a pale sandy color. It should dry out in the oven as much as possible, but the color should not become darker than pale, pale gold.

Turn off the heat, open the oven door slightly, and let the meringue cool in the oven. It will crack as it cools—don't worry—it is all right.

Filling

Grate the rind of the oranges fine (you can grate the lemon rind at the same time if you wish) and set aside. Peel and section the oranges (see page 15). Cut each orange section crossways in half and place the pieces of orange in a strainer set over a bowl. Let them stand to drain well. (The recipe will not use the drained-off juice.)

Place the yolks in the top of a small double boiler off the heat. Beat them with a small wire whisk to mix well. Stir in the sugar, grated orange and lemon rinds, lemon juice, and salt. Place over hot water on moderate heat and cook, stirring and scraping the bottom and sides constantly with a rubber spatula, until the mixture thickens to the consistency of a soft mayonnaise; it should take 8 to 10 minutes.

2 seedless oranges
5 egg yolks
½ cup granulated sugar
Finely grated rind of 1 lemon
2 tablespoons lemon juice
⅛ teaspoon salt
1 cup heavy cream

6 TO 8 PORTIONS

Remove the top of the double boiler, stir in the well-drained, cut-up oranges, and let stand until cool. Then refrigerate briefly to chill slightly.

Meanwhile, in a small chilled bowl with chilled beaters, whip the cream until it is quite firm. Fold a large spoonful of the orange mixture into the cream, fold in another large spoonful, and then fold the remaining orange mixture and the cream together, handling as little as possible—they do not have to be completely blended.

Spoon this filling into the cooled meringue shell.

Refrigerate overnight. After an hour or so, cover the top loosely with plastic wrap.

Before serving, prepare the topping. (If you want to section the oranges for the topping when you make the shell and filling, refrigerate them overnight in their juice, then drain them well in a strainer before using.)

Topping

Peel and section the oranges (see page 15) and place them in a strainer set over a bowl to drain. If you have room in the refrigerator, place the oranges in the strainer in the refrigerator to chill for half an hour or more before serving.

3 seedless oranges
1 cup heavy cream
½ teaspoon vanilla extract
2 tablespoons confectioners sugar

In a small chilled bowl with chilled beaters whip the cream with the vanilla and sugar until it just barely holds a shape but not until it is really stiff. Refrigerate it until you are ready to assemble the pie. (If it stands too long it will separate slightly; just beat it or stir it a bit right before using.)

Shortly before serving (either right before or an hour or two before) place large spoonfuls of the whipped cream around the outer edge of the filling, and cover the center space with a mound of the orange sections.

(This should be easy to serve. But if you have any trouble cutting it, dip the knife in hot water before making each cut.)

VARIATIONS: I have had this pie with a generous sprinkling of shredded coconut all over the whipped cream. And I have heard of it being made with about ¼ cup finely cut-up pecans folded into the meringue just before it is placed in the pie plate. A caterer I know, who says that this pie is her most popular item, uses drained, crushed pineapple on top instead of the sectioned oranges. It lends itself to many of your own ideas.

Colorado High Pie

This has a crumb crust, a layer of sautéed apples, a mountainous topping of especially light and airy rum Bavarian, and a thin layer of whipped cream—divine! The crust can and should be made ahead of time and frozen; the apple filling can be made a day or two ahead; the topping should be made 3 to 10 hours before serving.

Apple Filling

Peel, quarter, and core the apples. Cut each piece in half the long way, and then cut crossways into slices ½ to ¾ inch wide.

Melt the butter in a frying pan with a tight cover. Add the apples and sugar, stir to mix, cover tightly, and cook over moderate heat for a few minutes until the apples have given off their juice. Then uncover and stir over high heat until the apples are tender and all of the liquid has evaporated. The mixture should be like a chunky applesauce. If the liquid evaporates before the apples are tender, cover the pan again, reduce the heat a bit, and let the apples steam, then uncover and stir over high heat again to dry a bit if necessary. Do not overcook.

Set aside the pan and let the apples cool or spread them in a thin layer on a large plate to cool. The apples can be used soon or they can be transferred to any container and refrigerated until you are ready for them.

1 9-inch baked *crumb crust (see page 22)*

2 pounds firm and tart apples *(3 to 4 large apples; Granny Smith are very good)*

2 tablespoons unsalted butter

3 tablespoons granulated *sugar*

6 TO 8 PORTIONS

Rum Chiffon Bavarian

Sprinkle the gelatin over the water in a small cup and let stand. Heat the milk, uncovered, over moderate heat until scalded. In the top of a double boiler, off the heat, stir the yolks just to mix. When the milk has formed a slightly wrinkled skin on its surface, gradually add it to the yolks, stirring as you do. Then stir in ¼ cup of the sugar (reserve remaining ¼ cup).

Place the top of the double boiler over hot water and cook the custard on moderately high heat, scraping the bottom and sides continuously with a rubber spatula until the mixture thickens enough to coat a spoon; that will be 180° on a candy thermometer. Add the softened gelatin and stir to dissolve.

Transfer the mixture to a medium-size bowl and stir in the vanilla and rum. Place the bowl of hot custard into a larger bowl of ice and water.

Using a rubber spatula, scrape the bottom and sides constantly until the mixture has cooled—test it on your wrist—do not let it start to thicken. Remove from the ice water (but reserve the ice water) and set aside.

In a chilled bowl with chilled beaters whip the cream until it holds a definite shape but not until it is really stiff, and set aside.

In the small bowl of the electric mixer beat the 4 egg whites with the salt until they hold a soft shape. Reduce the speed to moderate, gradually add the reserved ¼ cup of sugar, increase the speed to high, and continue to beat only until the whites hold a definite shape, but be careful not to overbeat or they will be too stiff to be folded in. Set aside.

Now, return the custard mixture to the ice water and stir constantly until it barely begins to thicken. Then gradually fold it (about one-third at a time) into the whipped cream; fold this mixture and the whites together. (It is best to do this last folding in a larger bowl. However, do not handle any more than necessary—keep it light and airy.)

To assemble the pie, begin by spreading the apples in the crust.

It will look as though you have more Bavarian than the crust will hold. Indeed you do. Here's how to make it fit. Create some temporary room for the pie in the freezer. Pour about half of the Bavarian (or as much as the crust will hold) over the apples. Place the pie in the freezer for about 5 minutes, just until the Bavarian is slightly set. (Reserve the remaining Bavarian at room temperature.) Then, after about 5 minutes, when the Bavarian on the pie is slightly set, pour or spoon on about one-quarter or one-third of the remaining Bavarian, or as much as it will hold without running over. Replace in the freezer. Continue until all the Bavarian is safely mounded on the pie. Do not allow it to freeze; it will take only a few minutes in the freezer each time. Refrigerate for at least a few hours.

1 envelope unflavored gelatin
¼ cup cold tap water
¾ cup milk
3 eggs, separated, plus 1 additional egg white (the white may be one that was left over from another recipe, frozen, and then thawed)
½ cup granulated sugar
1 teaspoon vanilla extract
¼ cup dark rum
1 cup heavy cream
Pinch of salt

Whipped Cream Topping

A few hours before serving, place the cream, vanilla, and sugar in a chilled bowl and, with chilled beaters, whip only until the cream is stiff enough to hold a shape—be careful not to whip it any more than necessary.

Place the cream by spoonfuls over the top, starting at the edges. Then use the back of the spoon to shape the cream into swirls and peaks.

Sprinkle the middle of the top with the optional bit of shaved chocolate.

1 cup heavy cream
½ teaspoon vanilla extract
2 tablespoons granulated or confectioners sugar
Optional: a bit of shaved semisweet chocolate

Savannah Banana Pie

This has a crumb crust made of Amaretti (Italian macaroons), a layer of sliced bananas, a layer of divine caramel (which is nothing but baked condensed milk), whipped cream, and buttercrunch candy. It is soft/chewy/creamy and crisp/brittle/crunchy—all wonderful. The combination of flavors and textures is out of this world.

This has several parts to it—all easy and fun—but they do take time; start this the day ahead or about 8 hours before serving.

This recipe is adapted from one in Savannah Style, a cookbook by the Junior League of Savannah, Georgia (Kingsport Press, 1980).

Macaroon Crust

This is an irresistibly delicious crust that you can use with any other cooked filling.

Adjust a rack to the middle of the oven and preheat oven to 375°. Prepare a 9-inch pie plate for a crumb crust by lining it with aluminum foil (see Crumb Crust, page 22).

To crumb the macaroons, I place them, still in their tissue paper wrappings, on a firm surface, pound them briefly with my hand or with a cleaver just to break them up, then unwrap and process them in a food processor until they become crumbs. Add the melted butter and process to mix. (Or crumb them any other way and mix them with the butter.)

Turn the mixture into the foil-lined pie plate and press it into place.

Bake for 10 minutes. Cool, then freeze for at least an hour until completely firm. Remove the foil and set aside. See Crumb Crust on how to remove the foil from the plate.

8 ounces Amaretti (see Notes), to make a generous 1½ cups crumbs
3 ounces (¾ stick) unsalted butter, melted

Filling

Adjust a rack to the middle of the oven and preheat oven to 425°.

Pour the condensed milk into an 8- or 9-inch Pyrex pie plate. Cover it airtight with aluminum foil, pressing the edges over the rim of the plate to seal. Place the plate in a large, shallow pan. Pour hot water about ½ inch deep into

1 14-ounce can sweetened condensed milk
3 to 4 ripe but not overripe bananas

8 PORTIONS

the large pan and bake for 1 hour and 20 to 30 minutes. The condensed milk will bake to a rich caramel color. During baking, add more water to the large pan if necessary. Remove the pie plate from the larger pan, then remove the foil covering and set the caramel aside to cool completely.

From 4 to 8 hours before serving, peel the bananas and cut them crosswise into ¼-inch slices. Do the cutting over the crust and let the slices fall into the crust. Flatten the layer of bananas a bit.

With a teaspoon, place small spoonfuls of the cooled caramelized milk all over the bananas (if you place too much in any one spot you will not have enough to go around). Then, with the back of the spoon, smooth the top a bit to cover the bananas completely.

Refrigerate from 4 to 8 hours.

Whipped Cream Topping

About 3 ounces Almond Roca (see Notes)
1½ cups whipping cream
2 tablespoons confectioners sugar
½ teaspoon vanilla extract
1 or 2 drops (only) almond extract

Unwrap the candy and on a cutting board cut down on the candy bars with a small sharp knife to slice the candy thin. Set it aside.

In a small chilled bowl with chilled beaters whip the cream with the sugar and vanilla and almond extracts only until the cream holds a definite shape but not until it is really stiff. (To prevent overwhipping, I whip with an electric mixer until the cream holds a soft shape and then finish the whipping with a wire whisk.)

Place the cream by tablespoonfuls in a circle around the rim of the pie—do not cover the middle of the filling.

Sprinkle the candy over the whipped cream.

Refrigerate and serve very cold.

NOTES: Amaretti, Italian macaroons, are now in almost every "gourmet" store and in many not so "gourmet," as well as in many of the overabundance of mail-order catalogs that have recently flooded our country. The brand I buy is Amaretti di Saronno, Lazzaroni & Company, made with apricot kernels, not almonds.

Almond Roca is a wonderful buttercrunch candy with a crisp center and a chocolate coating made by Brown & Haley in Tacoma, Washington. It comes in a pink tin can and is usually available at any fine food store. English toffee candies or Heath Bars can be substituted.

Old-Fashioned Butterscotch Pie

This old Southern recipe makes a velvety smooth and creamy pie with a rich butterscotch flavor. Make this early in the day to serve that night. (If you wish, the pie crust may be made ahead of time and may be frozen, unbaked, in the pie plate.)

Sprinkle the optional nuts over the bottom of the baked pie shell and set aside. Place the yolks in a medium-size mixing bowl and set aside. Place the butter in a 10- to 12-inch frying pan over moderate heat to melt and begin to brown slightly. (The browned butter adds more flavor.)

Add the brown sugar, stir to mix, and cook over moderate heat, stirring occasionally. After bubbles form all over the surface, continue to boil for 2 minutes, stirring occasionally with a wooden spoon.

Now, be careful with this next step. Have ready a long-handled wooden spoon or rubber spatula. Add the boiling water all at once to the boiling sugar mixture; it will all bubble up furiously and give off steam. Stir over heat until smooth. Remove from the heat and set aside.

Sift together the flour, cornstarch, and salt into a 3-quart saucepan. Gradually stir in the milk. If there are any lumps in the mixture press on them with a rubber spatula to dissolve them. When the mixture is smooth, stir in the hot brown sugar mixture.

Place over medium-low heat and cook, scraping the bottom and sides of the pan constantly with a rubber spatula, until the mixture comes to a boil. Then continue to scrape the pan and let the mixture boil for 1 minute.

Remove from the heat and add a few large spoonfuls of the hot mixture to the egg yolks, mixing well with a small wire whisk. Whisk in a few more spoonfuls. Then pour the yolk mixture into the remaining hot milk mixture, stirring well.

Place over low heat and cook, stirring, until the mixture comes to a low boil. Continue to stir and scrape the pan, and let simmer for 1 minute.

Remove from the heat. Stir in the vanilla. Pour into a large mixing bowl. Stir frequently, very gently, folding the mixture to allow steam to escape, until the mixture is cool.

Turn into the prepared pie shell and refrigerate for several hours.

1 9-inch baked *pie shell (see page 17)*
Optional: 2 ounces (½ cup) pecans, cut or broken into medium-small pieces
3 egg yolks
3 ounces (¾ stick) unsalted butter
1 cup dark brown sugar, firmly packed
1 cup boiling water
2 tablespoons unsifted all-purpose flour
3 tablespoons cornstarch
Scant ½ teaspoon salt
1⅔ cups milk
1¼ teaspoons vanilla extract

6 TO 8 PORTIONS

Whipped Cream Topping

In a chilled bowl with chilled beaters whip the ingredients until the cream holds a firm shape. Place the whipped cream by spoonfuls all over the top of the pie, placing the spoonfuls around the rim first and on the center. If you have a cake-decorating turntable place the pie plate on it. With a long, narrow metal spatula smooth the whipped cream. Then, if you wish, use the back of a spoon to form a few large swirls in the cream.

1 cup heavy cream
2 tablespoons granulated or confectioners sugar
½ teaspoon vanilla extract

Coconut Cream Pie

This is a very old-fashioned, traditional Southern pie that is creamy-thick and full of coconut. When it has been refrigerated enough, the filling will be just barely thick enough to hold its shape (that is the way it should be); it must be refrigerated at least 5 to 6 hours before it is served.

Sift the flour, sugar, and salt together into the top of a large double boiler off the heat. Add the milk very gradually at first, whisking it in with a small wire whisk, until the mixture is smooth. With a rubber spatula stir in the coconut.

Put a little hot water in the bottom of the double boiler, place the top over it, and cook on moderate heat. (It is all right if the water boils.) Stir and scrape the bottom and sides frequently with the spatula for about 10 minutes until the mixture thickens. Then continue to cook, stirring occasionally for 10 minutes more.

Place the egg yolks in a mixing bowl. Add a bit of the hot coconut mixture, stirring well as you do. Con-

1 9-inch baked pie shell (see page 17)
6 tablespoons unsifted all-purpose flour
½ cup granulated sugar
¼ teaspoon salt
2 cups milk
1 cup shredded coconut
2 egg yolks
1 tablespoon unsalted butter
¾ teaspoon vanilla extract
Scant ¼ teaspoon almond extract

8 PORTIONS

tinue, gradually mixing in about half of the coconut mixture. Then stir the yolk mixture into the remaining coconut mixture.

Replace over the hot water on moderate heat and cook, stirring, for 2 minutes more.

Remove from the heat. Add the butter, vanilla and almond extracts, and mix gently.

Transfer to a wide bowl to cool, occasionally stirring gently.

Pour the cooled coconut mixture into the pie shell.

Whipped Cream Topping

In a chilled bowl with chilled beaters whip the cream, sugar, and vanilla until the cream holds a definite shape. Spoon the cream over the top of the filling and spread it smoothly or form it into swirls and peaks. Sprinkle generously with the coconut.

Refrigerate for at least 5 or 6 hours. (It is a good idea to set the refrigerator control to coldest for a few hours before serving the pie.)

1 cup heavy cream
2 tablespoons granulated or confectioners sugar
½ teaspoon vanilla extract
About ½ cup shredded coconut

Coffee and Cognac Cream Pie

This is positively wonderful! It is a small pie (made in an 8-inch plate) with a wonderfully crunchy crust of crumbled Amaretti and butter… with a smooth, creamy, dreamy, barely set filling of coffee, cognac, and whipped cream… topped with more whipped cream and chocolate shavings or grated chocolate.

Although it can be cut into six small portions, it is not too much for four. Or maybe two.

The crust can be made way ahead and frozen, or it can be made about 2 hours before you use it. The filling is best if you make it the day you serve it, but it can be made early. And I suggest that you put the whipped cream on top no earlier than necessary, but a few hours ahead is okay.

Get ready for a treat.

Pie Crust

Prepare an 8-inch glass pie plate as follows: Turn the plate upside down, cover it with a large square of aluminum foil, press down on the sides of the foil to shape it, then remove the foil, turn the plate right side up, and place the foil in the plate. Press it smoothly into place and fold the corners and the edge of the foil back over the rim of the plate.

In a bowl mix the crumbs and butter.

Turn the crust mixture into the plate. With your fingertips distribute it loosely over the bottom and then the sides of the plate. Press it firmly into place (it must be firm), first pressing the sides and then the bottom. (This crust does not get baked.)

Place the crust in the freezer for at least an hour or two, or as much longer as you wish. (If you leave it longer, wrap it in plastic wrap.)

When you are ready to use the crust (or anytime after it is frozen) remove the foil as follows: Turn the edges of the foil up. Carefully lift the foil and the frozen crust. Slowly and carefully peel the foil away, holding the crust upright on your left hand as you peel with your right hand. When the foil is removed, gently replace the crust in the plate, holding a knife or a small spatula under the crust to ease it in slowly.

Now the crust can wait at room temperature or in the refrigerator while you prepare the filling.

4 to 5 ounces Amaretti (to make 1 cup of crumbs, see Note)

3 ounces (¾ stick) unsalted butter, melted

Filling

In a small heatproof cup sprinkle the gelatin over the water. Dissolve the coffee in the boiling water. Set aside.

In the small bowl of an electric mixer beat the yolks with the sugar at high speed for about 5 minutes until the mixture is thick and almost white. Mix in the salt and vanilla.

Place the cup of gelatin in a little hot water in a small pan over low heat until the gelatin is dissolved.

Then mix the gelatin with the coffee and cognac and, gradually, on very low speed, add the mixture to the yolks, scraping the bowl with a rubber spatula and beating only until smooth. Set aside.

In a small chilled bowl with chilled beaters whip the cream only until it holds a shape, not until it is really stiff. Let the whipped cream stand now until you are ready for it.

Place the bowl containing the egg yolk mixture into a larger bowl half filled with ice and water, and scrape the

1½ teaspoons unflavored gelatin

2 tablespoons water

1½ tablespoons instant espresso or other instant coffee

2 tablespoons boiling water

3 egg yolks

½ cup granulated sugar

¼ teaspoon salt

½ teaspoon vanilla extract

¼ cup cognac

1 cup heavy cream

6 PORTIONS

yolks' bowl constantly with a rubber spatula until the mixture thickens to the consistency of a heavy cream sauce.

Fold about half of the egg yolk mixture into the whipped cream and then fold the cream into the remaining yolk mixture.

Very carefully pour the filling into the prepared crust. Watch the edges to be sure it doesn't run over. There will probably be more filling than the crust will hold. If so, do not use it all at once. Place the filled crust in the freezer or the refrigerator briefly only until the filling begins to set. Then add the remaining filling, pouring it carefully onto the center of the pie.

Refrigerate for at least 2 hours.

Whipped Cream Topping

In a chilled bowl with chilled beaters whip the cream with the sugar and vanilla only until the cream holds a shape but not until it is really stiff.

Fit a pastry bag with a large star-shaped tube. Fold down a deep cuff on the outside of the bag. Transfer the whipped cream to the bag. Close the top and press from the top, forming large rosettes of cream in a border around the rim of the pie. Sprinkle the chocolate shavings or grated chocolate on the filling in the middle. Or, if you prefer, simply spread the cream all over the top.

Refrigerate.

1 cup heavy cream
1 tablespoon plus 1 teaspoon
*   granulated sugar*
½ teaspoon vanilla extract
Chocolate shavings or grated
*   chocolate*

NOTE: Amaretti are Italian macaroons—extra dry and crunchy with a very special taste and texture. They are made in two sizes: The large size comes wrapped two together in tissue paper; the small size is called Amarettini. (They are available at specialty food stores.) To make 1 cup of crumbs you will need about 8 tissue-paper packages, or a scant 4 ounces. To crumble them, place the packages on a board or work surface, whack them with a heavy cleaver, then unwrap the papers and grind the Amaretti in a food processor or a blender until the crumbs are fine. The Amarettini do not have to be crumbled before they are processed or blended. Or you can place them in a bag and crush them with a rolling pin. Either way, they must be fine crumbs.

Amaretti do make an extraordinary crust, but the pie can be delicious even if you don't have Amaretti. Any other kind of crumbs may be substituted—either graham crackers, chocolate wafers, zwieback, or Oreo cookies (crumble the Oreo cookies and the filling together), etc.

Frozen Peanut Butter Pie

This is served frozen; it may be made many days or even a week or two ahead. It is something like chocolate peanut butter ice cream. The crust is made with chocolate cookies and salted peanuts; the filling has milk chocolate, cream cheese, peanut butter, and whipped cream. It never freezes too hard to serve easily.

This is adapted from a non-chocolate pie that is served at Mary Mac's Tearoom in Atlanta.

Chocolate Wafer Crumb Crust

Make crumbs of the cookies; break them coarse and crumble in a food processor or a blender until fine. Set aside in a bowl. In the processor or blender grind the nuts until fine. Add the nuts to the crumbs. Melt the butter and add it to the nut and crumb mixture; stir to mix thoroughly.

Line a 9-inch pie plate with foil and shape and bake the crust, following the directions for a crumb crust (see page 22).

6 ounces (24 wafers)
  chocolate wafers (to make
  1¼ cups crumbs)
¼ cup salted peanuts
3 ounces (¾ stick) unsalted
  butter

Filling

Break up the chocolate and place it in the top of a small double boiler over shallow warm water on low heat. Cover the pot with a folded paper towel (to absorb steam) and with the pot cover. Let stand until almost melted, then uncover and stir until completely melted and smooth.

Meanwhile, in the large bowl of an electric mixer, beat the cream cheese and peanut butter until soft and perfectly smooth. Beat in the chocolate. On low speed gradually beat in the milk, scraping the sides of the bowl as necessary. Beat in the sugar. Remove the bowl from the mixer.

In the small bowl of an electric mixer with clean beaters whip the cream until it holds a shape.

Add the whipped cream all at once to the peanut butter mixture and fold together gently only until just incorporated.

Pour as much of the filling into the crust as it will hold comfortably. Let the remaining filling stand at room temperature. Place the filled crust in the freezer for

8 ounces milk chocolate
8 ounces Philadelphia brand
  cream cheese, at room
  temperature
½ cup smooth peanut butter
¾ cup milk
1 cup confectioners sugar,
  strained or sifted
1 cup whipping cream

8 PORTIONS

about 10 minutes. Then pour on about half of the reserved filling. Freeze again for about 10 minutes. Then add all of the remaining filling to the pie, and return it to the freezer.

Freeze until the top is firm and then cover airtight with plastic wrap. Store in the freezer.

Transfer to the refrigerator for 10 to 15 minutes before serving.

Marbleized Chiffon Pie

This is a very old recipe that the Hershey company used to print on the labels of large bars of milk chocolate. Why did they stop? The filling is similar to a Bavarian mixture, but just before it is turned into the crust it is mixed (only slightly) with melted milk chocolate (giving a marbleized effect).

The combinations of light, airy, and fluffy with crisp, crunchy, chewy, and milk chocolate with whipped cream are sensational. It is a fabulous pie.

Break up the chocolate and place it in the top of a double boiler over warm water on low heat. Cover the top of the pot with a folded paper towel (to absorb steam), then with the pot cover, and let cook very slowly until the chocolate is melted. Then uncover, remove from the hot water, and set aside to cool to room temperature, stirring occasionally with a rubber spatula.

Place the cold tap water in a small custard cup, sprinkle the gelatin over the top, and let stand.

Place the milk in the top of a small double boiler over warm water on moderate heat and let cook, uncovered, until scalded (or until there is a lightly wrinkled skin on the top of the milk).

Meanwhile, place the yolks in a small bowl and beat them with a whisk until well mixed. (Place the bowl on a folded towel to prevent slipping.) While beating with the whisk, gradually add 3 tablespoons of the sugar (reserve the remaining 2 tablespoons of sugar). Whisk briskly until pale.

1 9-inch baked crumb crust (see page 22)
8 ounces milk chocolate
¼ cup cold tap water
1 envelope unflavored gelatin
⅔ cup milk
2 eggs, separated
5 tablespoons granulated sugar
½ teaspoon vanilla extract
1 cup whipping cream
Pinch of salt

8 PORTIONS

Gradually add the hot scalded milk to the egg yolk mixture, whisking constantly. Then return the mixture to the top of the small double boiler over warm water on moderate heat. Cook, scraping the bottom and sides with a rubber spatula, until slightly thickened. (When it is just right it will register 180° on a candy thermometer.)

Remove the top of the double boiler. Add the softened gelatin, stir until melted, add the vanilla, and transfer to a rather large mixing bowl. Let stand for a few minutes.

Meanwhile, in a chilled bowl with chilled beaters, whip the cream until it holds a shape but not until it is really stiff. Set aside.

In a small bowl with clean beaters whip the egg whites with the salt until the whites hold a soft shape. Gradually add the remaining 2 tablespoons of sugar, and beat only until the whites just barely hold a firm shape but not until they are stiff or dry. Set aside.

Place the bowl of milk and egg yolk mixture into a larger bowl of ice and water. Stir and scrape the bottom and sides constantly until the mixture cools, chills, and then just barely begins to thicken. Do not let it actually set. Remove from the ice and water.

In three or four small additions fold half of the chilled mixture into the whipped cream and the other half into the beaten egg whites.

In the large bowl that the milk and egg yolk mixture chilled in, fold together the whipped cream mixture and the egg white mixture.

Add the room-temperature melted chocolate. Fold together (with a large rubber spatula) very briefly (only two or three foldings) until the mixtures are roughly marbleized. Do not overdo it. (When you serve the pie you will see that the chocolate and filling have formed a fascinating layered effect.)

Pour as much of the marbleized mixture into the crusts as it will hold. Place in the freezer or refrigerator for only a few minutes to harden slightly, then pour the remaining marbleized mixture on the top.

Refrigerate for at least 3 to 4 hours.

Whipped Cream Topping

In a chilled bowl with chilled beaters whip the cream with the sugar and vanilla until it holds a shape.

Either spread the cream to cover the top of the pie or put it in a pastry bag fitted with a star tube and press out in a design over the top of the pie.

If you like, sprinkle the top generously with coarsely grated milk chocolate or with milk chocolate curls made with a vegetable parer.

Use a rather long, heavy knife to cut portions.

1 cup whipping cream
2 tablespoons granulated or
  confectioners sugar
½ teaspoon vanilla extract
Optional: milk chocolate

Salted Almond Chocolate Pie

When a new taste sensation hits the nation it doesn't take long to spread from coast to coast. All over the country, people are discovering the taste appeal of chocolate that is both sweet and salty. It's new, it's tantalizing, it's delicious.

This has a crisp, crumb crust made of chocolate wafer cookies (I use Nabisco). The soft and gooey milk chocolate filling has marshmallows and coarsely chopped, chunky, roasted salted almonds. It is served frozen, at which point it is similar to ice cream (when the pieces of marshmallow in the filling are frozen they become wonderfully deliciously chewy).

The crust can be made ahead of time and stored in the freezer, if you wish. The filling is quick and easy. The pie should be frozen for at least 3 hours before serving—although it can wait in the freezer for days.

Chocolate Wafer Crumb Crust

Adjust a rack one-third up from the bottom of the oven and preheat oven to 300°. Line a 9-inch pie plate with aluminum foil (see Crumb Crust, page 22).

6 ounces bought chocolate wafer cookies (to make 1½ cups crumbs)

3 ounces (¾ stick) unsalted butter, melted

Coarsely break up the chocolate wafers and spin them in a food processor—or pound them in a bag—to make crumbs. Mix the crumbs with the melted butter and turn into the lined pie plate; press into shape. Bake for 15 minutes. (This chocolate crumb crust should be baked longer and slower than the usual crumb crust; it will become especially dry, crisp, and crunchy.) Then turn off the heat, open the oven door, and let the crust stand in the oven to cool off slowly.

When it is cool, place the crust in the freezer for at least an hour and then remove the foil lining. Refrigerate until ready to fill. See Crumb Crust for directions on how to shape the crust, bake, cool, and freeze it, and how to remove the foil from the plate.

Salted Almond Chocolate Filling

This is a new version of an old favorite called Chocolate Mallow.

With wet scissors (dipped in cold water) cut 16 marshmallows into quarters (reserve the remaining 4 marshmallows). Place cut marshmallows in the top of a large double boiler. Break up the chocolate and add it, then add the light cream. Place over hot water on medium heat. Cover and cook, stirring occasionally, until the marshmallows and chocolate are melted.

Meanwhile, with wet scissors, cut the remaining 4 marshmallows into pieces about ½ inch in size. Set them aside.

Chop the nuts very coarsely; they should not be fine. I use a small rounded wooden chopping bowl with a round-bladed knife. Or you can chop them on a board with a heavy chef's knife. (Cutting each nut into 4 or 5 pieces is about right, but they should be uneven, with some larger pieces.) Set the nuts aside.

In a small bowl with chilled beaters whip the cream until it just holds a shape. Refrigerate the whipped cream until you are ready for it.

When the chocolate mixture is melted and smooth, remove it from the hot water and set it aside, stirring occasionally until completely cool. (To save time place the top of the double boiler into a bowl of ice and water and stir constantly until cool.) The cooled chocolate mixture will be quite stiff. Fold in the nuts, the reserved marshmallows, and then the whipped cream in several additions. Do not fold any more than necessary: It is all right if some of the cream is not completely incorporated.

Turn the mixture into the crust. Smooth the top. Freeze for at least 3 hours.

Unless you plan to freeze the pie for days, do not cover it, because the wrapping might stick. If you are freezing for longer, place the pie in a box.

20 marshmallows
8 ounces milk chocolate
½ cup light cream
⅓ cup roasted salted almonds (in the nut section of most supermarkets; I buy Blue Diamond brand)
1 cup heavy cream

6 TO 8 PORTIONS

Chocolate Mousse Pie

This is from the Wine Cellar restaurant in Charleston, South Carolina. It has a crumb crust made of chocolate wafers and a dense rum-flavored chocolate mousse filling. Whipped cream and chocolate curls or grated chocolate are on top.

The crust can be made ahead of time and frozen, if you wish. The filling should be refrigerated overnight after it is in the crust. The whipped cream can be fixed at the last minute or a few hours before serving.

Chocolate Wafer Crumb Crust

Adjust a rack one-third up from the bottom of the oven and preheat oven to 375°. Line a 9-inch pie plate with aluminum foil (see Crumb Crust, page 22).

Coarsely break up all but 9 of the cookies (you will not use them for this recipe) and place them in a food processor fitted with the metal chopping blade. Add the coffee and process until you have even crumbs. (The cookies can be crushed by placing them, with the coffee, in a double or triple plastic bag and rolling over them with a rolling pin.) Place the crumbs in a mixing bowl.

Melt the butter and stir it into the crumbs with a rubber spatula.

Turn the mixture into the prepared pie plate. See Crumb Crust for directions on how to shape the crust, bake, cool, and freeze it, and how to remove the foil from the plate.

18½-ounce package of chocolate wafer cookies (Oreo sandwich cookies can be substituted, filling and all) to make 1½ cups crumbs

1 teaspoon powdered (not granular) instant coffee or espresso

3 ounces (¾ stick) unsalted butter

Chocolate Mousse Filling

Break up the chocolate and place it in the top of a large double boiler over hot water on moderate heat. Cover with a folded paper towel (to absorb steam) and the pot cover. Let cook until the chocolate is almost all melted. Then uncover and stir until smooth. Remove the top of the double boiler and set it aside to cool.

Separate 2 of the eggs; set aside the whites. In a rather small bowl place 1 egg and the 2 egg yolks. Beat or whisk until mixed. Mix in the rum and set aside.

6 ounces semisweet chocolate (see Note)

3 eggs

3 tablespoons dark rum

1 cup whipping cream

8 PORTIONS

In a small chilled bowl with chilled beaters whip the cream until it just holds a point when the beaters are raised. Set aside.

In a clean small bowl with clean beaters beat the 2 egg whites until they hold a firm shape when the beaters are raised but not until they are stiff or dry. Set aside.

Add the egg and the rum mixture to the chocolate and mix briskly with a small wire whisk until smooth.

Very gradually at first, fold about half of the chocolate mixture into the beaten whites. Then, in a larger bowl, fold together the remaining chocolate and the whites.

Now, very gradually at first, fold about half of the chocolate mixture into the whipped cream. Then fold the whipped cream into the remaining chocolate mixture. Do not handle any more than necessary during any of this folding together.

Pour the mousse into the prepared crust, smooth the top with the back of a spoon, and refrigerate, uncovered, overnight.

Whipped Cream Topping

In a chilled bowl with chilled beaters whip the ingredients until the cream is stiff enough to hold its shape. It should be firm enough not to run when the pie is served, but a bit too soft is always nicer than a bit too stiff.

Place the cream evenly by large spoonfuls over the filling, and then smooth the top. Leave it smooth or form peaks with the bottom of a large spoon.

1½ cups whipping cream
3 tablespoons granulated or confectioners sugar
2 tablespoons rum
½ teaspoon vanilla extract

Chocolate Topping

Work directly over the pie or over a length of wax paper. Form milk chocolate curls with a vegetable parer or grate semisweet chocolate with a cheese grater onto the pie.

Refrigerate for a few hours, if you wish, or serve immediately.

Milk chocolate curls or grated semisweet chocolate

NOTE: I generally reach for Tobler Tradition or Lindt Excellence when a recipe calls for semisweet chocolate. Lately, I have also been using a lot of Poulain. However, a neighbor of ours recently made this pie with semisweet chocolate morsels and it was delicious.

Florida Cream Cheese Pie

This delicious pie is adapted from Jane Nickerson's Florida Cookbook (University of Florida Press, 1973). Mrs. Nickerson was food editor for The New York Times for many years.

The pie is filled with a light and fluffy cream cheese/gelatin mixture that is full of fresh orange sections; biting through the bland/sweet cheese mixture and at the same time the sweet/tart/juicy orange is a taste thrill.

This makes a lovely dessert, even after a large meal. It can be served a few hours after it is made or it can wait overnight.

Drain the orange sections in a large strainer set over a large bowl and set aside. Place the ½ cup of juice in a small custard cup. Sprinkle the gelatin over it and let stand for 3 to 5 minutes. Then place the cup in a little hot water in a small pan over low heat. Let stand for a few minutes until the gelatin is dissolved. Then remove it from the water and set aside briefly.

Meanwhile, place the cheese in the large bowl of an electric mixer and beat until smooth and soft. Add the sugar and then the milk and beat well. Then stir the gelatin mixture and gradually add it to the cheese mixture, scraping the bowl with a rubber spatula, and beating until perfectly smooth.

In a small chilled bowl with chilled beaters whip the cream until it holds a definite shape when the beaters are raised but not until it is really stiff. Set aside.

Put some ice and water in a large bowl, filling it about one-quarter full. Place the bowl of cream cheese mixture in the ice and water. Stir with a rubber spatula until the mixture thickens just so that it barely mounds when dropped from the spatula. Remove from the ice water, saving the ice water.

Immediately fold about half of the cheese mixture into the whipped cream. Then fold the whipped cream into the remaining cheese mixture.

Replace the bowl of cheese mixture in the larger bowl of ice and water. Stir very gently until the mixture begins to hold a shape. Then gently fold in the drained orange sections and turn it all into the pie crust, mounding it high in the middle.

Refrigerate.

1 9-inch baked *extra-deep* pie shell (*see page 17*)

1½ cups orange sections (*see page 15; you will need 4 or 5 large seedless oranges*)

½ cup fresh orange juice (*may be drained from the oranges or may be additional*)

1 envelope unflavored gelatin

8 ounces Philadelphia brand cream cheese at room temperature

½ cup granulated sugar

½ cup milk

1 cup heavy cream

6 TO 8 PORTIONS

NOTE: Mrs. Nickerson also makes this in a graham cracker crust. It is delicious, but since a crumb crust is not as deep as a baked crust, there is always some filling left over. If you use a crumb crust, pour the extra filling into one or two wine glasses or custard cups to serve separately.

Creamy Coconut Cream Cheese Pie

This easy pie, in a spicy crumb crust, is filled with a mixture of coconut, cream cheese, whipped cream, and cognac and crème de cacao, which makes it a sort of a Brandy Alexander cheese pie (if you use gin in place of the cognac you will have a Gin Alexander pie). It has an optional chocolate sauce. All in all, it is a delicious and unusual dessert.

Crumb Crust

Mix together the ingredients and follow the directions for a crumb crust (see page 22), using a 9-inch pie plate.

1¼ cups graham cracker crumbs
1 tablespoon granulated sugar
1 teaspoon ginger
1 teaspoon cinnamon
2 ounces (½ stick) unsalted butter, melted

Filling

Place the cream cheese, sugar, milk, coconut, cognac, and crème de cacao in the bowl of a food processor or in the jar of a blender. Process or blend for 30 seconds. The mixture should be thoroughly mixed and the coconut shreds should be cut into smaller pieces but should not be too fine. Transfer this mixture to a large mixing bowl.

Sprinkle the gelatin over the water in a small heatproof cup. Let stand for about 5 minutes to soften. Then place the cup in a little hot water in a small saucepan or frying pan over low heat. Let stand only until the gelatin is dissolved. Then remove from the hot water and set aside for a moment.

Meanwhile, as the gelatin is dissolving, remove and set aside about 2 tablespoons of the heavy cream. In a chilled bowl with chilled beaters (it can be the small bowl of the electric mixer if you wish) whip the remaining cream only until it holds a very soft shape. Quickly stir the reserved 2 tablespoons of cream into the gelatin and quickly, while beating, add the gelatin all at once to the partially whipped cream, and continue to beat until the cream holds a definite shape, but not until it is really stiff.

Fold the whipped cream mixture and the cheese mixture together. If the mixture is runny, place some ice and water in a large bowl, place the bowl of filling in the ice water, and stir or fold very gently only until the mixture thickens enough so it can be slightly mounded in the crust.

Pour the filling into the crust, mounding it slightly.

Refrigerate for 4 to 10 hours.

Serve just as it is, or with the following sauce.

6 ounces Philadelphia brand
  cream cheese, at room
  temperature
2 tablespoons granulated
  sugar
¼ cup milk
3⅓ ounces (1 to 1⅓ cups)
  shredded coconut
2 tablespoons cognac or
  brandy
2 tablespoons crème de cacao
1 envelope unflavored gelatin
¼ cup cold tap water
2 cups heavy cream

8 PORTIONS

Bimini Chocolate Sauce

Place all the ingredients in a small, heavy saucepan over low heat. Stir occasionally until the chocolate is melted. Then stir the sauce briskly with a small wire whisk until it is as smooth as honey.

The sauce should be served at room temperature, poured or spooned over the top of the pie. (If you serve this sauce with ice cream, it may be served cool or warm.)

If the sauce thickens too much while it stands, stir it with a wire whisk to soften, or, if necessary, stir over hot water to soften.

NOTE: I use Tobler or Lindt extra-bittersweet, or Tobler Tradition or Lindt Excellence (both semisweet)—you can use any semisweet.

½ cup heavy cream
6 ounces semisweet chocolate,
  coarsely chopped or broken
  (see Note)
2 tablespoons unsalted butter

Apple Cream Cheese Pie

Cheesecake is so popular in America that some people believe we should change "as American as apple pie" to "as American as cheesecake." How about a combination of the two?

This is a cream cheese pie in a graham cracker crust. But under the cheese is a surprise: a generous layer of apples, walnuts, raisins, ginger, cinnamon, brown sugar, and butter. The combination is delirious, delicious, delovely. The whole experience—that's American.

P eel, quarter, and core the apples. Cut them into about ¾-inch chunks. Melt the butter in a large frying pan.

Add the apples, sugar, and lemon juice. Stir to mix. Cover and let steam for a few minutes, stirring occasionally until the apples are barely tender. Then uncover and cook, stirring until the liquid is almost all evaporated. Stir in the cinnamon, nutmeg, raisins, walnuts, and the ginger, and continue to cook, stirring, for a few minutes until the liquid has evaporated and the apples are just tender. Set aside to cool.

Prepare the cheese mixture.

1 9-inch baked crumb crust
(see page 22)
2 large or 3 medium tart
cooking apples (preferably
Granny Smith)
1 tablespoon butter
3 tablespoons dark or light
brown sugar, firmly packed
1 to 2 teaspoons lemon juice
(depending on the tartness
of the apples)
1 teaspoon cinnamon
¼ teaspoon nutmeg
¼ cup raisins
½ cup walnuts, broken into
medium-size pieces
3 to 4 tablespoons candied or
preserved ginger, cut into
¼-inch pieces

6 GENEROUS PORTIONS

Cheese Mixture

Adjust a rack one-third up from the bottom of the oven and preheat oven to 350°.

In the small bowl of an electric mixer beat the cheese until it is soft and smooth. Beat in the vanilla and sugar until mixed, then beat in the cream and finally the eggs one at a time, scraping the bowl with a rubber spatula and beating until smooth. (Do not beat any more than necessary after adding the eggs; this should not become airy.)

Turn the apple mixture into the crust and smooth the top.

12 ounces Philadelphia brand
cream cheese, preferably at
room temperature
1 teaspoon vanilla extract
½ cup granulated sugar
⅓ cup whipping cream, sour
cream, or Crème Fraîche
(see page 255)
2 eggs

Pour the cheese mixture very slowly over the center of the apples. Do not add it quickly or all at once. Depending on the size of the apples and on the depth of the crust, you might or might not have room for all of the cheese mixture. Don't take a chance. If it looks as though the cheese mixture might run over the edge, do not use it all.

Bake for 25 minutes.

Cool to room temperature, and then refrigerate for several hours or overnight.

Blueberry Cream Cheese Pie

When blueberries are at the height of their season and you can find big beautiful ones, this is the dessert to make. It is scrumptious and easy, and it can be made hours or a day ahead, if you wish. You must make the crust ahead of time. (If you have a graham cracker crust all baked and ready to go in your freezer, then making this pie is a snap.)

Adjust a rack one-third up from the bottom of the oven and preheat oven to 350°. In the small bowl of an electric mixer beat the cheese until it is soft and smooth. Add the vanilla and sugar and beat until mixed. Beat in the cream and then the eggs one at a time, scraping the bowl with a rubber spatula and beating until smooth. (Do not beat any more than necessary after adding the eggs; this should not become airy.)

Pour the filling into the crust and bake for 25 minutes.

Remove from the oven and let stand until cool. Refrigerate for about an hour, or overnight, if you wish.

1 9-inch baked *crumb crust*
   (see page 22)
12 ounces Philadelphia brand
   cream cheese, preferably at
   room temperature
1 teaspoon vanilla extract
½ cup granulated sugar
⅓ cup whipping cream, sour
   cream, or Crème Fraîche
   (see page 255)
2 eggs

6 GENEROUS PORTIONS

Topping

Wash the berries (see To Wash Blueberries, page 14) and drain to dry.

In a small, shallow pan melt ½ cup of the jelly over moderate heat, stirring occasionally. Bring the jelly to a boil and simmer gently for a minute or two.

With a pastry brush, brush a thin layer of the jelly over the top of the pie (directly onto the cream cheese filing). Set the remaining jelly aside to cool a bit and thicken slightly.

When the jelly has just barely begun to thicken and the berries are thoroughly dry (and the cream cheese filling is cold), place the berries and the jelly in a bowl and very gently, with a rubber spatula, fold the berries and the jelly together until the berries are thoroughly coated.

Turn the mixture out over the top of the pie. With your fingers, carefully move the berries around, as necessary, so that they touch the crust on the sides and they cover the top nicely.

A bit of the jelly should run out between the berries to fill in the spaces between the berries and the rim. If it does not, melt a few more tablespoons of the jelly and, with a small spoon, gradually drizzle on a bit more jelly, until there is just enough to cover the cheese where it shows next to the rim, but be careful not to use so much that it runs out over the crust.

Refrigerate for a few hours, or all day, or overnight.

3 cups fresh blueberries
About ½ cup red currant jelly

Peach Cream Cheese Pie

Peaches and blueberries are in season at the same time. That poses a serious problem: which cheesecake to make? Should it be the preceding blueberry one, or this? They are equally fabulous. It probably depends on which fruit is nicer. But there is one other consideration. This peach recipe does not hold up overnight. However, you can have the crust all made and in the freezer, you can make the cream cheese filling the day before serving, and then finish the peach part just an hour or two before serving (it only takes a few minutes). For a party make both and let your guests have their choice.

djust a rack one-third up from the bottom of the oven and preheat oven to 350°. In the small bowl of an electric mixer beat the cheese until it is soft and smooth. Add the vanilla and sugar and beat until mixed. Beat in the cream and then the eggs one at a time, scraping the bowl with a rubber spatula and beating until smooth. (Do not beat any more than necessary after adding the eggs; this should not become airy.)

Pour the filling into the crust and bake for 25 minutes.

Remove from the oven and let stand until cool. Refrigerate for an hour, or overnight if you wish.

1 9-inch baked crumb crust
(see page 22)
12 ounces Philadelphia brand
cream cheese, preferably at
room temperature
1 teaspoon vanilla extract
½ cup granulated sugar
⅓ cup whipping cream, sour
cream, or Crème Fraîche
(see page 255)
2 eggs

Peach Topping

Peel the peaches (see page 178) and place them in a bowl of acidulated water (water mixed with the juice of a lemon to keep the peaches from discoloring).

Place the preserves in a small, shallow pan over moderate heat. Stir occasionally until the preserves come to a boil, simmer for a minute or two, and then force the preserves through a strainer. Stir in the almond extract.

Brush a thin layer of the preserves over the top of the pie (directly onto the cream cheese filling).

Then drain the peaches on a large, heavy towel. Cut each peach in half, remove the pit, and then cut each half into about six lengthwise slices. Drain the slices briefly on the towel. Then arrange the slices so that they overlap slightly and make a nice, even ring at the right angles to, and touching, the crust. Cut the remaining peaches into ⅓- to ½-inch chunks. Place the chunks in the middle of the pie.

With a pastry brush, gently and generously brush the remaining preserves all over the peaches and over any spaces between the peaches. If you do not have enough, melt and strain a bit more.

Refrigerate.

If the pie stands for more than an hour or two, the glaze will dry and the peaches will become dull. If this happens, just before serving, melt and strain still more preserves and brush over the peaches again.

About 3 large, just-ripe fresh
freestone peaches
About ½ cup apricot preserves
¼ teaspoon almond extract

6 GENEROUS PORTIONS

Lemon Cream Cheese Pie

The smooth and creamy filling is a combination of cream cheese and cottage cheese or ricotta, which makes a slightly lighter mixture than many others. And the smooth and creamy topping is a mixture of half sour cream and half sweet cream.

A sensational dessert. It is easy and you will love it.

Crumb Crust

Mix together the ingredients and follow the directions for a crumb crust (see page 22), using a 9-inch pie plate.

1¼ cups graham cracker crumbs
1 tablespoon granulated sugar
1 teaspoon cinnamon
½ teaspoon nutmeg
½ teaspoon ground ginger
Pinch of allspice
3 ounces (¾ stick) unsalted butter, melted

Filling

Adjust a rack to the middle of the oven and preheat oven to 350°.

Mix the rind and juice and set aside. In a processor fitted with the metal chopping blade or in a few additions in a blender process or blend the cottage cheese or ricotta cheese until it is as smooth as honey (it takes a full minute in a processor).

In the small bowl of an electric mixer beat the cream cheese until it is perfectly smooth. Add the smooth cottage cheese or ricotta cheese and beat to mix. Then add the sugar, vanilla, and the eggs one at a time, scraping the bowl with a rubber spatula and beating until smooth after each addition.

When the filling is perfectly smooth, remove the bowl from the mixer, stir in the lemon rind and juice, and pour into the prepared crust.

Bake for 30 minutes.

Remove from the oven and cool completely. Then prepare the topping.

Finely grated rind of 1 lemon
3 tablespoons lemon juice
¾ cup creamed cottage cheese or ricotta cheese (may be large or small curd, regular or low fat)
8 ounces Philadelphia brand cream cheese, at room temperature
¾ cup granulated sugar
½ teaspoon vanilla extract
2 eggs

6 TO 8 PORTIONS

Topping

In a chilled bowl with chilled beaters whip the whipping cream until it holds a firm shape when the beaters are raised (but be careful not to overbeat).

In a bowl stir the sour cream until it is soft and smooth. Stir in the sugar. Then gently fold the sour cream and the whipped cream together.

Just pile the topping loosely on top of the pie, letting some of the filling show around the edges. Or, if you prefer, smooth it all over the filling.

Refrigerate for at least a few hours.

I like this plain, but I have sprinkled a few chopped green pistachio nuts (see Pistachio Nuts, page 6) right on the center before serving, and I liked that too.

1 cup whipping cream
1 cup sour cream
2 tablespoons granulated sugar
Optional: a few green pistachio nuts, chopped (to sprinkle on top)

Date Pecan Pie

On a recent trip by car from California to Florida we drove through Palm Springs and Indio, California, which is where dates grow. We stopped at a stand to drink date shakes (see Note) and to buy dates to take home. I realized that all the dates I had ever eaten were, literally, dried and dry. In Indio even the dried dates are so fresh that they are as soft and moist as a fresh juicy plum. Eating them is a thrill; I couldn't stop.

This is the way they make pecan pie in Indio, and it has to be the world's best. (Even with supermarket dates, we still say the pie is the best.) The dates are barely distinguishable in the pie, but they add an incredible chewy, caramel quality.

When you shop for dates, buy the softest ones you can find. If they are dry and hard when you begin, they will stay that way. Do not use the cut-up, sugared dates.

The pie will be thick, gooey, very chewy, crunchy, and yummy—wonderful. It should be served cold to be at its best.

Adjust a rack one-third up from the bottom of the oven and preheat oven to 350°. Have the prebaked pie shell ready. With scissors or a knife cut the dates into medium-size pieces, cutting each date into about six pieces, and set aside. Melt the butter in a small pan over low heat.

Meanwhile, in the small bowl of an electric mixer beat the eggs for a minute or two until they are very foamy. Add the sugar, flour, salt, and vanilla and beat to mix well. Beat in the melted butter (either warm or cooled) and the corn syrup. Remove the bowl from the mixer. Stir in the dates.

Using a slotted spoon, remove the dates, letting most but not all of the liquids run off them, and place them in an even layer in the prepared pie shell. (Reserve the liquids.)

Sprinkle the pecans evenly over the dates. Slowly and carefully pour the reserved liquids over the nuts, covering them all, even though they will rise to the top.

Bake for 45 minutes. The pie will be well browned although the center will still be shaky and soft. Do not bake longer—the center will become firm as it cools and still firmer when it is refrigerated.

Cool on a rack and then refrigerate for a few hours. If you do not have time for that, place the pie in the freezer for 30 minutes, or a bit longer. Any way you do it, get it really cold or the filling might be a little too runny and not so chewy (although it will still taste fabulous).

Use a strong, heavy, sharp knife for cutting the pie. If the pie resists the knife and feels tough, that means it is just right—and will feel perfect in your mouth.

Everyone seems to agree that as wonderful as this is plain, it is better still with whipped cream or vanilla ice cream.

1 9-inch baked *extra-deep pie shell (see page 17)*

8 ounces (1 cup, packed) pitted dates

4 ounces (1 stick) unsalted butter

4 eggs

1 cup granulated sugar

1 tablespoon all-purpose flour

⅛ teaspoon salt

1 teaspoon vanilla extract

1 cup light corn syrup

6 ounces (1½ cups) pecan halves

8 TO 10 PORTIONS

Indio Whipped Cream

In a chilled bowl with chilled beaters whip the ingredients only until the cream holds a soft shape, not until it is stiff or dry. If you whip the cream ahead of time refrigerate it and then, if it has separated a bit, whisk it lightly with a wire whisk just before serving. Pass the cream separately or spoon it onto the individual plates alongside the pie.

2 cups whipping cream

3 tablespoons maple syrup or honey

3 tablespoons rum or bourbon

NOTE: If you would like to order dates directly from a date grower in Indio, write for a catalog from Jensen's, 80-653 Highway 111, Indio, CA 92201, or from Shields Date Garden, 80-225 Highway 111, Indio, CA 92201.

Pumpkin Pie

This has a smooth, light, creamy, custardy filling with a delicious, delicate blend of spices and flavors.

This is easy to prepare, and although it is traditional for Thanksgiving and Christmas, it is equally appreciated all year.

To eat this at its very most delicious, make it a few hours or less before serving. But with the unbaked crust waiting in the pie plate in the freezer, it takes only a few minutes to put the filling together. (When the pie stands overnight the filling is still fine but the crust loses its fresh flaky quality.)

Adjust a rack one-third up from the bottom of the oven and preheat oven to 450°. Have the prepared unbaked crust in the freezer. It must be in the freezer at least 20 to 30 minutes, although of course it can be there longer.

Place the cream (or heavy cream and milk) in a small saucepan, uncovered, on moderate heat. Let stand until a slightly wrinkled skin forms on top or tiny bubbles appear around the edge.

Meanwhile, in the large bowl of an electric mixer or any large bowl with a wire whisk, beat the eggs lightly just to mix. Beat in the vanilla, sugar, and salt. Through a fine strainer add the spices. Then add the pumpkin and mix well. (If you have been using a whisk, it will be better to mix in the pumpkin with a rubber spatula or wooden spoon.) Gradually stir in the hot cream.

Do not remove the pie crust from the freezer until you are ready to bake it. Pour the pumpkin mixture into the frozen crust.

Bake for 10 minutes at 450°, then reduce the oven temperature to 350° and bake for 30 to 40 minutes longer (total baking time 40 to 50 minutes) until a small sharp knife gently inserted into the middle of the pie comes out clean. (Every time you test the pie with the knife it will leave a scar that will increase in size as the pie cools. Do not cut more than necessary. Having made this many times, I know that in my oven it takes a total of 45 minutes to bake—I don't test.)

Place the baked pie on a rack.

Serve while still barely warm or at room temperature.

1 9-inch extra-deep pie shell (see page 17), frozen, unbaked

1¾ cups light cream (or 1 cup heavy cream and ¾ cup milk)

3 eggs

½ teaspoon vanilla extract

¾ cup light brown sugar, firmly packed

½ teaspoon salt

¼ teaspoon finely ground black pepper

½ teaspoon ginger

¼ teaspoon mace

¼ teaspoon nutmeg

1 pound (2 cups) canned pumpkin (buy the kind labeled "solid pack," not "pumpkin-pie filling," or to use fresh pumpkin, see Notes)

8 PORTIONS

Whipped Cream

In a chilled bowl with chilled beaters whip together all the ingredients.

2 cups heavy cream
¼ cup granulated or confectioners sugar
1 teaspoon vanilla extract

    If the pie is still slightly warm when you serve it, it is best to serve the whipped cream separately (the heat of the pie would melt the cream). Whip the cream until it is not too stiff; it should barely hold a shape and should be more like a thick sauce. But if the pie has cooled to room temperature, the cream can be whipped until it holds a definite shape, and can be spread over the top of the pie. Either way, the cream can be whipped a few hours ahead, refrigerated, and then whisked a bit with a small wire whisk just before using.

NOTES: If you are serving the pie while it is still slightly warm, place the whipped cream in the freezer for about 20 minutes before you serve it. The slightly warm, spicy pie and the icy cold, bland cream are a wonderful combination.

    To use fresh pumpkin: With a large, heavy knife, cut the pumpkin into chunks. With a small paring knife, cut away the rind and the seeds and the membranes. Cut the meat into pieces 2 or 3 inches in diameter. Place in a heavy saucepan with 1 inch of boiling water. Cover and simmer until the pumpkin is tender when tested with a small sharp knife. Drain the pieces on a towel. Purée through a food mill or (a few pieces at a time) in a food processor. (The puréed pumpkin should be smooth, but do not process long enough to liquefy it.) This may be frozen.

Honey Yam Pie

This is an old Creole recipe from New Orleans. The pie is delicate, light, more like custard than potatoes—but you will know it is sweet potatoes you are eating. It is not too rich or too sweet, and is easily made with canned yams (or sweet potatoes).

While the crust is baking, heat the preserves and strain them. As soon as the crust is done brush the hot preserves on the hot crust, and return to the oven to bake 2 minutes more to set the preserves. Set aside to cool.

Leave the oven on. The rack should be one-third up from the bottom of the oven and the temperature should be 450°.

Drain the yams and reserve the liquid. Purée the yams in a food processor or a blender, adding a spoonful (or a bit more) of the reserved liquid (you will not need the remaining liquid), just enough to moisten the yams sufficiently to make a purée.

In a bowl beat the eggs lightly just to mix. Mix in the honey, orange juice, cream, salt, and vanilla.

Gradually stir the egg mixture into the yams. Then strain through a large strainer set over a large bowl.

Now, very slowly pour the filling into the crust, pouring against the rim rather than in the center (a safety precaution to keep the apricot glaze unbroken—the glaze protects the bottom crust so it doesn't become wet or limp). Either grate the nutmeg over the top or sprinkle it on.

Carefully place the pie in the oven and immediately reduce the temperature to 350°.

Bake for 40 minutes or until the filling is just set. You can test it by tapping the rim of the plate; when the filling barely moves, but does not shake, it is done.

Cool completely.

1 9-inch baked *extra-deep pie shell (see page 17)*
2 tablespoons apricot preserves
1 1-pound, 1-ounce can yams or sweet potatoes, in syrup
4 eggs
⅓ cup honey
⅓ cup orange juice
⅔ cup heavy cream
⅛ teaspoon salt
1 teaspoon vanilla extract
¼ teaspoon nutmeg

8 PORTIONS

Whipped Cream

In a chilled bowl with chilled beaters whip together all the ingredients until the cream holds a definite shape. It is best not to place the cream on the top of the pie much ahead of time. If you whip it ahead of time, refrigerate it. Whisk it briefly with a small wire whisk just before using.

Shortly before serving, either spread the cream all over the top or, with a pastry bag and a star-shaped tube or with a teaspoon, form a border of whipped cream and leave the center uncovered.

Or serve the whipped cream separately, spooning it over individual portions.

Refrigerate the pie and serve it cold.

1⅓ cups heavy cream
2 tablespoons honey
½ teaspoon vanilla extract
Optional: 2 tablespoons bourbon, rum, or brandy

Shoofly Pie

One day I received a mail-order catalog of stunning leather and wool clothes and handmade sweaters from The French Creek Sheep & Wool Company in Elverson, the heart of Pennsylvania Dutch country.

Soon after, on one of our car trips, we drove there. The clothes were spectacular, and Jean and Eric Flaxenburg, who own and run the business (which includes raising their own sheep for the wool), invited us to their charming museumlike home for Shoofly Pie and coffee.

What a way for me to be introduced to one of the oldest and most historic American desserts!

This recipe is from Michelle Swartz, who works at The French Creek Company and is quite famous locally for her wonderful baking. Recipes for this vary from a rather dry crumb cake (great for dunking) to a soupy, runny pie. And then there is this one: soft, tender, moist (but not runny), custardy (but not creamy), and not too sweet.

When our country was very young, word spread that the people of southeastern Pennsylvania were the best cooks in the colonies. In 1758 the Moravian citizens of Bethlehem built an inn called The Sun Inn. From the beginning it was famous for its food. The great men of the colonies all went there: George Washington (with Martha), Benjamin Franklin, John Hancock—everyone who was anyone ate and slept at The Sun Inn. It is possible that this was the start of basic American cooking.

Shoofly Pie was on the first menu at The Sun Inn.

You need a 10-inch pie plate, preferably Pyrex.

The crust can be made (but not baked) ahead of time and frozen; the crumb mixture of the filling can be made ahead of time. But the molasses mixture should be prepared immediately before baking and the pie should be baked only 2 or 3 hours before serving.

Pie Crust

Sift together into a wide mixing bowl the flour, salt, and sugar. With a pastry blender cut in the butter until the particles are fine and the mixture resembles coarse meal (some of the particles may be the size of small kernels of corn). Mix the lemon juice with 3 tablespoons plus 1 teaspoon of ice water and very gradually drizzle it over the flour mixture, stirring constantly with a fork (stir even more than you might think necessary). The dry ingredients should all be just barely moistened. If necessary, stir a bit longer, and if the mixture is still too dry stir in a few more drops of water.

Turn the mixture out onto a board or counter top. Handle

it very little now. Press it together into a ball; if absolutely necessary you may knead it once or twice, and then form it into a ball. Flatten it into a 5- or 6-inch round, wrap in plastic wrap, and refrigerate for an hour or longer (overnight or a few days is all right too).

Remove the chilled dough from the refrigerator about 10 or 15 minutes before rolling it out; let it stand, wrapped, at room temperature.

Carefully flour a pastry cloth and rolling pin. Place the dough on the floured cloth. (It is considered taboo ever to turn pastry over while you are rolling it out because—the experts say—the dough will absorb too much flour and will become tough. But if you are careful and if you don't use too much flour on the cloth, I think it is all right to turn the dough over once while you are rolling it out. It might handle better if you do.)

Carefully roll the dough into a 14-inch circle.

Drape the dough over the rolling pin and carefully transfer it to the pie plate, centering it as well as you can. If you have a cake-decorating turntable place the pie plate on it. Trim and flute the edge (see page 19); it is not necessary to make an extra-deep crust.

Place the lined pie plate in the freezer or refrigerator. (If you are going to freeze it for any more than an hour or so, wrap it airtight in plastic wrap after it is frozen solid.)

1⅓ cups sifted all-purpose flour
½ teaspoon salt
1 tablespoon granulated sugar
4 ounces (1 stick) unsalted butter, cold and firm, cut into ½-inch squares (it is best to cut the butter ahead of time and refrigerate it)
1 teaspoon lemon juice
About 3 tablespoons plus 1 teaspoon ice water

Filling

Adjust an oven rack one-third up from the bottom and preheat oven to 450°.

Stir the flour and sugar together in a wide bowl to mix. Add the butter and rub the ingredients together with your fingertips to make coarse crumbs. (There is not enough butter to absorb all of the dry ingredients; therefore some of the flour and sugar will remain powdery—and some of the butter may remain obvious and only partially mixed with the dry ingredients. That is as it should be.)

In the small bowl of an electric mixer beat the egg just to mix. On low speed beat in the molasses. Pour the hot water into a 1-cup glass measuring cup; add the baking soda and stir to dissolve. On low speed gradually add the water mixture to the molasses mixture, beating until incorporated.

Stir half of the crumb mixture (1 cup) into the molasses mixture and without

1 cup unsifted flour
⅔ cup dark brown sugar, firmly packed
2 ounces (½ stick) unsalted butter, cut into ½-inch squares
1 egg
1 cup molasses (see Note)
¾ cup very hot water
1 teaspoon baking soda

8 TO 10 PORTIONS

waiting, pour it into the chilled crust (which may be frozen). Sprinkle the remaining crumb mixture evenly on top and place in the oven (most of the top crumb mixture will sink into the filling during baking). ***Immediately reduce the oven temperature to 350°.***

Bake for about 30 minutes or until the filling is set and does not quiver when the pie plate is shaken gently from side to side. Do not overbake. (And do not be disappointed when you see that the fluted rim of the crust has shrunk and settled itself onto the edge of the filling—it happens.)

Cool to room temperature. Serve at room temperature, or even slightly warm. It is more tender/delicate/delicious than if it is refrigerated.

Serve plain or with softly whipped cream. (For 1 cup of cream add ½ teaspoon vanilla extract or 1 tablespoon brandy and 2 tablespoons granulated sugar.)

NOTE: You can use any dark or light molasses; however, I have recently discovered Plantation Brand Barbados Unsulphured Molasses, which I buy in health food stores, and it has a delicious, mild flavor. In Pennsylvania Dutch country they use Turkey Table Syrup.

Prune and Apricot Turnovers

These were a specialty of my mother's. All the years I lived at home it was a special treat for me if my mother let me decorate the turnovers. But she was artistic and creative and she liked decorating them herself, so usually we each did half. And we tried to outdo each other.

Although these are wonderfully delicious, the first things I think of when I think "turnovers" are fun—and gorgeous. If you do craft work of any kind you will love making these; it can become a hobby.

The pastry is flaky, the filling is sweet and tart and almost-but-not-quite runny.

The prunes and apricots should be soaked overnight before they are stewed. Then the prune and apricot filling and the pastry should both be refrigerated for several hours or overnight before they are used.

Prune and Apricot Filling

In a covered 2-quart container or saucepan soak the prunes and apricots in the water overnight.

The next day, combine the first three ingredients and bring them to a boil, uncovered, over moderate heat. Reduce the heat, allowing the mixture to simmer slowly. Cook the fruit only until it is tender and until the water is almost completely absorbed or evaporated but do not mash the fruit or allow it to disintegrate. This needs almost constant stirring to prevent burning, but in order not to break up the fruit any more than necessary, stir only gently, with a wooden spatula. And do not really stir; all you are trying to do is keep the fruit on the bottom from burning, so just push the spatula around the bottom slowly, as necessary. After about 5 minutes of simmering add the sugar and salt and continue to simmer and stir until there is only a little liquid remaining but do not cook until too dry. Total cooking time (including the first 5 minutes) is about 20 minutes. The mixture will continue to thicken as it cools.

Then cool and refrigerate.

6 ounces (1 cup) dried pitted prunes
6 ounces (1 cup) dried apricots
1½ cups water
½ cup granulated sugar
½ teaspoon salt

9 OR 10 LARGE TURNOVERS

Pastry

Prepare a double amount of pie pastry for a 9-inch pie (see page 17). On a lightly floured surface knead gently only two or three times until the ingredients just barely hold together, wrap, and refrigerate overnight or for several hours.

When you are ready to bake, adjust two racks to divide the oven into thirds and preheat oven to 425°. Line two cookie sheets with aluminum foil shiny side up.

Lightly flour a pastry cloth and a rolling pin. Cut the pastry in half, return one piece to the refrigerator, and place the other piece on the pastry cloth.

With a floured rolling pin gently pound the firm pastry until it is soft enough to roll. Roll it out until it is ⅛ inch thick, reflouring the pin as necessary and sprinkling and then spreading a bit of flour over the surface of the dough occasionally if necessary; it is generally not necessary to reflour the pastry cloth while rolling, if it has been well floured.

The rolled-out dough will be cut with a 5-inch round cookie cutter. (That's a large one.) Or it can be cut with a knife into 5-inch squares. If you are going to cut it into squares you should plan ahead and roll out the dough into a 5- or 10-inch width. Cut out the rounds or squares. Reserve remaining scraps but do not press or knead them together; just place them on top of each other and reroll and recut. Reroll the scraps only once (the pastry would not be flaky after further rerolling); reserve them to make cut-out decorations for the tops of the turnovers. You should have 9 or 10 rounds or squares.

Place the rounds or squares on wax paper or foil.

Divide the filling among the rounds or squares, placing it to one side of center but not too close to the edge. Use a rounded tablespoon of the filling for each turnover. (You will have a few spoonfuls of leftover filling; it is a delicious spread for toast or crackers.)

Place a small cup of cold water next to your work area.

Fold over one turnover at a time. With a soft brush wet a border about ½ inch wide around one-half of the round or square (the squares can be folded to make rectangles or triangles). Fold the dry half of the pastry over the wet border and press the borders together gently. Place the folded turnovers on the foil-lined cookie sheets.

With the backs of the tines of a fork, floured if necessary, press around the borders to seal the edges together and to make a ridged design.

Shape all of the turnovers.

Now roll out the remaining pastry scraps; it is best to roll this a bit thinner than the dough for the turnovers themselves. Cut out designs using small cookie cutters, truffle cutters, the tip of a knife or scissors. Use cold water as a paste to fasten the design on; just brush or finger a bit of water where you want it on the turnover before applying the design.

Egg Wash (glaze)

In a small cup stir the yolk and water together. Strain through a fine strainer.

1 egg yolk
1 teaspoon water

Then, with a soft brush, brush the egg wash gently all over the top, including the design and the rim. But do not use so much that it runs down on the sides; it would make the turnovers stick. Two thin coats are best (if you allow the wash to form puddles on the turnovers they will not brown evenly).

With a four-pronged fork pierce the top once, avoiding the design, to allow steam to escape.

(At this point these can be frozen to bake later on. Let them stand until the egg wash dries. Then place the cookie sheet in the freezer. When the turnovers are frozen, peel the foil away from the backs of the turnovers and wrap each individually in plastic wrap. When you are ready to bake, unwrap, place on foil-lined sheets, and put into the preheated oven frozen. They seem to bake in the same time even if they are frozen.)

Bake for about 30 minutes, reversing the sheets top to bottom and front to back as necessary to ensure even browning. Bake until nicely browned; do not underbake. (If you bake only one sheet at a time, bake it in the middle of the oven: one sheet takes less time.)

Cool the turnovers on a rack. However, if you can arrange to serve these warm, by all means do so.

If the turnovers are frozen after they are baked, they can quickly be thawed and reheated, unwrapped, in a 350° oven.

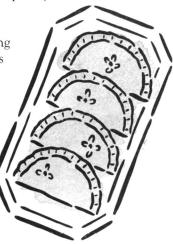

VARIATIONS: My mother never added anything to the filling so this is the way I think it should be. But I have at times added a few coarsely chopped walnuts and it was wonderful. Also, when I added 3 tablespoons cognac to the cooked and cooled filling, I thought that was the best.

Tarts

French Tart Pastry

The pastry can be prepared in a processor, a mixer, or by hand.

In a food processor: Fit the bowl with the metal blade. Place the flour, sugar, salt, and butter in the bowl. Process on/off for 10 seconds (ten 1-second pulses) until the mixture resembles coarse meal. Place the egg and water in a small bowl and beat to mix. Then, through the feed tube, add the egg and water and continue to process briefly (about 20 seconds) only until the mixture barely (but not completely) holds together.

In an electric mixer: The same procedure can be followed, using the large bowl of the mixer and low speed; use a rubber spatula to keep pushing the butter pieces into the beater.

By hand: Place the dry ingredients in a mound on a large board or work surface, form a well in the middle, place the pieces of butter with the egg and water in the well. With the fingertips of your right hand work the center wet ingredients together, gradually incorporating the dry ingredients until the two mixtures are all mixed. It helps to use a dough scraper or wide metal spatula to push the dry ingredients in toward the center as necessary.

1¾ cups unsifted *all-purpose flour (stir to aerate before measuring)*

2 tablespoons granulated sugar

¼ teaspoon salt

4 ounces (1 stick) unsalted butter, cold and firm, cut into small pieces (see Notes)

1 cold egg

1 tablespoon ice water

However you have arrived at this stage of the pastry, now turn the mixture out onto a large unfloured board or smooth work surface. Knead briefly (only a few seconds) until the mixture is smooth and holds together and press the mixture together to form a ball. Smooth the sides and flour it lightly. Unless the kitchen is terribly hot, or unless you have handled the mixture too much (enough to melt the butter), it is not necessary to refrigerate this before using. If you must, refrigerate it for only about an hour or less. If it is refrigerated too long it will crack when you roll it out.

NOTES: Cut the stick of butter lengthwise, then cut each half lengthwise again, and slice all four quarters into ½-inch slices. It is best to cut and refrigerate the butter ahead of time.

After shaping this pastry, if you have any leftover scraps, make cookies. Press the scraps together, roll on a floured pastry cloth with a floured rolling pin to about ¼-inch thickness, cut with cookie cutters, sprinkle with granulated sugar, and bake at 350° only until the cookies are slightly colored. They are delicious.

Tart Tatin
(Upside-Down Apple Pie)

Technically, a tart is considered a sort of pie with an undercrust only—no crust covering the filling. While this tart is baking it has a top crust only, then it is turned over, making a bottom crust only.

There is a theory that this recipe originated when a waitress dropped a pie. When she returned the damaged upside-down pie to the kitchen, it inspired someone there to perfect this. And then there is another story: Tart Tatin was not the result of an accident but was carefully planned in order to eliminate a wet or soggy bottom crust. It is generally believed that the recipe was originally from the Hotel Tatin run by the two Tatin sisters in the town of Lamotte-Beuvron in France. But some historians recall that the Tatin sisters did not really create this. They say it was an easy, inexpensive peasant dessert and that everyone in the locality was making it. However, when word of this recipe spread to other areas, it was the Tatin version that they spoke about.

When I had this at Maxim's in Paris it looked like a pizza, very large and very thin. I make it in a 10-inch Pyrex pie plate that is 1¾ inches deep, and makes a Tart Tatin that is deeper than the usual. You can use any shallow round baking dish or tart pan that measures about 10 inches in diameter. And if it is shallower than the pie plate, simply use fewer apples, and you will have a thinner tart.

For many years, before I ever made this, I heard dire warnings about the difficulty of getting it all out of the inverted plate without some of the apples sticking to the plate. I was gun-shy before trying it. So I lined the plate with aluminum foil. And it worked like a charm. I have done it that way ever since.

I have successfully prepared this early in the day and refrigerated it. But this is best if it is baked about 3 or 4 hours before serving. Don't turn it out onto the plate, however, until just before you serve it. (See Note.)

*I*f you wish, the crust may be prepared ahead of time and refrigerated. Or it can be mixed immediately before using. Adjust a rack one-third up from the bottom of the oven and preheat oven to 400°. Prepare a 10 x 1¾-inch pie plate as follows: Turn the plate over, center a 12-inch square of foil over the plate, fold down the sides of the foil to shape it to the plate, and then remove the foil and turn the plate right side up. Place the foil in the plate, pressing it carefully into place. Smooth over the foil with your fingers, a pot holder, or a folded towel. Fold the corners (and extending edges, if there are any) back over the rim of the plate. Butter sides only, with additional butter, melted, using a pastry brush or wax paper.

Peel the apples. Cut them into quarters and remove

the cores. Cut each quarter into four lengthwise slices and set aside.

Place 3 tablespoons of the butter and ⅓ cup of the sugar in a small pan over moderate heat to melt the butter. Set aside.

Mix 3 tablespoons of the sugar with the cinnamon and set aside.

Place the remaining 5 tablespoons butter (it must be soft but not melted) in the bottom of the foil-lined plate. With the back of a teaspoon spread it carefully to cover the bottom. Sprinkle the remaining sugar evenly over the butter.

Now place some of the apple slices neatly and carefully overlapping each other, first around the outer edge and then in the center. Sprinkle with about half of the cinnamon-sugar. Cover with the remaining apple slices and the remaining cinnamon-sugar. Then pour the melted butter and sugar mixture over the surface.

Cover the top with a piece of wax paper and, with your hands, press down on the paper to press the apples into a compact, rather smooth layer. Remove the wax paper.

Now, on a floured pastry cloth with a floured rolling pin, roll the dough into a circle as wide as the plate. Use something the size of the plate as a pattern and trim the pastry with a pizza cutter, a pastry wheel, or a small sharp knife.

Carefully fold the pastry in half, then lift it, center it over the apples, unfold it, and that is all. Do not press it down on the edge of the plate.

Bake for about 35 minutes until the crust is a nice golden color.

Let stand in the pan on a rack for 2 or 3 hours until the bottom of the pan has cooled.

You will need a cake plate with a slight rim to turn this out onto. Cover the tart with the cake plate. There may be a considerable amount of juice; therefore it is important to invert the pie plate quickly before the juice runs all over. If you are quick, none will run out, but just in case, hold it over the sink while you quickly turn the cake plate and the pie plate over, carefully holding them firmly together.

If the juice runs onto the plate, use paper towels to absorb it and leave the plate clean.

Pastry for 1 10-inch pie crust (see page 17)

5 medium-size tart cooking apples (I like Granny Smith)

4 ounces (1 stick) unsalted butter, at room temperature

¾ cup granulated sugar

1 tablespoon cinnamon (this is not traditional but it is wonderful)

6 GENEROUS PORTIONS

Glaze

Apply the glaze as close to serving time as is comfortable.

Melt about ½ cup of apricot preserves in a small saucepan or frying pan over moderate heat, stirring with a wooden spoon. Press it through a strainer. Return to the pan and bring to a boil; let boil for about half a minute. Then brush it all over the top of the apples.

In France this is served alone, or with Crème Fraîche (see page 255) or whipped cream. If you serve the whipped cream, use 1 cup heavy cream, 2 tablespoons sugar, and ½ teaspoon vanilla extract. In a chilled bowl with chilled beaters whip only until the cream holds a soft shape but not until it is stiff. If you whip the cream ahead of time, refrigerate. It will probably separate slightly while standing. Just beat it a bit with a small wire whisk right before using. Serve the cream separately, ladling a spoonful over the side of each portion.

Or serve it with ice cream.

NOTE: Some wonderful restaurants where Tart Tatin is a *spécialité* prepare it ahead of time, but bake it to order and serve it HOT, right out of the oven. It is delicious.

Apricot Tart

This is a favorite dessert that I taught in many cities around the country where I gave cooking classes. And, when Food & Wine Magazine *asked me for a recipe for their cover, this was it. It is a wonderful tart made of the best pastry I know. It can be beautifully plain, or creative and artistic with a design on top made of some of the pastry. It is great fun to make and you will be proud to serve it. Plan it for a party (or a magazine cover).*

The filling can be made days or weeks ahead—the apricots soak overnight, but if you are in a rush, they need not be soaked, just simmer them longer to soften them. The pastry is best made right before using it. In cooking classes I served this warm, even hot. I have also frozen it for weeks and thawed it to serve. Or I have made it several hours ahead of time and let it cool to room temperature. Any of these ways is fine.

You will need a plain flan ring measuring 9½ inches in diameter and ¾ inch in depth (see Notes).

The filling should be made first.

Filling

Soak the apricots overnight in the water.

    Then place the apricots and water in a heavy saucepan. Add the sugar and stir to mix. Place over moderately high heat and stir until the mixture comes to a boil. Reduce the heat slightly, cover, and simmer for about 10 minutes—stir occasionally to be sure it is not sticking or burning. Then uncover, raise the heat to moderately high again, and stir almost constantly until the apricots are very tender and are beginning to fall apart and the liquid has thickened—reduce the heat if necessary to avoid spattering—and remember that the mixture will thicken more as it cools; do not cook until it becomes too dry. It usually takes about 8 to 10 minutes, but apricots vary considerably and some may take longer. You can help them along by cutting the apricots with the side of a wooden spoon as you stir them. Do not purée them—you should have thick, chunky apricot preserves.

12 ounces dried apricots (see Notes)
2 cups water
1¼ cups granulated sugar
½ teaspoon vanilla extract
¼ teaspoon almond extract
Optional: 1 tablespoon rum, cognac, or kirsch
Optional: about 2 tablespoons thinly sliced toasted almonds

8 TO 10 PORTIONS

    Remove from the heat. Cool a bit and then stir in the vanilla and almond extracts and the optional liquor. If you wish, stir in a few thinly sliced toasted almonds.

    This can be used as soon as it has cooled, or it can be refrigerated for weeks. (Many of the people who came to the cooking classes told me they liked this apricot preserve so much that they made it to serve with toast—I agree.)

Rich Flan Pastry (pâté sablée)

This may be put together in a food processor or, traditionally, on a board.

In a food processor: Fit the processor with the steel blade. Place the flour, salt, and sugar in the bowl of the processor. Add the butter and process on-and-off (like pulse beats) for about 10 seconds until the mixture resembles coarse meal.

    In a small bowl mix the egg, yolks, rind, and juice. Then, with the processor going, add these mixed ingredients through the feed tube and process only briefly (just a few seconds) until mixed, not until it all holds together—it should be dry and crumbly.

    Traditional method: Place the flour on a large board, marble, or smooth counter top. Form a well in the center and add all the remaining ingredients. With the fingertips of your right hand work the center ingredients together. Then gradually incorporate the flour, using a dough scraper or a pancake turner in your left hand to help move the flour in toward the center. When all of the flour has been absorbed, knead briefly only until the dough holds together.

For either method: Turn the pastry out onto a large board, marble, or counter top. Press together to form a ball. Then "break" the dough as follows: Start at the far end of the ball of dough and, using the heel of your hand, push off a small piece (it should be a few tablespoonfuls), pushing it against the work surface and away from you. Continue until all the dough has been pushed off.

Form the dough into a fat sausage shape, cut it in half, and then form into two balls. Lightly flour the balls of dough. With your hands flatten them slightly into rounds 6 to 8 inches in diameter. Wrap them in plastic wrap and let them stand at room temperature for 20 to 30 minutes. (If the room is very warm, or if the pastry was handled too much, it may be refrigerated for about 10 minutes, but no longer. If it is too cold when it is rolled out it will form small cracks on the surface and the filling might run out.)

To shape and bake: Place two racks in the oven, one one-third up from the bottom and one in the center, and preheat oven to 375°. Butter the inside of a 9½ x ¾-inch flan ring and place it on an unbuttered flat cookie sheet (the sheet should have at least one flat edge so you can slide the baked tart off the sheet).

Flour a pastry cloth and a rolling pin. Place one round of the dough on the cloth and roll it into a 12-inch circle.

Drape the dough over the rolling pin and transfer it to the flan ring, centering it carefully as you unroll it.

With your fingertips carefully press the dough into place without stretching it. The dough will stand about ½ inch above the ring on the sides. If necessary, straighten it with scissors, leaving ½ inch of dough above the rim.

If the dough cracks or tears while you are working with it, it can be patched with a little additional dough.

Spoon the cold apricot filling into the shell and smooth the top of it—it should be flat, not mounded.

Flour the fingers of your right hand. Hold a spot on the rim of the dough, holding it with your thumb and the sides of your bent-under index finger. Press on the raised edge of the dough to flatten it and make it thinner. Work all the way around. Then fold the thinner rim of dough down over the filling, pulling it in toward the center a bit in order to keep it slightly away from the flan ring.

Roll the remaining half of the dough until it is a scant ¼ inch thick, then trim it into a circle about 10 or 10½ inches in diameter (use anything that size as a pattern and cut around it with a pizza cutter, a pastry wheel, or a small sharp knife).

With a pastry brush dipped in water or with your fingertips wet the rim of the bottom dough that is folded over the filling. Now, to transfer the top crust, drape it loosely over the rolling pin and unroll it over the filling.

With your fingertips press down on the edges to seal both crusts together. Then

2½ cups unsifted *all-purpose flour*
Scant ½ teaspoon salt
½ cup granulated sugar
8 ounces (2 sticks) unsalted butter, cold and firm, cut into ½-inch pieces (it is best to cut the butter ahead of time and refrigerate it)
1 egg plus 2 egg yolks
Finely grated rind of 1 lemon
2 teaspoons lemon juice

cut around the rim with a table knife to remove excess dough; the edge of the dough must not extend over the flan ring or the dough might stick and it will be difficult to raise and remove the ring after the tart is baked. Then press around the edge of the pastry with the back of the tines of a fork to seal it. Again, keep the upper edge of the pastry slightly away from the flan ring.

Glaze

Beat the yolk and water just to mix and strain it through a strainer. Brush it over the top of the tart but be careful not to let it run down the sides—that could make it stick to the flan ring. With the back of a table knife score a diamond

1 egg yolk
1 teaspoon water

pattern in the dough, being very careful not to score the dough deeply; make shallow lines about ½ inch apart, first in one direction and then, on an angle, in the opposite direction.

To make a design on the top, press together all leftover scraps of the dough and roll them out on the pastry cloth with the rolling pin. Roll this a little thinner than the crusts. Cut with a long, sharp knife or a pastry wheel into ½-inch-wide strips. Place them on the tart in a bow design. Then cut the remaining dough with a small scalloped or plain round cutter, or with a heart-shaped cutter, and place these around and on top of the bow.

(When *Food & Wine Magazine* made this, it was for their Valentine's Day issue. They cut out the additional dough with large heart-shaped cutters, and placed one heart in the middle and six in a circle around it. It was gorgeous!)

Brush it all well with the egg wash.

With the tip of a small sharp knife, cut a few small slits (air vents), cutting right up against the bow or other design so the cuts do not show.

Bake low in the oven for about 30 minutes. Then reduce the oven temperature to 350°, raise the tart to the center of the oven, and bake for 20 to 30 minutes more (total baking time is 50 to 60 minutes) until the top is beautifully browned.

When the tart is removed from the oven , if any of the pastry has run out under the flan ring, use a small sharp knife to trim and remove it.

It is easiest to remove the flan ring if you do it immediately, while the pastry is hot, before it cools and becomes crisper. Use pot holders that are not too thick and bulky (or use a folded towel or napkin) and, very gently, slowly, and carefully, raise the ring to remove it.

(If you have trouble removing the ring, let it stand until the tart is cool. Then slide the tart [still in the flan ring] onto an inverted 8- or 9-inch round cake pan. The ring will then slide down, and the tart can be transferred to a serving plate. All of these directions are "HANDLE WITH CARE.")

If you were able to lift the flan ring up off the hot tart, then let the tart cool completely on the cookie sheet.

When cool, use a flat-sided cookie sheet as a spatula, and carefully transfer the tart to a flat serving plate. Or carefully loosen the tart by sliding a long, narrow metal spatula under it and, if it moves easily, just use your hands to slide it off the flat side of the cookie sheet. But don't force it; if it feels as though the tart might crack, use something large and flat (i.e., the bottom of a loose-bottomed quiche pan) to transfer it.

Apricot Glaze

In a small pan over moderate heat stir the preserves and water until the mixture comes to a boil. Strain through a strainer, then brush the glaze carefully all over the top of the tart. (If you plan to freeze the baked tart, do not glaze the top until the tart is thawed—glaze it shortly before serving.)

¼ cup apricot preserves
2 teaspoons water

This tart is delicious as it is, but it is still better with vanilla ice cream; the slightly sour taste of the apricots with the smooth, sweet ice cream is gorgeous!

NOTES: This can be made in a 9-inch loose-bottomed cake pan in place of the flan ring. Even though the cake pan is deeper, you can make a tart only ¾ inch deep in it.

I use plain supermarket apricots; they have a nice tart flavor and they generally work better for this recipe than some of the fancier, more expensive apricots. (Some of the more expensive ones do not fall apart as they should, even after long cooking.)

Sour Cream Apple Tart

This is an unusual variation on apple pie. It has the advantage of a crust that does not demand the delicate, careful handling of standard pie crust. So tender and flaky and buttery that I could eat it with no filling, this is a cream cheese pastry that can be mixed in an electric mixer; if the mixer continues a bit after it is all done, it does not hurt the delicious pastry one bit. The crust is baked empty, then the apple slices are sautéed in a frying pan and placed in the baked shell. There is a creamy caramel sauce over the apples, and a thick layer of sour cream on top. Gorgeous, dramatically simple looking, and mouth-watering.

If you would like to prepare some of this ahead of time, the unbaked shell can be frozen in the tart pan. (Then be prepared to spend about 1½ hours to finish the tart.)

You will need an 11 x 1-inch two-piece tart pan, preferably made of black or dark blue metal.

Cream Cheese Pastry Crust

This fabulous crust can also be used with other fillings—anything that does not have to be baked in the crust.

It is best to chill the dough for an hour or two before rolling it out or chill it overnight or longer and then let stand at room temperature for 30 to 60 minutes, or as necessary.

In the large bowl of an electric mixer beat the cheese and butter until they are softened and incorporated. Then, on low speed, add the flour and beat, frequently scraping the bowl with a rubber spatula, until the ingredients hold together. (This will take several minutes of beating—if they do not want to hold together, turn the mixture out onto a work surface and knead a bit and press together.)

4 ounces Philadelphia brand cream cheese
4 ounces (1 stick) unsalted butter
1 cup sifted all-purpose flour

With your hands form the mixture into a smooth ball, flatten it slightly (if you intend to chill this for more than an hour or two, flatten it to about ½-inch thickness), wrap airtight in plastic wrap, and refrigerate.

On a floured pastry cloth with a floured rolling pin roll out the dough into a circle 13 inches, or a bit more, in diameter. Drape the dough over the rolling pin and transfer it to a loose-bottomed 11 x 1-inch tart pan.

Ease it into the pan, do not stretch it, and press it gently into place. Trim the edge with scissors, leaving a generous ½ inch of dough beyond the rim of the pan. It is important to have a high rim with no low spots; if necessary, the dough can be patched to fill in any low spots or cracks (use a drop of water as paste).

To form a narrow hem, roll or fold over the edge of the dough, turning it in toward the middle; let the doubled hem extend about ¼ inch above the rim of the pan.

With pastry pincers form a design around the edge of the dough, or score it lightly every ¼ inch, making lines at an angle with the dull edge of a table knife.

With a fork prick holes all over the bottom of the crust, moving the fork ¾ to 1 inch apart each time.

Place the pan in the freezer for at least 10 to 15 minutes, or longer if you wish. (If it is to remain in the freezer for a longer time, wrap it airtight after it is frozen.)

Before baking, adjust a rack one-third up from the bottom of the oven and preheat to 450°. Line the frozen pastry shell with a 12-inch square of foil shiny side down and fill the foil at least halfway with pie weights or dried beans.

Bake at 450° for 13 minutes, then reduce the temperature to 350° and gently remove the foil and weights from the shell; continue to bake 7 to 10 minutes more (total baking time is 20 to 23 minutes) until the shell is well browned on the edges and lightly browned on the bottom. Do not underbake.

Filling

While the crust is baking, place the preserves (it is not necessary to strain them) in a small pan over moderate heat and stir occasionally to bring to a boil. The preserves should be boiling when the pastry shell comes out of the oven. Brush or spread the hot preserves over the bottom of the baked shell and return the pan to the oven for a minute or two to dry the preserves a bit; set aside.

Peel, quarter, and core the apples. Cut each quarter into five lengthwise slices.

Melt about half of the butter in a wide frying pan. Cover the bottom of the pan with some of the apple slices. Sprinkle with just a bit of the sugar. Cook, uncovered, over moderate heat, turning the slices occasionally with two forks until they are tender. Place them on a large plate and set aside as you continue to sauté all of the slices, using all of the remaining sugar and butter (and a bit more of either or both if necessary). The cooked slices may be piled on top of one another on the plate.

Then, with your fingers, place all of the cooked slices over the preserves in the shell. The way they are placed is not terribly important since they will not show, but you want to have a rather even layer of apples. Here's how I do it.

Start in the middle of the shell and form a rosette (a sunburst? a pinwheel?) of slices overlapping one another right in the middle. Then place slices at right angles to the ones in the middle (these go lengthwise following the line of the rim of the pan), overlapping one another lengthwise. Then you will find that the best way to fill in the remaining space and to use up all of the slices is to form the outside row of ap-

⅓ cup apricot preserves
4 large (about 2 pounds) pie apples—Granny Smith (wonderful) or Jonathan
About 2½ ounces (5 tablespoons) unsalted butter
About 2 tablespoons granulated sugar

8 TO 10 PORTIONS

ples at a 45° angle to the rim (not parallel to the rim and not on a right angle to it). They should all overlap one another deeply. Set aside.

Caramel Sauce

Place the cream in a small pan and cook, uncovered, over medium heat until almost boiling.

⅔ *cup whipping cream*
½ *cup granulated sugar*

At the same time, place the sugar in a frying pan over high heat and stir constantly with a long-handled wooden spatula until the sugar starts to melt and turn brown. Reduce the heat a bit to prevent burning. Continue to stir until the sugar is smooth and a rich caramel color. Remove from the heat, let cool for 1 minute, and then slowly stir the hot cream into the caramelized sugar. Return to the heat and stir again for a minute or so until perfectly smooth.

Let cool for 1 minute and then, with a large spoon, drizzle the caramel sauce over the apples in the crust. Set aside.

Sour Cream Topping

Preheat oven to 350°. Stir the ingredients in a bowl until combined. Pour over the tart. (If there are any low spots along the rim of the crust, do not use all of the sour cream mixture or it will run over.)

3 *cups sour cream (see Note)*
1 *tablespoon plus 2 teaspoons granulated sugar*
1 *teaspoon vanilla extract*

With the back of a spoon spread and smooth the sour cream layer carefully. Be careful not to get any of the caramel sauce into the topping; it should be pure white. And be careful to keep the topping just within the rim of the crust; don't let it get on top of it.

Bake for 7 minutes; remove from oven and cool to room temperature.

Refrigerate for at least several hours, or all day. (Do not serve this too soon or the sour cream will be a little runny—although yummy.)

NOTE: Sour cream keeps well, refrigerated, for a long time. The local dairy says 6 weeks. But after several weeks, although the cream still looks fine, it seems more sour than it was at first. For this particular recipe I recommend that you buy the freshest sour cream available.

Orange Tart

This consists of a shallow pastry shell brushed with apricot preserves, filled with fresh orange sections, and covered with a thickened orange juice mixture. It is light, tart, wonderfully refreshing, but should only be made when the oranges are delicious. It is best the day it is made, but the crust can be prepared ahead and placed in the freezer unbaked until you are ready for it. And, if you wish, the oranges can be sectioned a day ahead. Then there is not too much left to do. You will need a 9-inch flan ring only ½ or ¾ inch deep (a pie plate is too deep).

Pastry

Prepare the French Tart Pastry (see page 88). Flour the ball lightly, flatten it to a 6- or 7-inch circle, and put it on a floured pastry cloth. With a floured rolling pin roll the pastry into a 12-inch circle.

Place a 9 x ½- or ¾-inch flan ring on a cookie sheet. Roll the pastry loosely on the rolling pin, and unroll it over the flan ring, centering it carefully. With your fingers, press it into place. With scissors, trim excess, allowing ½- to ¾-inch overlap. Fold excess inside to form a double thickness on the rim and press together firmly. The rim should be upright a scant ¼ inch above the flan ring. If you wish, form a design on the folded edge by pressing the back of a knife blade at an angle across the top of the rim, at ¼-inch intervals all around the edge, or crimp it with a dough crimper.

Place the pastry shell on the cookie sheet in the freezer at least until it is frozen or longer if you wish (if you do leave it in the freezer longer, cover it well with plastic wrap or foil after it is frozen).

When you are ready to bake, adjust a rack to the center of the oven and preheat oven to 375°. Line the frozen shell with aluminum foil and fill it with dried beans or pie weights (aluminum pellets made for that purpose) to keep the shell in place.

Bake for 20 minutes. Remove from the oven and carefully remove the foil and beans by lifting the four corners of the foil. Return the shell to the oven and continue to bake for about 10 to 15 minutes more until the shell is thoroughly dry and lightly browned. (The pastry will shrink away from the sides of the pan.) After removing the foil, keep an eye on the pastry; if the bottom puffs up, prick it immediately and gently with a cake tester.

Remove the shell from the oven and let stand until completely cool. Remove the flan ring by lifting it off.

Orange Filling

Peel and section the oranges (see page 15), placing the sections and the juice in a bowl. Add the sugar and stir gently to mix without breaking the fruit. Let stand about 15 minutes.

Then pour it all into a large strainer set over a large bowl, and let drain for about 15 minutes.

Measure the juice. You need 1 cup; if there is less, add water, kirsch, rum, or cognac to make 1 cup.

In a small, heavy saucepan stir the 1 cup of liquid with the cornstarch and salt until smoothly blended. Place over moderate heat and stir gently until the mixture comes to a low boil, thickens, and becomes clear (it will take about 5 minutes). Then reduce the heat to low and stir gently for a minute or two. Add the 2 teaspoons kirsch, rum, or cognac, or the 1 teaspoon lemon juice and mix gently. Set aside and let stand, stirring occasionally, until cool.

Meanwhile, *very carefully* transfer the pastry shell (the safest way is to use a flat-sided cookie sheet or the bottom of a quiche pan as a spatula) to a large, flat cake plate or a board and make room for it in the refrigerator.

In a small pan over moderate heat stir the preserves until they come to a boil. Turn the hot preserves into the pastry shell and brush or spread them to cover the bottom.

Then place the drained orange sections over the preserves in a neat pattern as follows: Place one slice at a right angle to the rim of the right-hand side of the shell (three o'clock), with the thick (curved) side facing the top (twelve o'clock). Place another slice closer to you, slightly overlapping the first. Continue to form a circle of orange sections all around the shell, overlapping each other slightly more toward the center of the pie than on the outside, rather like a fan pattern. Then form another similar circle inside the first. Fill in the space in the center by placing the slices any way they fit or by cutting them into smaller pieces if that seems easier.

Carefully spoon the cornstarch mixture all over the oranges.

This should be refrigerated for at least 2 or 3 hours, or as long as 10 hours (but after that the cornstarch mixture begins to dry out).

Before serving this may be decorated with a few seedless green grapes, either mounded in the center or in a ring around the outside. And if you wish, the grapes can be brushed with a bit of additional melted apricot preserves.

About 10 seedless oranges
⅔ cup sugar
Water, kirsch, rum, or cognac (if needed)
2 tablespoons cornstarch
Pinch of salt
2 teaspoons kirsch, rum, or cognac, or 1 teaspoon lemon juice
¼ cup apricot preserves
Optional: seedless green grapes
Optional: additional apricot preserves

8 PORTIONS

Strawberry Tart

This crisp, cookielike shell, baked in a flan ring or a quiche pan, is filled with strawberries and generously covered with a glaze made of puréed strawberries. It is a picture. And very delicious.

If you wish, the pastry shell may be shaped in the flan ring and frozen for days or weeks. It is best to bake it when you are ready to use it; that should be the day you serve it.

You will need a 9- or 10-inch flan ring, ¾ or 1 inch deep. Or a similar-size, loose-bottomed quiche pan.

Prepare the French Tart Pastry (see page 88). Flour the ball lightly, flatten it to a 6- or 7-inch circle, and put it on a floured pastry cloth. With a floured rolling pin roll the pastry into a 12-inch circle. If you use a 10-inch flan ring or quiche pan, roll the pastry out to a 12½- to 13-inch circle.

Place the flan ring on a cookie sheet. Roll the pastry loosely on the rolling pin, and unroll it over the flan ring, centering it carefully. With your fingers, press it into place. With scissors, trim excess, allowing ½- to ¾-inch overlap. Fold excess inside to form a double thickness on the rim and press together firmly. The rim should be upright a scant ¼ inch above the flan ring. If you wish, form a design on the folded edge by pressing the back of a knife blade at an angle across the top of the rim, at ¼-inch intervals all around the edge, or crimp it with a dough crimper.

Place the pastry shell on the cookie sheet in the freezer at least until it is frozen or longer if you wish (if you do leave it in the freezer longer, cover it well with plastic wrap or foil after it is frozen).

When you are ready to bake, adjust a rack to the center of the oven and preheat oven to 375°. Line the frozen shell with aluminum foil and fill it with dried beans or pie weights (aluminum pellets made for that purpose) to keep the shell in place.

Bake for 20 minutes. Remove from the oven and carefully remove the foil and beans by lifting the four corners of the foil. Return the shell to the oven and continue to bake for about 10 to 15 minutes more until the shell is thoroughly dry and lightly browned. (The pastry will shrink away from the sides of the pan.) After removing the foil, keep an eye on the pastry; if the bottom puffs up, prick it immediately and gently with a cake tester.

Remove the shell from the oven and let stand until completely cool. Remove the flan ring by lifting it off.

Filling

Place the berries in a large bowl of cold water, agitate them briefly, and then immediately remove them from the water. The sand will settle to the bottom—do not disturb it while you remove the berries. Pick off the stems and hulls and drain on towels.

In a blender or a food processor purée 1 box of the berries to make 2 cups purée. Strain the purée through a large strainer set over a large bowl. Place the strained purée in a heavy 2-quart saucepan and add the sugar and salt.

In a small custard cup sprinkle the gelatin over 2 tablespoons of the water, and let stand.

Place the remaining ½ cup minus 1 tablespoon of water and the lemon juice in a small bowl with the cornstarch and stir to dissolve. Add the cornstarch mixture to the strained berries.

Place over moderate heat. Stir constantly but gently with a rubber spatula for about 6 or 7 minutes until the mixture comes to a low boil, thickens, and becomes rather clear. Then reduce the heat to low, add the softened gelatin, and stir to dissolve. Continue to cook and stir gently for 3 minutes more.

Remove from the heat and gently transfer to a wide bowl to cool.

While the cornstarch mixture cools, place the berries in the baked shell. They may stand upright, in a pattern of concentric circles. Or, if they are large, they may be cut in half and placed on their cut sides, overlapping one another in concentric circles. Either way they should completely fill the shell.

With a teaspoon, gently spoon the cooled gelatin mixture evenly all over the berries and the spaces between. If the berries were halved and are overlapping, it may be necessary to raise some of them a bit to allow the mixture to run under and around them, and to fill up all the space.

Refrigerate the tart for at least a few hours.

If the tart was made in a quiche pan, place it over a bowl that has a narrower diameter than the opening in the bottom of the pan. The sides of the pan will slide down away from the tart. Now, either serve the tart on the bottom of the pan on a large serving plate, or remove it from the bottom by using a flat-sided cookie sheet, or the bottom of another quiche pan, or two wide spatulas, and carefully transfer it to a serving plate or board.

OPTIONAL DECORATION: Just before serving, peel a kiwi fruit (with a vegetable parer), slice it crossways in very, very thin circles, and place them, overlapping, in a ring around the top. If there are not enough slices, cut them in half and use half slices.

2 or 3 pint boxes (2 or 3 pounds) fresh strawberries, depending on the size of the berries and the size of the flan ring (if you use the berries whole you will need a large number; but if they are very large, you can cut them in half, and use only half as many)

1 cup granulated sugar
⅛ teaspoon salt
2 teaspoons unflavored gelatin
½ cup plus 1 tablespoon water
1 tablespoon lemon juice
3 tablespoons cornstarch

8 PORTIONS

Whipped Cream

In a chilled bowl with chilled beaters whip all the ingredients until the cream holds a soft shape but not until it is stiff.

Serve the cream separately, placing a generous spoonful alongside each portion.

2 cups heavy cream
¼ cup granulated or
    confectioners sugar
1 teaspoon vanilla extract

Strawberry and Blueberry Tart

This is a four-star red, white, and blue production for the Fourth of July, or whenever both strawberries and blueberries are in season. It has a crisp pastry shell baked in a shallow flan ring and a layer of cream cheese that is covered with a beautiful pattern of strawberries and blueberries all coated with currant jelly. The crust may be frozen, if you wish, before it is baked. The crust should be baked and the tart should be assembled from 2 to 10 hours before serving.

You will need a flan ring no more than ¾ or 1 inch deep, and 9, 10, or 11 inches wide. If you have a choice, use the largest size—you will have room for more filling—but the ring must be shallow.

Prepare the French Tart Pastry (see page 88). Flour the ball lightly, flatten it to a 6- or 7-inch circle, and put it on a floured pastry cloth. With a floured rolling pin roll the pastry into a 12-inch circle. If you use a 10- or 11-inch flan ring, roll the pastry 3 to 3½ inches wider than the ring.

Place the flan ring on a cookie sheet. Roll the pastry loosely on the rolling pin, and unroll it over the flan ring, centering it carefully. With your fingers, press it into place. With scissors, trim excess, allowing ½- to ¾-inch overlap. Fold excess inside to form a double thickness on the rim and press together firmly. The rim should be upright a scant ¼ inch above the flan ring. If you wish, form a design on the folded edge by pressing the back of a knife blade at an angle across the top of the rim, at ¼-inch intervals all around the edge, or crimp it with a dough crimper.

Place the pastry shell on the cookie sheet in the freezer at least until it is frozen or longer if you wish (if you do leave it in the freezer longer, cover it well with plastic wrap or foil after it is frozen).

When you are ready to bake, adjust a rack to the center of the oven and preheat oven to 375°. Line the frozen shell with aluminum foil and fill it with dried beans or pie weights (aluminum pellets made for that purpose) to keep the shell in place.

Bake for 20 minutes. Remove from the oven and carefully remove the foil and beans by lifting the four corners of the foil. Return the shell to the oven and continue to bake for about 10 to 15 minutes more until the shell is thoroughly dry and lightly browned. (The pastry will shrink away from the sides of the pan.) After removing the foil, keep an eye on the pastry; if the bottom puffs up, prick it immediately and gently with a cake tester.

Remove the shell from the oven and let stand until completely cool. Remove the flan ring by lifting it off. The baked but empty pastry shell will be fragile—if you freeze it for at least half an hour it will be safer to transfer. Transfer it to a flat cake plate or serving board.

Filling

Beat the cheese until it is soft and smooth. Add the sugar and cream and mix thoroughly.

Spread the filling in a smooth layer over the bottom of the crust. Refrigerate.

8 ounces Philadelphia brand cream cheese, at room temperature
2 tablespoons granulated sugar
¼ cup heavy cream

Topping

Place the preserves in a small, heavy saucepan over low heat and stir until they are smoothly melted and come to a boil. Set aside.

If the strawberries are small, place a circle of them standing upright around the outer edge of the tart. If they are very large, cut them in half lengthwise and make a circle of halves, cut side down, each half overlapping the previous one.

With a teaspoon spoon a thin layer of the preserves over the berries to coat them completely.

Now, depending on the size of your pastry shell, you will use all or only some of the blueberries. Start by placing about half of them in a bowl with about half of the melted preserves. Mix gently with a rubber spatula. With a teaspoon, spoon the berries into the space left in the middle of the tart. If you have room for more (they may be mounded a bit but not too high or it will be difficult to serve), mix as many as you want with more of the preserves and

12 ounces (1 cup) seedless red currant preserves
1 pint box (1 pound) fresh strawberries, washed, hulled, and drained
1 pint box (1 pound) fresh blueberries, washed and drained (see page 14)

6 TO 10 PORTIONS
(DEPENDING ON THE SIZE OF THE TART SHELL)

mound them. Then spoon a few teaspoons of the melted preserves over the top of the blueberries.

How about that!

Okay. Right into the refrigerator for at least 2 hours, preferably not more than 10.

NOTE: You will see that this is not an exactly precise recipe as far as just how much fruit or preserves you will use. You may not have room to use it all. If so, use only as much as looks good, and save the rest for something else.

Blueberry Custard Tart

This has a buttery, cookielike crust and a creamy custard filling full of fresh blueberries. A wonderful summer dessert. The crust can be prepared in the pan way ahead of time and frozen, if you wish. The filling is quick and easy.

The crust can be partially baked earlier in the day or just before using. But the final baking—with the filling—should be done about 4 hours before serving, if possible.

You will need an 11 x 1-inch loose-bottomed quiche or tart pan, preferably black or blue-black metal, rather than shiny silver colored; the dark color makes the crust brown.

Pastry

Prepare the French Tart Pastry (see page 88). Flour the ball lightly, flatten it to a 6- or 7-inch circle, and put it on a floured pastry cloth. With a floured rolling pin roll the pastry until it forms a circle about 13½ to 14 inches in diameter. The dough will become very thin; it is important to keep it the same thickness all over.

Place the rolling pin over one edge of the dough, roll up one side of the dough onto the rolling pin, lift it, and unroll the dough over the tart pan, centering it carefully. Quickly ease the dough on the sides down into the pan, making the sides a little thicker. If you have a cake-decorating turntable place the pan on it. Then, with scissors, trim the edges, leaving an even ½- to ¾-inch border standing up over the rim of the pan. If the pastry is not wide enough in some places and too wide in others, trim the excess and use it where you need it. Wet the edges of the patch with a bit of water, turn it upside down, and press it securely where you need it.

Now fold in a narrow hem—about ¼ inch wide—folding toward the middle (not toward the outside) and leaving the rim of the pastry raised a bit above the edges of the pan. With pastry pincers, form a design on the rim or, with the dull side of a knife blade, form shallow ridges on an angle to decorate it.

(Prick fork holes about ½ inch apart in the bottom of the pastry.)

Place the quiche pan lined with the dough in the freezer for at least 15 to 20 minutes, or as much longer as you wish. (If you freeze it longer, wrap it airtight after it becomes firm. It can be baked frozen.)

To bake, adjust a rack one-third up from the bottom of the oven and preheat oven to 400°.

Center a 12-inch square of foil shiny side down over the frozen shell, press the foil into place in the shell, and fill it with dried beans or pie weights. Bake for 15 minutes, remove the shell from the oven, and slowly and gently remove the foil (with the beans or weights) by raising all four corners at once.

Return the shell to the oven and continue to bake for 5 to 10 minutes more, until it is dry and the bottom barely begins to color.

Remove the shell from the oven and let cool for about 10 minutes. Meanwhile, lower the oven temperature to 325° and prepare the filling.

Blueberry Custard

Wash and thoroughly dry the berries (see To Wash Blueberries, page 14). Set aside.

Sift or strain together the sugar, cinnamon, and nutmeg. In a large bowl beat the eggs and yolks lightly just to mix. Stir in the dry ingredients, vanilla, and cream.

Place the blueberries evenly in a layer in the prepared pastry shell. Gently and slowly pour part of the cream mixture over the berries. Do not fill the shell all the way or it might spill on the way to the oven. With the back of a large spoon tap any berries that are on top of the custard just to wet the tops a bit.

2 cups fresh blueberries
¼ cup granulated sugar
¼ teaspoon cinnamon
¼ teaspoon nutmeg
2 eggs plus 2 egg yolks
1 teaspoon vanilla extract
1 cup whipping cream

8 PORTIONS

Place the pan in the oven, then reach in and pour in the remaining custard. (If there are any low spots on the rim of the pastry, the custard would run over; watch it carefully and, if necessary, do not use the full amount.)

Bake for about 35 minutes, until the custard no longer shakes if you tap the pan, and until a small sharp knife gently inserted into the middle of the custard comes out clean. (The knife test leaves a scar; use it only if you are not sure otherwise.)

Let the tart cool to room temperature. Remove the sides of the pan by placing

the pan on a shallow custard cup; the sides will slip down.

I always prefer to remove desserts from the bottom of a quiche pan or springform, rather than serve on the bottom. In this case removing the tart is a bit touchy because it is so wide, so tender, and so fragile; however, it can be done. But you decide. If the tart looks gorgeous and you do not want to chance hurting it, do not attempt to transfer it. (Just place it on a folded napkin on a wide, flat serving plate.) But if you do decide to transfer it, here's how. Do it now, after the tart has reached room temperature and before it is refrigerated. (When it is refrigerated it might stick to the bottom because of the butter in the pastry.) Use a flat-sided cookie sheet as a spatula. Gently ease it under the tart, holding your left hand at the opposite side of the tart to help it up onto the cookie sheet. Transfer over a flat plate or a board you will serve it on. Now move your left hand to the side of the tart that is closest to you and very gently—without any real pressure—ease the tart off the sheet onto the plate or board.

Refrigerate the tart for 1 to 3 hours before serving.

OPTIONAL DECORATION: Place a row of fresh strawberries on the filling around the circumference of the tart. Or form a circle of small rosettes of whipped cream around the circumference.

Pear and Almond Tart

This is festive and gorgeous and should be photographed for the cover of a food magazine. It is wonderful for Thanksgiving, Christmas dinner, or a New Year's Eve party. Or any time you can get good pears. (They are generally best in the fall and winter. Three favorite varieties are Comice, Anjou, and Bartlett.)

You will need a 12½ x 1-inch metal quiche pan with a loose bottom.

The pastry can be made and shaped in the pan days or weeks ahead (freeze it), but it should be baked and the tart should be finished the day it will be served.

Prepare the French Tart Pastry (see page 88). Flour the ball lightly, flatten it to a 6- or 7-inch circle, and put it on a floured pastry cloth. With a floured rolling pin, roll the dough out to a circle 15½ to 16 inches in diameter.

This is such a wide circle of tender and delicate pastry that it might crack or tear while you transfer it to the quiche pan. If so, don't get upset. You can patch it. Or you can press it all together and reroll it.

Fold the rolled-out dough in half and then in half again, forming a triangle. Very quickly, very carefully, place it in the pan with the point of the triangle in the center of the pan. Quickly and carefully unfold the dough and press it into place. If it is too large anywhere, and too small somewhere else, remove the excess and place it where you need it. When you patch the dough it is best to wet the edges with a bit of water and be sure to press it securely.

With scissors trim excess, allowing ½- to ¾-inch overlap. Fold excess inside to form a double thickness on the rim and press together securely. The rim should be upright only about ⅛ inch above the pan. If you wish, form a design on the folded edge by pressing the back of a knife blade at an angle across the top of the rim at ¼-inch intervals all around the edge, or crimp it with a dough crimper.

Place the pastry shell in the freezer until it is firm. Or if you wish, this can be frozen for weeks (but cover it with plastic wrap or foil after it is frozen).

When you are ready to bake, adjust a rack one-third up from the bottom of the oven and preheat oven to 375°.

Line the pastry shell with aluminum foil; the regular 12-inch foil is too narrow, but that is the kind to use—the wider one is too stiff. Use one long piece, and then another, crossing the first piece, at a right angle to it. Press the foil into place in the frozen shell. The ends of the foil should extend a few inches above the rim of the pastry. Fill the foil with dried beans or pie weights (aluminum pellets made for this purpose).

Do not place the quiche pan on a cookie sheet—it keeps the bottom from browning. Bake for 20 minutes. Then remove the pan from the oven and carefully remove the foil and beans by lifting the bottom piece of foil from opposite sides, and return the pastry to the oven to bake 10 to 15 minutes longer until the pastry is lightly colored on the edges and slightly colored on the bottom. When the pastry shell is baked, remove it from the oven. Raise the oven temperature to 400°.

While the pastry is baking (or after it has been baked, if you prefer) prepare the filling.

Almond Filling

The almonds must be ground to a fine powder; it can be done in a food processor (see To Grind Nuts in a Food Processor, page 14) or a nut grinder, but make them fine. Set aside.

In a small bowl beat the egg and yolk just to mix. Stir in the almond extract, rum, sugar, melted butter, and the ground almonds.

Set the filling aside and prepare the pears.

*5 ounces (1 cup) blanched
  almonds
1 egg plus 1 egg yolk
¼ teaspoon almond extract
1 tablespoon dark rum,
  cognac, or bourbon
½ cup granulated sugar
2 ounces (½ stick) unsalted
  butter, melted*

10 GENEROUS PORTIONS

Pear Filling

With a vegetable parer peel the pears, then cut each one in half the long way, and with the tip of a small paring knife cut out the cores and the seeds and remove the stems. After each pear is ready, brush it all with lemon juice and set it aside on a large plate.

6 to 7 medium-size firm pears (about 3¼ pounds)—the pears must not be soft or overripe
Juice of 1 large lemon
¼ cup granulated sugar

Make sure that the shell has stood for at least 10 minutes (but it is fine if it cools completely) before filling. Spread the almond filling in an even layer over the bottom of the shell.

Place about 10 pear halves, flat sides down and pointed ends in toward the middle, touching one another around the outer edge of the tart. (If the pears are too wide, trim a small slice off the sides.)

Now, to fill the center space with pears: Cut 2 halves the long way to make 4 pieces. Then cut each quarter the long way into 4 or 5 thin slices.

Place the slices in a fanlike pattern, overlapping one another, to fill in the center. The slices will overlap more in the middle and fan out at the outside. You will probably still have a small empty spot in the middle; cut a piece of pear into a square shape to fill that in.

Brush and sprinkle any remaining lemon juice over the pears. Sprinkle the sugar over all. Bake one-third up from the bottom in the preheated 400° oven for 50 minutes. While the tart is baking, prepare the glaze.

Glaze

Stir the preserves and liquor over moderate heat until melted. Force through a strainer set over a bowl. Return to the saucepan. About 8 to 10 minutes before the tart is finished baking, bring the preserves to a boil and let them simmer slowly for about 5 minutes.

1 cup apricot preserves
1 tablespoon dark rum, cognac, or bourbon

Remove the baked tart from the oven. Brush the hot preserves over the hot tart (if you are careful not to allow it to run down the sides, you can brush it over the top edge of the pastry). It will be a generous amount of glaze. After you have covered everything well, drizzle the remaining glaze slowly over all the fruit.

Immediately return the glazed tart to the hot oven for 3 minutes—it sets the glaze.

Remove from the oven and cool to room temperature.

Place the cooled quiche pan over a bowl that is narrower than the diameter of the rim of the pan. The sides of the pan will slip down. Then, either serve the tart on the bottom of the pan, or transfer it to a large, flat serving plate or board. Use a flat-sided cookie sheet or the bottom of a quiche pan like a spatula to transfer the tart.

Refrigerate until serving time.

Purple Plum and Almond Tart

This is a large, colorful, mouth-watering, French fruit tart. You will need an 11 x 1-inch metal quiche pan with a separate bottom, or an 11 x 1-inch flan ring placed on a cookie sheet. The pan will be lined with pastry, prebaked, then covered with a ground almond filling and then with purple plum halves. It will all be baked together and then brushed with apricot preserves. The purple juices from the plums run over the almond filling and, if they are juicy, a bit might run over the rim of the pastry, making a gorgeous picture.

This should be served within 6 hours after it is made; after that it loses its fresh look.

Pastry

Prepare the French Tart Pastry (see page 88). Flour the ball lightly, flatten it to a 6- or 7-inch circle, and put it on a floured pastry cloth. With a floured rolling pin, roll the dough into a circle 14 to 14½ inches in diameter.

Drape the pastry over the rolling pin and unroll it over the quiche pan or the flan ring on a cookie sheet. Ease the pastry down on the sides to fit into the pan where the sides and bottom meet. With scissors trim excess, allowing ½- to ¾-inch overlap. Fold excess inside to form a double thickness on the rim and press together. The rim should extend only about ⅛ inch above the pan or ring.

If you wish, score a design on the edge by pressing the back of a table knife at an angle at ¼-inch intervals across the rim all around.

Place the pastry shell in the freezer until it is firm. Or, if you wish, this can be frozen for weeks (but cover it with plastic wrap or foil after it is frozen).

When you are ready to bake, adjust a rack one-third up from the bottom of the oven and preheat oven to 375°. Line the frozen pastry with a 12-inch square of aluminum foil. Let the corners of the foil stand up; do not fold them over the sides of the pastry. Fill the foil with dried beans or with pie weights.

Bake for 20 minutes, then remove the pastry from the oven, carefully remove the foil and beans by lifting the four corners, and return the pastry to the oven to bake for 10 to 15 minutes more until the shell is thoroughly dry and lightly browned. (The pastry will shrink away from the sides of the pan.) After removing the foil, keep an eye on the pastry; if the bottom puffs up, prick it immediately and gently with a cake tester.

The filling can be made while the pastry is baking or after it has been removed from the oven.

Almond and Plum Filling

The almonds must be ground to a fine powder; this can be done in a food processor (see To Grind Nuts in a Food Processor, page 14), or a nut grinder, but grind them fine. Set aside.

In the small bowl of an electric mixer beat the egg and the yolk with the almond extract, cognac, and ½ cup of the sugar (reserve remaining ¼ cup). Mix in the melted butter and the ground almonds.

If you have just baked the pastry shell, let it stand for about 10 minutes (it does not have to cool completely but it can if you wish). Raise the oven rack to one-third down from the top. Preheat the oven to 375°.

Cut the plums in half and remove the pits.

Spread the almond filling in an even layer over the bottom of the pastry shell. Cover the filling with the plums, placing them cut side down. Start with a circle of 12 halves on the outside (more or less, depending on the size of the plums), touching each other. Then, inside them, a circle of 6 halves (again, more or less, depending on the size), touching each other. And 1 half in the middle. With medium-size plums there will be 1 half of a plum left over.

Sprinkle with the reserved ¼ cup sugar. Drizzle with the 1 tablespoon kirsch or cognac.

It is generally best not to place a quiche pan on a cookie sheet (it might prevent the bottom from browning). In this recipe the plum juice may run over; therefore, place a cookie sheet or a jelly-roll pan on a rack below to catch any overflow.

Bake for 30 to 45 minutes, depending on the ripeness of the fruit. It should be tender but not too soft. Test it with a cake tester. While the tart is baking, prepare the glaze.

5 ounces (1 cup) blanched almonds
1 egg plus 1 egg yolk
¼ teaspoon almond extract
1 tablespoon cognac or brandy
¾ cup granulated sugar
2 ounces (½ stick) unsalted butter, melted
10 medium-size or large plums (about 2½ pounds; I do not use the small blue plums for this)
1 tablespoon kirsch, cognac, or brandy

10 TO 12 PORTIONS

Glaze

Stir the preserves in a small pan over low heat until they are completely melted and come to a boil. Force them through a strainer. Return to the pan. Just before you remove the tart from the oven, bring the glaze to a boil again.

When the tart is removed from the oven it should stand for 2 or 3 minutes (no more) before the glaze is applied. (The fruit will be a little wrinkled now, but unless the tart was overbaked it won't be too shriveled.)

With a pastry brush, brush the hot glaze all over the fruit and over the space between the fruit and on the rim.

½ cup apricot preserves

Return the tart to the oven for 2 to 3 minutes. (It helps to set the glaze.)

If some of the juice ran over the pastry it might make it difficult to remove the sides of the quiche pan or the flan ring after the tart has cooled. Therefore, do not wait until it cools. After about 5 minutes, remove the tart as follows: Place the pan over a bowl that is smaller in diameter than the opening in the bottom of the pan. As you do, the sides of the pan should slide down. If it needs a little help, easy does it. Use a cookie sheet as a spatula to transfer the tart very carefully from the bottom of the pan to a serving platter. If it is stuck to the bottom, release it gently with a knife or a long, narrow spatula.

To remove the tart from a flan ring, lift the ring to remove it, and use a flat-sided cookie sheet as a spatula to transfer the tart very carefully to a serving platter.

Peach and Almond Tart

This variation of the previous Purple Plum and Almond Tart should be prepared only when peaches are at the height of their season. The pastry with its almond filling can be baked a day ahead if you wish and the peaches can be poached a day ahead if you wish. But an hour to two before serving, the peaches should be drained, placed on the tart, and glazed—it will take only about 10 minutes. And will be gorgeous.

Pastry

Follow the recipe for the Purple Plum and Almond Tart through the directions to place the almond filling in the partially baked tart shell. Bake on the center rack of a preheated 375° oven for 25 minutes until the filling is golden brown and barely firm to the touch. Set aside to cool.

Peach Topping

Blanch the peaches and peel them (see page 178). Cut them in half, separate the halves, remove the pits, and cut each into six even lengthwise slices.

Place the sugar, water, vanilla, and kirsch in a large, wide frying pan that has a tight

cover. Stir over moderate heat until the sugar melts and the mixture comes to a boil.

Add the sliced peaches, reduce the heat to low, cover, and simmer gently, stirring the peaches very carefully a few times with a rubber spatula. Cook for only 3 to 5 minutes—more or less, depending on the ripeness of the peaches. They must not be over-cooked or become limp. When they are just barely tender, use a slotted spoon and transfer them to a large, flat dish. (If you prepare the peaches a day ahead, cover the plate with plastic wrap and refrigerate overnight. Then continue with the next step.)

5 large freestone peaches, ripe but firm
½ cup granulated sugar
¼ cup water
½ teaspoon vanilla extract
2 tablespoons kirsch, rum, or cognac
½ cup apricot preserves

10 TO 12 PORTIONS

When the peaches are cool, place them carefully on several thicknesses of paper towels to drain well.

Meanwhile, remove the flan ring or the sides of the quiche pan.

Boil the syrup remaining in the pan for a few minutes over high heat until it thickens to a thick jelly. Watch it carefully and stir it occasionally with a wooden spoon.

Place the apricot preserves in a small, heavy saucepan over moderate heat. Add a scant tablespoon of the reduced peach syrup (see Note), stir occasionally until the preserves are melted, and then force through a strainer. Return the preserves to the saucepan, bring to a boil, then reduce the heat to low and keep the preserves warm.

Place the drained peaches on top of the almond filling as follows: Place one slice at a right angle to the rim on the right side of the tart (three o'clock) with the thick (curved) side facing up (twelve o'clock). Place another slice closer to you, slightly overlapping the first. Continue to form a circle of slices all around the tart, overlapping each other slightly more toward the center of the tart than on the outside, rather like a fan pattern. Then form another similar circle inside the first. And continue until there is just a small space left in the center; it might be easiest to fill that if you dice a few of the slices. Or, if the peaches are really large, there might not be any space left in the center.

Brush the warm strained apricot preserves over the top to cover the peaches completely.

Transfer the tart, using a flat-sided cookie sheet or the bottom of a quiche pan as a spatula, to a large, flat serving plate or a board. Or, if you have baked this in a quiche pan, it may be served on the bottom of the pan if you wish.

It is best to serve this within an hour or two. The beautiful glaze on the peaches begins to fade.

NOTE: The little bit of thick jelly that remains in the pan after boiling down the peach syrup may be scraped out and used as a jelly on toast.

Lemon and Almond Tart

This has a prebaked pastry crust and two fillings: one almond (like marzipan) and one lemon (with juice, grated rind, and pieces of diced fresh lemon). Both fillings are poured into the baked crust and it is all baked into a creamy, semifirm, custardy mixture.

Although this is still delicious after standing all day (and even overnight), here's how to serve it fresh, and yet not have any last-minute fuss. The pastry can be made ahead of time and frozen, unbaked, in the pan. Then it can be baked early in the day for that night. At the same time, the two fillings can be prepared (this does not take long). Cover the fillings and let the empty baked crust and the two fillings stand at room temperature until 3 or 4 hours (more or less) before serving. Then put it all together (it only takes a minute or two) to bake.

You will need a 12½ x 1-inch fluted metal quiche pan with a separate bottom, or a 12½ x 1-inch flan ring. And be prepared with a large enough flat serving platter or a serving board. Or, if you have used a quiche pan, serve the tart right on the bottom of the pan (placed on a tray or a board or whatever you have that is large enough).

Pastry

Prepare the French Tart Pastry (see page 88). Flour the ball lightly, flatten it to a 6- or 7-inch circle, and put it on a floured pastry cloth. With a floured rolling pin, roll it out to a circle 15½ to 16 inches in diameter. If you are using a flan ring place it on a cookie sheet. (Do not place a quiche pan on a cookie sheet—it might keep the bottom from browning.)

Now, caution: This is such a wide circle of pastry that if you drape it over a rolling pin to transfer it, the weight of the pastry is very likely to cause it to come apart. It is safer to fold this loosely in half and then in half again to make a triangle and, with your hands, put it in the pan, placing it carefully to cover only one-quarter of the pan with the point in the middle. Then, carefully (try to keep your fingernails away), unfold and press it into place. If it is too large anywhere, and too small somewhere else, remove the excess and place it wherever you need it. If you patch the pastry, wet the ends a bit with water and be sure to press it securely; the patch must not open during baking. If you have a disaster while placing the pastry in the pan, either patch it or form it into a ball again and reroll (it might even behave better if it is rolled twice).

With scissors trim excess, allowing a generous ½-inch overlap. Fold excess inside to form a double thickness on the rim and press together to form a strong rim that stands ⅛ to ¼ inch above the pan or ring. There must not be any low spots.

Place the pastry shell in the freezer until it is firm. Or, if you wish, this can be frozen for weeks. (Wrap after it becomes firm.)

When you are ready to bake, adjust a rack one-third up from the bottom of the oven and preheat oven to 375°.

Since the regular 12-inch aluminum foil will not be wide enough to line this pan, and the wider foil is too heavy to work with comfortably, use two pieces of the 12-inch foil, each about 17 inches long. Place them in the pastry, crossing each other at right angles. Press the foil into place in the pastry.

Fill the foil with dried beans or with the aluminum pellets that are made for that purpose.

Bake for 20 minutes. Remove from the oven and carefully remove the foil and beans by lifting the bottom piece of foil (lift from opposite sides), and return the pastry to the oven to bake 10 to 15 minutes longer until it is lightly colored on the edges. (The pastry will shrink away from the sides of the pan.) After removing the foil, keep an eye on the pastry; if the bottom puffs up, prick it immediately and gently with a cake tester.

While the pastry crust is baking, or after it has baked, prepare both fillings.

You will use the same oven rack position and oven temperature to bake this tart with the filling; therefore do not turn off the oven after baking the crust.

Almond Filling

The almonds must be ground to a fine powder; this can be done in a food processor (see To Grind Nuts in a Food Processor, page 14) or a nut grinder. In the small bowl of an electric mixer beat the egg and the yolk with the almond extract and cognac or kirsch. Add the sugar and beat until it is pale. Mix in the melted butter and the ground almonds. Set aside.

5 ounces (1 cup) blanched almonds
1 egg plus 1 egg yolk
¼ teaspoon almond extract
1 tablespoon cognac or kirsch
½ cup granulated sugar
2 ounces (½ stick) unsalted butter, melted

Lemon Filling

Grate fine the rind of 1 extra-large or 2 medium-size lemons. Squeeze the juice of 1 extra-large or 1½ medium-size lemons to make 3 tablespoons juice. Mix the juice with the rind. Set them aside. With a small sharp paring knife, peel 1 extra-large or 1½ medium-size lemons. Carefully and completely remove every bit of white. Section the lemons by cutting down on either side of the membrane to loosen the sections. Remove all the pits. Place the wedge-shaped sections on a flat plate or board and cut them lengthwise and then crosswise, making pieces about ¼ to ⅓ inch in diameter. However, if the lemons are small it will not be necessary to cut the wedges lengthwise—just crosswise. You should have approximately 3 tablespoons of pieces. (Use more or larger

2 extra-large or 3 medium-size lemons
1 cup granulated sugar
2 teaspoons unsifted all-purpose flour
4 eggs
1 cup light corn syrup
1½ tablespoons unsalted butter, melted

12 TO 16 PORTIONS

pieces if you wish.) Mix the pieces with the juice and rind.

In a small bowl stir the sugar and flour to mix.

In the small bowl of an electric mixer, or in any bowl with an eggbeater or a wire whisk, beat the eggs just to mix. Beat in the sugar-flour mixture just to mix. Then mix in the corn syrup and the melted butter. With a rubber spatula stir in the lemon juice mixture.

Now pour the almond filling into the prebaked crust and smooth it with a rubber spatula or the back of a spoon. It will be a very thin layer.

Place the tart on a rack one-third up from the bottom in the preheated 375° oven.

With a ladle, gently ladle the lemon filling over the almond filling. It will not stay in separate layers; the lemon will run down into the almond—it is okay. CAU-TION! Be extremely careful when you pour the lemon filling into the tart; if any of it runs over the sides of the crust it will cause the tart to stick to the pan as though it were the strongest glue in the world—you will probably break the tart in trying to re-move it from the pan. (Guess how I know?)

Bake for 35 to 40 minutes until a small sharp knife inserted into the middle comes out clean. The top will become brown. Do not cover it with foil during baking (it would stick).

If it looks as though some filling might have run over, it is best to remove the tart immediately while everything is hot, before it cools and hardens. Carefully remove the sides of the quiche pan (by placing the pan on a bowl that is narrower than the opening in the bottom of the pan) or if you have used a flan ring, raise it gently with your fingers. If the bottom is stuck, use a long, sharp knife to release it. Then use a flat-sided cookie sheet, or the bottom of a quiche pan, to transfer the tart to a flat serving plate.

If it does not look as though some filling has run over, let the tart cool before re-moving it to a serving plate.

Let the tart stand for at least a few hours. Serve at room temperature.

Sugar Topping

Sprinkle the top generously with confectioners sugar through a fine strainer held over the tart.

Lemon Tartlets

These are tiny, bite-size pastries with a light and flaky buttery crust and a tart, creamy lemon filling. They are fancy, classy, elegant; make them for your most important occasions. They should be refrigerated or frozen until they are served; serve them like cookies—they are finger food. Both the pastry and the filling recipes may be doubled. You will need small, round tartlet pans that measure 2¾ inches in diameter and are ½ inch deep, and a cookie cutter that fits them (3¹⁄₁₆ inches in diameter).

Pastry

Prepare the French Tart Pastry (see page 88). Divide the dough in half and form it into two balls, flatten them slightly, wrap in plastic wrap, and refrigerate for an hour or so.

Adjust a rack one-third up from the bottom of the oven and preheat oven to 350°. Lightly flour a pastry cloth and a rolling pin. Roll one piece of the pastry at a time, rolling until it is a scant ¹⁄₁₆ inch thick (very thin!); it is more delicate, crisp, and flaky if it is thin.

Cut the rolled-out pastry with a plain or scalloped round cutter that is 3¹⁄₁₆ inches in diameter. With a small metal spatula or with a table knife transfer each round of pastry into a tartlet pan. With your fingers press the pastry into place in the pans. (If you don't have enough pans, just do as many as you can at a time.) Place the pastry-lined pans in the freezer for a few minutes or longer.

Cut small squares of aluminum foil about 3¼ inches on a side. When the pastry is firm, press a square of foil into each tartlet. Place them on a cookie sheet. Fill with dried beans or with aluminum pellets to keep the pastry in place.

The pastry should be cold or frozen when it is baked. Bake for 13 minutes. Remove from the oven and quickly and carefully remove the foil and beans or pellets. Then return the pastry shells to the oven and continue to bake for a few minutes longer until the pastry is a light golden color; it should not be too pale—it looks and tastes better when it has some color.

Let the tartlet forms stand for a moment or so until you can remove the baked shells from the pans. Set aside to cool.

(If these are made ahead of time, wrap them airtight and freeze until you are ready to fill them.)

You will need 20 baked shells of the size indicated for the following amount of filling.

(If you have leftover pastry, roll it out, cut it into shapes, sprinkle with sugar, and bake thin cookies.)

Lemon Filling

This is an English recipe, called lemon curd or lemon cheese. It is used like a jam or jelly as a spread for toast or muffins, or as a filling for a layer cake or a sponge roll. It keeps for several weeks in the refrigerator. It is very easy to make a jar of this as a lovely gift.

This is not as temperamental as the usual egg custard. The large amount of sugar (or is it the lemon juice?) seems to protect the eggs from curdling. Stir frequently, but don't worry.

Place the eggs and the yolk in the top of a large double boiler. Add the sugar and whisk or beat lightly to mix. Add the butter, rind, and juice.

Place over hot water on moderate heat. Cook, uncovered, stirring frequently with a rubber spatula, for 20 to 25 minutes or until the mixture is as thick as a heavy cream sauce. Strain into a wide-topped pitcher.

Place 20 baked tartlet shells on a tray. Pour the warm filling into the shells, carefully filling each one almost to the top. The filling will set as it cools.

3 eggs plus 1 egg yolk
1 cup granulated sugar
4 ounces (1 stick) unsalted butter, cut into pieces
Finely grated rind of 2 large lemons
6 tablespoons fresh lemon juice

OPTIONAL DECORATION: These may be left completely plain. Or they may be topped while the filling is still soft with a light sprinkling of finely chopped, unsalted green pistachio nuts, or a bit of crumbled, toasted sliced almonds, or a sliver of preserved kumquat. Whatever, keep it small and simple. Or wait until shortly before serving and top each one with a rosette of whipped cream, or with a border of small rosettes of whipped cream.

Refrigerate or freeze until serving time—they may be eaten frozen. Refrigerated, they are tender and delicate; frozen, they are almost the texture of semifirm cheese.

To freeze, pack the tartlets in a single layer in a box that is shallow but deep enough so the cover does not touch the filling. Freezer paper or plastic wrap will stick to the filling unless the tarts are frozen firm before they are covered.

NOTE: If your pans are a different size from mine, the cookie cutter must be large enough to cut rounds of pastry that will reach just to the rims of the pans, or a tiny bit above the rim; the pastry may shrink slightly in the baking.

Rancho Santa Fe Lemon Tart

A tender and crisp crust and a wondrously creamy lemon filling covered with an apricot glaze—looks like a million dollars. It is easy, but because the dough is rolled quite thin it takes a light touch and TLC.

You will need an 11 x 1-inch loose-bottomed quiche or tart pan made of black metal because black metal browns the crust better than shiny metal does.

Pastry

It is best to make the pastry ahead of time; it should be refrigerated for 2 to 24 hours before it is rolled out. It can also be frozen, but if it is, refrigerate overnight (to thaw) before using.

The pastry can be made in a food processor or by hand. Either way, start by combining the yolk, ice water, whipping cream, and the vanilla and almond extracts in a small container (preferably with a spout if you are going to use a food processor). Refrigerate.

In a food processor: Fit the bowl with the metal chopping blade, place the flour, salt, and sugar in the bowl, turn the machine on/off once, add the butter and process on/off about 10 to 12 times (for a total of 10 to 12 seconds) only until the mixture resembles coarse crumbs. With the machine running quickly pour the cold egg yolk mixture through the feed tube and then process on/off only until the dough barely begins to hold together and just leaves the sides of the bowl (but not until it forms a ball).

By hand: Place the dry ingredients in a wide mixing bowl, add the butter, and with a pastry blender cut it in until the mixture resembles coarse crumbs. Then with a fork stir in the cold egg mixture.

Whichever way you have mixed the ingredients, now turn the dough out onto a work surface and press it together to form a ball, then place it on plastic wrap and pat into a 6-inch circle. Wrap in plastic wrap and refrigerate for 2 hours or more.

When you are ready to shape the crust, have an 11 x 1-inch black metal quiche pan at hand. Place the round of dough on a floured pastry cloth. With a floured rolling pin roll out the dough carefully (it will become quite thin) to form a circle about 14 inches in diameter. (Reflour the rolling pin occasionally while you are working with it and spread a tiny bit of flour over the top of the dough once or twice to prevent sticking.)

Hold the rolling pin across the dough (from twelve o'clock to six o'clock) and raise the left side of the pastry cloth to lift about half of the dough and flip it over the

1 egg yolk
1 tablespoon ice water
1 tablespoon plus 1 teaspoon
   whipping cream
½ teaspoon vanilla extract
¼ teaspoon almond extract
1½ cups sifted all-purpose
   flour
¼ teaspoon salt
1½ tablespoons granulated
   sugar
4 ounces (1 stick) unsalted
   butter, cold and firm, cut
   into 8 to 10 pieces

rolling pin. Using the rolling pin, carry the dough over to the quiche pan, center it as well as you can, then lower and unroll it over the pan. Remove the rolling pin and with your fingers ease the sides of the dough down into the pan. (If necessary, the dough can be patched; you can cut some off one part, dampen the top edge of the patch with a bit of water, turn it upside down [because the top probably has less flour on it and will therefore stick better], and place it over another part. Press the edges securely to seal.)

Trim the edge with scissors, leaving a ½-inch overhang. Fold ¼ inch of the over-hang in toward the center of the circle to make a narrow hem extending about ¼ inch above the rim. Press gently to made it neat and smooth. Then, with pastry pin-cers, make a design on the rim or, with the dull side of a knife blade, score the rim gently with little lines on a slant, about ¼ inch apart.

Prick fork holes in the bottom of the pastry about ½ inch apart.

Refrigerate or freeze the pastry shell for at least 30 minutes (or longer) before baking.

To bake, adjust a rack to the middle of the oven and preheat oven to 400°.

Line the chilled pastry shell with a 12-inch square of foil shiny side down. Fill the foil with dried beans or pie weights and bake for 5 minutes more until the bottom of the shell just begins to color slightly.

Remove the shell from the oven and reduce the oven temperature to 250°. (If there are any cracks or holes in the bottom of the pastry shell, see Patching the Pas-try, page 20.)

Let the shell stand to cool while you prepare the filling.

Lemon Filling

Place the cream in a saucepan over moderate heat, stirring occasionally, until the cream just comes to a boil.

Meanwhile, in a wide bowl, beat the yolks lightly with a wire whisk, just to mix. In a small bowl stir the cornstarch and sugar together and then gradually whisk them into the yolks, just to mix. Gradually whisk in the lemon juice. When the cream comes to a boil add it gradually, whisking to mix but not enough to make the mixture foamy.

Pour about 2 cups of the filling into a small, wide pitcher (a plastic 2-cup measuring cup, for instance). Pour the remaining filling into the pastry shell, carefully place the shell in the oven, then reach into the oven and slowly pour the 2 cups of filling from the pitcher (this prevents spilling).

Bake for 1 hour at 250°. The filling will still appear slightly soft but it will firm as it cools. Remove from the oven and let stand until completely cool.

1½ cups whipping cream
7 egg yolks
1 tablespoon cornstarch
¾ cup granulated sugar
⅔ cup lemon juice (see Note)

12 PORTIONS

Apricot Glaze

Heat the preserves in a small pan to soften. Strain to re-move any coarse pieces. Return to the pan and stir in the cognac.

½ cup apricot preserves
1 tablespoon cognac

When the tart has cooled completely heat the glaze un-til it comes to a boil. Pour the hot glaze gently over the tart and tilt the pan to run the glaze all over the top. It must touch the crust all around; if necessary, use a brush very gently.

Refrigerate.

Remove the sides of the pan and, using a flat-rimmed cookie sheet as a spatula, transfer the tart gently and carefully to a wide, flat serving plate.

Whipped cream is optional.

Whipped Cream (optional)

In a chilled bowl with chilled beaters whip the cream with the sugar and vanilla only until the cream holds a soft shape, not until it is stiff.

2 cups whipping cream
¼ cup confectioners sugar
1 teaspoon vanilla extract
Optional: fresh cherries or
*   berries*

Serve the cream separately, spooning or pouring it alongside each portion.

This does not need a thing but if you just happen to have some fresh black cherries with long stems or fresh strawberries with bright green hulls or fresh blackberries or raspberries, arrange a cir-cle of them around the top of the pie.

NOTE: The amount of lemon juice can be increased to ¾ cup if you love a sour lemon taste; I consider ⅔ cup a happy medium.

Grape Tart

This has a marvelous crust made of a rich ground almond butter-cookie dough that resembles Linzer Torte. You press it into the pan with your fingertips; it is baked empty and then filled with concentric rings of grapes in a variety of colors and kirsch-flavored apricot preserves. It is a most delicious dessert, and gorgeous. It is festive and partyish; serve it any time you can get beautiful grapes and you want to make a big impression. Have you seen the candles that look like French fruit tarts? That's what this tart looks like.

The crust may be prepared ahead of time and frozen if you wish. Finish the tart from 4 to 12 hours before serving.

The seeds must be removed from the grapes, a slow process. If you like detail work, you will enjoy doing it. I do. Otherwise, it would be good to have someone help. (This can be made with seedless grapes; it won't be as dramatic all in one color, but it will still be an exciting dessert.)

You will need an 11- or 12-inch loose-bottomed quiche pan that must not be more than 1 inch deep.

Almond Crust

To prepare the pan, place the rim of an 11 or 12 x 1-inch loose-bottomed quiche pan in the freezer. Melt 2 to 3 tablespoons of butter (in addition to the butter in ingredients—this is for buttering the pan). With a pastry brush, brush it all over the inside of the chilled rim (the cold pan will set the butter and keep it from running). Then butter the bottom of the pan and place it inside the rim. Use a generous amount of fine, dry bread crumbs to sprinkle all over the bottom and the sides. Then, carefully, holding the bottom in place with your fingertips, shake out excess crumbs over paper. (If the pan is not buttered and crumbed, the crust will stick; do it thoroughly.) Set aside.

The almonds must be ground to a fine powder. This can be done in a food processor (see To Grind Nuts in a Food Processor, page 14) or a nut grinder. If you use a processor, leave them in the processor bowl and finish the crust as follows: Add the flour, salt, cinnamon, cloves and/or ginger, and sugar and process briefly only to mix. Cut the butter into pieces, add, and process to mix very well. Then, through the feed tube, add the yolks and process until the mixture holds together. Turn it out onto a board and work it a bit between your hands until it is thoroughly mixed.

Without a processor, cream the butter, add the sugar, and beat to mix. Mix in the

7½ ounces (1½ cups)
  blanched almonds
1 cup unsifted all-purpose
  flour
¼ teaspoon salt
¾ teaspoon cinnamon
Pinch of ground cloves and/or
  powdered ginger
½ cup granulated sugar
5 ounces (1¼ sticks) unsalted
  butter
2 egg yolks

12 PORTIONS

yolks and then the remaining dry ingredients. Mix or knead until thoroughly mixed.

Here's the best way to line this pan with this nut mixture: Take about 2 or 3 tablespoons of the dough and roll it between your hands into a short, fat cigar shape. Press it against the rim of the pan. Continue, overlapping the pieces slightly, all around the rim. Then divide the remaining dough into three or four pieces, flatten them slightly between your hands, and press into the bottom of the pan. Be sure that wherever the pieces meet all seams are pressed together well. Smooth the top of the rim; it must not be higher than the rim of the pan. Press the bottom firmly to make a smooth and compact layer. The bottom crust will be about ⅓ inch; the sides may be a bit thicker. Bend your index finger and press your knuckle into the angle where the sides and bottom meet—that section should not be too thick.

To decorate the rim, press the back of the blade of a table knife slightly at an angle across the top of the rim to score it. Repeat at ¼-inch intervals all around the rim. Or use pastry pincers; they work fine if you are careful.

Place the crust in the freezer until it is firm. To bake, adjust a rack one-third up from the bottom of the oven and preheat oven to 350°. Tear off a 12-inch square of aluminum foil. Brush one side of it with butter (it is not usually necessary to butter the foil for lining a crust, but it is advisable in this recipe) and place it, buttered side down, in the frozen crust. Press firmly into place. Fill with dried beans or pie pellets.

Bake for 35 minutes. Remove the crust from the oven and carefully remove the foil and beans by lifting the corners of the foil.

Continue to bake the crust. If the bottom puffs up, flatten it very gently and slightly with the bottom of a wide metal spatula. Bake for 15 to 20 minutes more until the crust is brown on the edges and done (although it will be soft to the touch) on the bottom.

Set aside to cool. When the crust has cooled to tepid or room temperature, remove the sides of the pan by placing the pan over a bowl that is narrower than the base of the quiche pan. The sides of the pan will slide down. You can either leave the pastry on the bottom of the pan or you can transfer it to a flat serving platter or a board. To transfer it, let it cool completely. Then, gently and carefully, transfer it with two wide metal spatulas, or use a flat cookie sheet or the bottom of a quiche pan as a spatula. If it seems too fragile to move, freeze it first. Either way, be careful.

Grapes

You will need about 3 pounds (9 cups) of grapes. If you can get red, green, and black grapes, it will make a stunning tart. But if you can get only one or two colors, it is okay. It will look best if the grapes are large. Remove the grapes from the stems and wash them in a bowl of cold water. Drain them in a strainer. Now, with a small sharp knife cut a grape in half from top to bottom, cutting through the stem end. With your fingernail remove the seeds. Then place the two halves next to each other, cut side down, on paper towels. Continue with all the grapes, keeping the halves in matched pairs.

Apricot Glaze

Stir the preserves in a saucepan over moderate heat until they melt. Meanwhile, sprinkle the gelatin over the kirsch in a small custard cup and let stand for 5 minutes. When the preserves have melted, pour them through a strainer set over a bowl; press on them with the back of a spoon to force them through the strainer. Return the strained preserves to the

18 ounces (1½ cups) apricot preserves
1 envelope unflavored gelatin
¼ cup kirsch

saucepan. Stir over heat, bring to a boil, add the softened gelatin, stir to dissolve, and then simmer gently for 3 minutes. Remove from heat.

Now, to assemble the tart, brush the hot glaze generously over the bottom and sides of the crust, and lightly over the top of the rim. The glaze will act as a glue for the grapes. Start by making a row of one kind of grape around the rim, placing the two halves together (it should look like the grapes were never cut), and placing each grape standing up, resting on its stem end or at a slight angle. Complete one circle of grapes and brush it generously with the glaze. Then make the next row, using another kind of grape (unless you have only one kind), fitting them compactly and brushing them generously with the glaze. With large grapes, I make five rows and fill in the center with more grapes. It will depend on the size of the grapes and how compactly you place them.

If the glaze starts to thicken while you are working with it, replace it over heat to melt again. When you have filled the tart with grapes, pour all the remaining glaze evenly over everything.

Refrigerate for 4 to 12 hours. You will need a strong, heavy, sharp knife for serving.

Individual Maple Pecan Tarts

Crisp, buttery crusts with a semifirm, chewy maple syrup filling that is loaded with pecans. Divine.

Shaping these pastry shells takes time and patience but is great fun. The crusts can be shaped in the pans ahead of time and frozen, if you wish. The filling is quick and easy to mix, but it can be done a day ahead and refrigerated if that fits your schedule better. These are best when they are fresh, but it is fine to bake them even in the morning for that evening.

You need special pans for making these. Kitchen shops call the pans either individual quiche or tartlet pans. They are made of black metal, they have loose bottoms and fluted rims, and they measure 4¾ inches (across the top) x 1 1/16 inches (in depth—inside).

Pastry

Place the flour, salt, and sugar in the bowl of a food processor fitted with the metal chopping blade. Turn the machine on/off two or three times just to mix the ingredients. Add the butter and let the machine run for about 5 seconds until the mixture resembles coarse meal.

(It is not necessary to mix the yolks.) With the machine running add the yolks and water through the feed tube and process just until the mixture forms a ball.

To make the pastry without a processor, mound the flour on a large work surface. Make a well in the center and place all the remaining ingredients in the well. With the fingertips of your right hand work the center ingredients together. Gradually incorporate the flour, using a dough scraper or a wide metal spatula in your left hand to help move the flour toward the center. When all the flour has been absorbed, knead briefly until the dough holds together, and finish by "breaking" the pastry as follows: Form it into a ball; then, starting at the side of the dough farthest from you and using the heel of your hand, push off small pieces (about 2 tablespoons), pushing the dough against the work surface and away from you. Continue until all the dough has been pushed off. Re-form the dough and "break" it off again.

Whichever way you have mixed the dough, now form it into a perfectly even fat sausage shape with flat ends, wrap it in plastic wrap, and refrigerate for a few hours or overnight.

When you are ready to roll out the dough, cut it into six equal pieces (they must be exactly the same size). The dough will be too firm to roll immediately. Let it stand for a few minutes. Flour a pastry cloth and a rolling pin.

Place a piece of the firm dough on the cloth and press down on it with the rolling pin to soften it a bit, then roll it into a circle 6 inches wide. This dough may be turned over once or twice during rolling, if you wish, to keep both sides lightly floured and to prevent sticking. The cloth and rolling pin should be lightly refloured as necessary.

After rolling out a circle of dough, use anything round and 6 inches in diameter as a pattern (I use a 6-inch flan ring), place it on the dough, and with a small sharp knife cut around the rim to form a perfect circle. Then fit the dough into the individual pans. (A slightly more complicated method, but one that also works, is to fit the round of dough into one of the individual pans, press it into place, and then with scissors trim the edge evenly, leaving ¼ to ½ inch of the pastry above the rim of the pan.

With your fingers gently turn in the edge of the pastry to form a narrow hem; the folded edge of the hem should be a bit higher than the top of the pan (with no low spots or the filling will run over). The top of the rim will crack slightly when the dough is folded; it is okay. Press the double thickness of pastry firmly together against the inside of the pan. (If your fingernails are in the way, bend a finger and use the

1¾ cups plus 2 tablespoons sifted all-purpose flour

¼ teaspoon salt

3 tablespoons granulated sugar

4 ounces (1 stick) unsalted butter, cold and firm, cut into small squares

3 egg yolks

1 tablespoon plus 1½ teaspoons ice water

6 INDIVIDUAL PIES

bent finger joint to press with—or use two bent finger joints together.)

With pastry pincers, or with tines of a fork, make a neat, ridged design on the rim. Place the lined pans in the freezer or refrigerator to become firm.

Filling

In the small bowl of an electric mixer beat the eggs to mix. On low speed, beating only to mix, add the maple syrup, sugar, vanilla, melted butter, and the rum.

2 eggs
⅔ cup maple syrup
⅔ cup light brown sugar, firmly packed
¾ teaspoon vanilla extract
1½ tablespoons unsalted butter, melted
2 teaspoons dark rum
7 ounces (2 cups) pecans, toasted (see To Toast Pecans, page 6), halves or large pieces

When you are ready to bake, adjust a rack one-third up from the bottom of the oven and preheat oven to 350°.

Place the individual pans lined with pastry on a jelly-roll pan or a cookie sheet.

Divide the pecans among the pans, placing them casually, but preferably with rounded sides up if you are using nut halves (instead of pieces). You can just estimate, or measure ⅓ cup of pecans for each pan.

Transfer the filling to a pitcher that is easy to pour from and pour the filling evenly into the pans, pouring in a slow stream to wet the tops of the nuts. Do not fill the pie shells completely at first—if you use too much filling in one shell, there might not be enough to go around. The filling should almost—but not quite—reach to the tops of the crusts.

Bake for 30 minutes, reversing the position of the jelly-roll pan or cookie sheet front to back once after about 20 minutes to ensure even browning. After 30 minutes the rims should be golden brown.

Remove from the oven and let stand for about 15 minutes. If some filling ran out of a tart, that tart should be removed from its pan as soon as possible; if you wait the filling hardens and it becomes more difficult.

To remove the tarts from the pans, place a pan on a small, narrow jar or other object; the sides should slip down easily, but they might need a little help from you. Then use a wide metal spatula to transfer the tart from the bottom of the pan to a rack to cool.

Many people like to serve whipped cream with pecan pie (especially in Texas, where the pecan is the state nut, and they eat a great many pecan pies). And many people think it is best with ice cream (at Spago, in Beverly Hills, California, they serve individual pecan pies—this size and shape—with a scoop of caramel ice cream on top). I think it depends on the occasion and the menu. But the tarts absolutely plain, with nothing, are perfect.

Cottage Cheese and Jelly Tart

This is a shallow cheese tart with a thin layer of jelly under the cheese. Cottage cheese makes a lighter cake than cream cheese, but with the same slightly tart flavor. This recipe was originally made in Virginia hundreds of years ago; versions of it have been popular since then. Traditionally it is made in a pie plate, but since the filling is so shallow (¾ inch deep) I suggest a shallow tart or quiche pan instead of a pie plate. It is quite easy and makes a delicious dessert.

It is best to serve this tart the same day it is made. You will need a food processor (a great time-saver over the original procedure of forcing the cheese through a linen towel) and a loose-bottomed tart or quiche pan 10 inches across the top and a scant 1 inch deep, preferably made of black or blue-black metal instead of a shiny silver-colored metal—the dark color encourages the pastry to brown.

Prepare pie pastry for a 10-inch crust (see page 17) and refrigerate it overnight, if possible, or for at least a few hours. On a floured pastry cloth with a floured rolling pin roll out the dough until it is 13 to 13½ inches in diameter (keep the thickness as even as possible). Drape the pastry over a rolling pin and unroll it over the tart or quiche pan, centering it carefully. Ease the sides down into the pan; do not stretch the pastry. If the pastry is too narrow in spots and too wide in other spots, cut away the part that is too wide, wet the edges of the pieces you have cut away with water, and place it where needed. Flour your fingertips and press the pieces together.

With scissors trim the edge, leaving a ½- to ¾-inch overhang. Fold the overhang over onto itself, folding in toward the center of the pan, to form a narrow hem at the top of the pastry, which should extend about ¼ inch above the sides of the pan.

If you have pastry pincers, use them to decorate the hem of the pastry; if not, use the dull edge of a knife and score little lines on an angle about ¼ inch apart around the hem. Then pierce the bottom at 12-inch intervals with a fork.

Place the pastry shell in the freezer for about 20 minutes (or for days or weeks, if you wish, in which case wrap it when it is firm).

To bake, adjust a rack one-third up from the bottom of the oven and preheat oven to 450°. Place a 12-inch square of foil shiny side down in the frozen pastry shell; press it into place (let the edges and corners stand up straight), and fill the foil at least ½ inch deep with dried peas or beans (which should be saved to be reused for the same purpose) or with aluminum pellets called pie weights.

Bake for 13 minutes. Then carefully remove the foil and beans or weights by lifting the four corners of the foil. (You may prepare the following cheese filling while the crust is baking, if you wish.)

Return the tart shell to the oven for only 2 to 3 minutes more, until the bottom looks dry. Watch the pastry; if it starts to puff up, pierce it carefully with a cake tester.

You will need an egg white now (to keep the crust crisp). If you have prepared the cheese filling while the crust was baking, you will have two leftover egg whites.

Beat the white until it is just barely foamy and, with a pastry brush, brush the white over the bottom of the hot baked shell. The heat will set the white quickly. After a few moments brush on another layer of egg white. This time, place the pastry shell in the oven for a moment or two to set the second layer of egg white. Remove the shell from the oven, but do not turn the oven off.

If the filling is ready, it may be poured into the hot shell and baked immediately. If not, set the shell aside while you prepare the filling.

Cottage Cheese Filling

Place the cottage cheese in a food processor bowl fitted with the metal chopping blade and process for a full minute until the cheese is as smooth and as thick as sour cream. Stop the machine once or twice and scrape down the sides. Then stop the machine, remove the top, add the salt, the ½ cup sugar, the vanilla, lemon rind, lemon juice, eggs and egg yolks, melted butter, and sour cream. Process again briefly until everything is smoothly blended.

Stir the jelly in a bowl until it is soft and spread it over the bottom of the pastry.

Very slowly pour the filling into the prepared shell without disturbing the jelly any more than necessary. The filling will almost fill the shell to the top; it is all right—it will not run over (unless you have some low spots on the shell, in which case do not use all of the filling).

Sprinkle the cinnamon-sugar over the top through a fine strainer.

Bake at 450° for 10 minutes; then reduce the temperature to 375° and bake for 20 minutes longer (total baking time 30 minutes). During baking the filling will rise very high and it will form cracks, but it will all settle down to its original height when it cools.

Let cool. Refrigerate for at least a few hours, and serve cold.

When the tart is cold, remove the sides of the pan and with a wide metal spatula ease the tart onto a flat cake plate.

Serve this plain or with any fresh or stewed fruit. It is delicious with a Raspberry Pear (see page 182) or a Stewed Peach (see page 178)—drained of its juice.

12 ounces large curd cottage cheese (preferably regular or 4 percent butterfat)
⅛ teaspoon salt
½ cup granulated sugar
1 teaspoon vanilla extract
Finely grated rind of 1 large lemon
1 teaspoon lemon juice
2 eggs plus 2 additional egg yolks
1½ tablespoons unsalted butter, melted
½ cup sour cream
½ cup black raspberry jelly (or any other smooth jelly; currant is good too)
1 teaspoon cinnamon and 1 teaspoon granulated sugar, mixed together

8 PORTIONS

Shortcakes, Cobblers, and More

Strawberry Shortcake

If it is made with sponge cake it is not shortcake. The dictionary says "a cake made short and crisp with butter—served with fruit usually between the layers." That's shortcake. Consider it if you invite friends for dessert and coffee, or for a Sunday brunch. I grew up with this as a frequent dinner dessert—my mother served it often—sometimes with her own home-grown berries. But home-grown or store-bought, Strawberry Shortcake always made the meal an occasion, a celebration, a festivity.

Strawberry Shortcake is certainly a traditional dessert, but this is an untraditional variation. It is spectacular, and I think easy enough for anyone.

Strawberries

The berries can be washed, hulled, and drained ahead of time, but wait until the last minute to finish their preparation. (When the berries stand after being mixed with the preserves they give off their juice, which causes them to lose their texture; they are more delicious if they are mixed just before serving.)

Wash, hull, and dry the berries (see To Wash Strawberries, page 14). Refrigerate the berries if they will have to wait more than an hour or so; otherwise they can wait at room temperature.

Place the preserves in a saucepan and let stand until you are ready to put the dessert together. Reserve the kirsch also.

3 1-pint boxes (3 pounds, or about 10 to 12 cups) fresh strawberries (or more if you wish)

12 ounces (1 cup) strawberry preserves

2 tablespoons kirsch

Shortcake

Part of this can be done early in the day or even a day ahead, although it takes only a few minutes from beginning to end. This should be served as soon as it is baked.

Before baking, adjust a rack to the middle of the oven and preheat oven to 450°. Butter two 8-inch layer cake pans and set aside.

Sift together into a wide bowl the flour, baking powder, salt, and sugar. With a pastry blender cut in the butter until the mixture resembles coarse crumbs (some of the pieces may be as large as corn kernels).

In a small bowl beat the egg to mix and beat in the milk.

(If you wish, the two mixtures may be refrigerated, separately, for hours or even overnight.)

To finish the shortcake, slowly drizzle the egg-milk mixture over the flour mixture and, with a table fork, stir vigorously to moisten all of the flour mixture. Stir well. If some dry ingredients remain dry in the bottom of the bowl and you need more liquid, drizzle in a bit of ice water (only about a teaspoonful at a time) where needed and stir to incorporate. When it is just right, the ingredients should be only damp enough to hold together when pressed together.

Turn the mixture out onto a lightly floured surface. Handle very little now. Flour your hands and press the ingredients lightly together to form a ball. Flour the ball lightly. With a sharp knife, cut the ball of dough in half. Form each half into a ball, flour lightly, flatten slightly, and place the balls in the buttered pans. Flour your fingertips and press out the dough to fill the pans; they will be thin layers.

Bake for about 12 minutes until just done—a medium golden color. Do not overbake.

While the cake is baking, place the preserves over medium-low heat just to melt. And slice the strawberries into a wide bowl, cutting each berry into three or four slices (or more if the berries are extra large). Drizzle the kirsch over the berries, toss gently with a rubber spatula, and set aside for a few minutes.

(If the cream has not been whipped ahead of time, do it now—see Whipped Cream, below.)

When the cakes are done, cover one with a rack, turn the pan and rack over, remove the pan, cover the cake with a wide platter, and turn the rack and platter over again, leaving the cake right side up. Move the cake to center it if necessary.

Without waiting, spread the top of the hot cake with room-temperature butter. It should melt and run into the cake, leaving only a shiny finish.

Pour the melted preserves (which may be warm or at room temperature) over the sliced berries and toss gently with a rubber spatula.

Place about half of the berries over the bottom layer of cake. With your bare hands press down on the berries to form them into a smooth and compact layer. If some of the berries or juices run over the edge of the cake it is all right—it looks nice—but you will have an easier time serving this if the layer of berries is not too thick.

Then cover the second cake with a rack, turn over, remove the pan, cover the cake with a cutting board or a cookie sheet, and turn over again, leaving the cake right side up. Lightly butter the top of this cake (do not use

2 cups sifted all-purpose flour
1 tablespoon plus 1 teaspoon baking powder
¼ teaspoon salt
¼ cup granulated sugar
4 ounces (1 stick) unsalted butter, cold and firm, cut into quarters the long way and then cut into ¼-inch slices (it is best to cut it ahead of time and refrigerate)
1 egg, cold
⅓ cup milk, cold
If necessary, a bit of ice water
Additional butter, at room temperature, to use after the cake is baked

8 PORTIONS

more butter than melts into the cake). And with a long sharp knife cut the cake into eight pie-shaped wedges. With a pie server transfer the wedges to re-form the layer and cover the berries.

Place the remaining berries in a pretty bowl. And place the whipped cream in another bowl. Bring both bowls and the cake plate to the table with a knife, a pie server, and two large serving spoons. Serve on wide plates, preferably dinner-size plates, a portion of cake in the middle with a mound of berries and their juice on one side of the cake and a mound of the whipped cream on the other side.

Whipped Cream

In a chilled bowl with chilled beaters whip the ingredients only until they hold a soft shape; this is better if it is not really stiff.

If you whip the cream ahead of time, refrigerate it. Then, just before serving, whisk it a bit with a wire whisk to bring it back to a smooth consistency (it separates a bit while standing).

2 cups whipping cream
¼ cup granulated or confectioners sugar
1 teaspoon vanilla extract

Washington State Cherry Cobbler

National Sweet Cherry Week is celebrated at the end of June because that is the beginning of the fresh cherry season in the northwest states of Washington, Oregon, Idaho, and Utah. The season is a short one and here in Florida, at the opposite side of the country, it comes and goes before I realize it. (The produce man says, "They're not in yet— come back next week." Then he says, "We had them last week but the season is over now.")

I will continue to wait but, while waiting, I have canned cherries on the shelf always ready to make this wonderful dessert.

It consists of a slightly thickened and mildly spiced cherry mixture in a shallow baking dish, topped with the lightest and tenderest old-fashioned buttermilk biscuits. I like it best very hot— straight from the oven—but it does hold its heat for about half an hour, and it is still delicious an hour or two later at room temperature.

The cherry mixture can be prepared hours ahead of time; the biscuits can be prepared up to an hour ahead of time, if you wish. If you want to prepare the biscuits ahead, place them on a tray covered with wax paper, loosely cover the biscuits with plastic wrap or wax paper, and refrigerate. Wait until you are ready to bake before placing the biscuits on the cobbler.

This recipe is written for one large baking dish, but it can also be made in individual onion soup bowls or similar ovenproof dishes, with one biscuit on top of each (in which case, cut the biscuits with a slightly wider cutter).

Cherry Mixture

Place a wide strainer or a colander over a large bowl. Pour the cherries and their syrup into the strainer or colander and let drain. Measure and reserve 2 cups of the syrup.

Sift together into a heavy 1½- to 2-quart saucepan the flour, salt, allspice, cinnamon, and sugar. Gradually add the 2 cups of cherry syrup, stirring with a rubber spatula (or a wire whisk if necessary) until smooth.

Place over moderate heat and cook, stirring and scraping the bottom and sides constantly with a rubber spatula, until the mixture comes to a gentle boil. Then reduce the heat to low and simmer, stirring gently, for 1 minute.

Remove from the heat. Add the butter and continue to stir gently until it is melted. Carefully mix in the lemon juice, then add the drained cherries and stir—always very gently.

Turn the warm mixture into an unbuttered shallow baking dish with at least a 2-quart capacity (11 x 8 x 1¾ or 2 inches). Smooth the top, and set aside.

2 cans (16 to 17 ounces each) pitted sweet cherries, packed in syrup (gorgeous with black Bing cherries, but light cherries may be used)
¼ cup unsifted *all-purpose flour*
⅛ teaspoon salt
¼ teaspoon allspice
¼ teaspoon cinnamon
⅓ cup granulated sugar
1 tablespoon unsalted butter
2 tablespoons lemon juice

6 PORTIONS

Buttermilk Biscuits

Adjust a rack one-third up from the bottom of the oven and preheat oven to 450°.

Sift together into a mixing bowl the flour, baking powder, salt, baking soda, and sugar. Add the butter and with a pastry blender cut it in until the mixture resembles coarse crumbs (small but visible pieces of butter make biscuits flakier than if the butter is cut in too fine). Up to this point the mixture can be made long ahead of time and refrigerated, if you wish.

Make a well in the middle of the ingredients in the bowl. Add the buttermilk all at once to the well and quickly stir with a fork for only 10 to 20 seconds until barely but not completely mixed.

Flour a work surface very lightly (good biscuits do not want any additional flour). Turn the mixture out onto the floured surface. With your hands press the mixture together gently, lightly, and quickly. Then knead it (fold part of the dough over onto itself) very briefly (only three or four times) until the mixture holds together but not until it becomes smooth.

If necessary, reflour the surface lightly, and lightly flour a rolling pin. Roll out the dough into a round shape about 7 inches in diameter and about ¼ to ⅜ inch thick.

Use a round cookie cutter 2 inches in diameter. Dip the cutter into flour before cutting each biscuit. Start cutting at the outside edge of the dough. Cut the biscuits as close to each other as possible. Each time, cut straight down (do not twist the cutter). When they are all cut use a metal spatula to transfer the biscuits to the top of the cherry mixture. Do not press the remaining scraps together (it would make tough biscuits). You can either use the scraps as they are, placing them any which way between the rounds, or place a few scraps next to each other and cut a round out of them, or cut a few half-moon shapes and place them between the rounds.

1 cup minus 2 tablespoons unsifted all-purpose flour
1 teaspoon baking powder
¼ teaspoon salt
¼ teaspoon baking soda
2 teaspoons granulated sugar
2½ tablespoons unsalted butter, cold and firm, cut into small pieces (it is best to cut the butter ahead of time and refrigerate it)
¼ cup plus 2 tablespoons buttermilk, cold

Glaze

Mix together the yolk and milk or cream (you will not use it all for this recipe) and brush it lightly over the tops of the biscuits (do not use so much that it runs down the sides). Sprinkle the sugar lightly all over the biscuits and exposed cherry mixture.

Bake for about 15 minutes until the biscuits are well browned and the cherry mixture is bubbling hot.

1 egg yolk
1 tablespoon milk or cream
2 to 3 teaspoons granulated sugar

NOTE: There are two schools of thought: those who push their biscuit topping down into the soupy part and wait for it to absorb the liquid (they're Southerners) and those who think the biscuits should be dry and should not become mushy (they're the Northerners). At least that's how it is with my husband and me (he's from Texas, I'm from New York).

VARIATION: This is the Cherry Cobbler made with fresh cherries. You need a cherry pitter for this. That is not a silly gadget; it is an essential tool. I don't know any other way to get the pits out. It is surprisingly quick and easy to pit a bowl full of cherries. Most kitchen shops sell cherry pitters.

Wash, dry, and pit the cherries, then set them aside. Sift together into a heavy 1½- to 2-quart saucepan the flour, salt, allspice, cinnamon, and sugar. Gradually stir in the water, pressing on any lumps of dry ingredients with a rubber spatula or briskly beating with a wire whisk until smooth.

Follow the preceding recipe to bring the mixture to a boil, simmer for 1 minute, stir in the butter and lemon juice, then add the optional food coloring to give the mixture a nice deep rosy hue. Stir in the pitted fresh cherries, turn the mixture into the baking dish, and then continue to follow the above recipe.

2 pounds (generous 6 cups) *fresh black Bing cherries*
¼ cup plus 1 tablespoon *unsifted all-purpose flour*
⅛ teaspoon salt
¼ teaspoon allspice
¼ teaspoon cinnamon
1⅓ cups granulated sugar
2 cups cool tap water
1 tablespoon unsalted butter
2 tablespoons lemon juice
Optional: red food coloring

New York State Apple Cobbler

This is unusual, and wonderful—you will love it. The secret is grated Cheddar cheese in the topping. It is best when it is hot, although it is also delicious after it has cooled. It can be prepared ahead of time and can stand at room temperature for a few hours, if you wish, before it is baked. It is one of the easiest recipes I know.

Topping

Grate the cheese either on a standing metal grater or in a food processor. (In a processor, use either the fine or medium grater blade. Or use the metal chopping blade, cutting the cheese into coarse chunks first and then processing it on/off for only a few seconds until coarsely processed.)

Place the cheese and butter in the large bowl of an electric mixer and beat until mixed. Add the salt, flour, and sugar and beat on low speed until mixed. Set aside.

6 ounces Cheddar cheese *(which may be mild or aged and sharp)*
4 ounces (1 stick) unsalted butter
¼ teaspoon salt
1 cup sifted all-purpose flour
½ cup light brown sugar, *firmly packed*

Apple Mixture

You will need an ovenproof baking dish that measures about 11 x 8 x 2 inches (2-quart capacity); butter the dish and set it aside.

Peel, quarter, and core the apples and cut each quarter into four to six lengthwise slices, depending on the size of the apples. You should have 8 to 10 cups of sliced apples.

Place the apples in a large mixing bowl with the sugar, cinnamon, nutmeg, and bourbon or brandy. Toss and mix with a rubber spatula until the ingredients are distributed evenly.

Turn the apple mixture into the buttered baking dish; arrange the apples slightly to make a rather smooth layer.

With your fingers crumble the topping over the apples, covering the fruit as completely as possible. Place a piece of wax paper over the surface and, with your hands, press down on the paper rather gently to press the topping into a fairly smooth layer.

Cover airtight with plastic wrap and let stand until you are ready to bake.

Before baking, adjust a rack to the middle of the oven and preheat oven to 350°.

Uncover the baking dish and bake for about 45 minutes until the apples are tender when tested with a toothpick and the topping is a beautiful golden-brown color.

Serve as is or with ice cream.

2½ to 3 pounds (4 large or 6 medium) tart cooking apples (I use Granny Smith)
½ cup light brown sugar, firmly packed
½ teaspoon cinnamon
¾ teaspoon nutmeg
2 tablespoons bourbon or brandy

6 PORTIONS

Down Home Apple Casserole

This is a bit like an apple pie without the crust, but this is creamy and has an almond and macaroon topping. It is, as they say, "a cup of tea" to prepare this. It can be prepared ahead of time, it can wait for hours, and then it can be baked (for only 15 minutes) during dinner and served bubbling hot right out of the oven. Or it can be baked ahead of time, refrigerated for several hours, and served very cold. I like it both ways. It is a simple country-style dessert, and at the same time it is elegant enough for almost any occasion.

*I*f you use Italian Amaretti (macaroons—usually available in all better food stores and kitchen shops), they do not have to be dried ahead of time in a slow oven until they are crisp. Crush them coarse and then grind them in a food processor, or place them between pieces of wax paper and pound with a wide cleaver or any similar tool. Place the ground macaroons in a bowl with the sliced almonds and stir to mix.

Adjust a rack one-third down from the top of the oven and preheat oven to 400°. You will need a shallow oven-proof baking dish with a 6-cup capacity. Butter it lightly and set aside.

Peel, quarter, and core the apples. Cut them into slices (if the apples are large, cut each quarter into four slices; if they are small, cut each quarter into two slices).

Place the apples, water, the ⅓ cup sugar, and the raisins in a large, heavy saucepan with a tight lid, but uncovered, over moderate heat. Stir occasionally until the liquid comes to a boil, then reduce the heat slightly, cover, and let cook for about 10 minutes until the apples are barely tender. Uncover again and let boil for a minute or two to reduce the liquid just a bit; do not cook longer than that—there should still be plenty of juice in the pan and the apples should not be overcooked.

Remove from the heat. Add the lemon juice, cinnamon, nutmeg, and optional mace. Stir or fold gently to mix.

In a small bowl whisk the cream and the flour together. Strain though a fine strainer, and then add to the apple mixture. Stir or fold again gently to mix.

Turn into the buttered baking dish. Smooth the top. Sprinkle with the macaroons and almonds, dot with small pieces of the butter, and sprinkle with the additional sugar.

This can be baked right away, or it can be covered and kept at room temperature for hours, or it can be refrigerated. If it is refrigerated, remove it from the refrigerator ahead of time to come to room temperature before baking.

Bake for about 15 minutes until it is bubbling hard around the edges. Then broil for a minute or two (that's all it takes) 7 or 8 inches below the broiler to caramelize the top a bit. Watch it carefully.

Serve this right away or let it cool, refrigerate it, and serve it very cold. Either way, serve it at the table on flat plates. If you serve it hot, the cream will

¼ cup crushed dried almond
  macaroons
⅓ cup thinly sliced
  unblanched (natural)
  almonds
2 pounds tart cooking apples
  (see Note)
½ cup water
About ⅓ cup granulated sugar
  (see Note)
¼ cup raisins
1 to 2 teaspoons lemon juice
  (see Note)
½ teaspoon cinnamon
¼ teaspoon nutmeg
Optional: pinch of mace
½ cup whipping cream
1 tablespoon all-purpose flour
1½ tablespoons unsalted
  butter, cold and firm
1 to 2 tablespoons additional
  granulated sugar

4 OR 5 PORTIONS

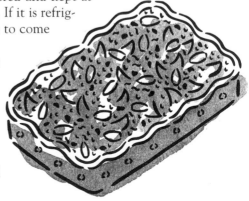

be thin and runny. If you cool and then chill it, the cream will thicken. Either way, spoon some of the cream onto each plate.

Serve just as it is, pass a bowl of cold Crème Fraîche or cold Sweet Sour Cream (see page 255), or serve ice cream with it.

NOTE: Granny Smith and Jonathan apples are considered best to use for pies or recipes like this one. Granny Smith are more tart. Adjust the amount of sugar and lemon juice depending on the sweetness of the apples. Taste before turning the mixture into the baking dish, and add more sugar if necessary.

Apple and Orange Cobbler

The year was 1937. My family was living on a dairy farm in Connecticut. When we drove into Danbury or New Milford, we passed a little roadside stand where a lady occasionally sold homemade bread. It was fabulous! We always tried to plan our shopping or driving at the time we thought her bread might be ready. Her name was Margaret Rudkin, and her farm was Pepperidge Farm.

She had started to bake bread, which she had never done before, because her son was allergic to certain ingredients in commercial bread. She said it was just as easy to bake several loaves at a time—she loved doing it—and she enjoyed selling the extra loaves. (Her bread sold for twenty-five cents a loaf, which seemed terribly extravagant; other bread cost less.) The first loaves were only whole wheat, and they were sold mainly to doctors, a few specialty stores, and a few lucky neighbors.

Mrs. Rudkin said that her first loaf should have been sent to the Smithsonian Institution as a sample of bread from the Stone Age because it was as hard as a rock and about an inch high.

This wonderful recipe has nothing to do with bread, but it was inspired by a recipe in The Margaret Rudkin Pepperidge Farm Cookbook (Atheneum, 1963), a beautiful book.

The filling for this can be made even a day or two ahead, and the biscuits can be prepared up to a few hours ahead, if you wish. If so, place the biscuits on a tray covered with wax paper, cover them loosely with plastic wrap or wax paper, and refrigerate. Wait until you are ready to bake before placing the biscuits on the cobbler.

If possible, serve this hot, right out of the oven.

*P*eel, quarter, and core the apples. Cut each quarter into four or five lengthwise strips. You should have 10 to 12 cups of loosely packed sliced apples.

Place the apples, orange rind, orange juice, 2 ounces (½ stick) of the butter (reserve the remaining ¼ stick), and the sugar in a wide, deep, heavy saucepan that has a tight-fitting cover.

Cover and cook over moderate heat, stirring a few times, for about 10 minutes until the apples have given off their juice and are just barely tender.

Pour the mixture into a wide strainer set over a wide bowl. Set aside the apples. Measure the strained syrup; you should have 1½ cups. (If you have less than that, add water or orange juice; if you have more, boil it, uncovered, over high heat to reduce, and set aside.)

In the saucepan that the apples cooked in, melt the remaining ¼ stick of butter over moderate heat, stir in the flour, reduce the heat to low, and simmer, stirring, for about 2 minutes.

Then over moderate heat add the drained 1½ cups of syrup (which should still be warm); pour it in all at once, stir briskly with a wire whisk, and then reduce the heat to low and scrape the pan with a rubber spatula, letting the syrup just simmer gently for about 2 minutes. Stir in the vanilla, let cool for a few minutes, then stir in the cooked apples and the orange sections.

Butter a wide, shallow 2-quart ovenproof baking dish (11 x 8 x about 2 inches). Turn the mixture into the baking dish, smooth the top, and set aside.

Continue with the recipe now or cover and refrigerate the fruit in the baking dish, and continue with the recipe later on.

3 pounds (6 to 7 large)
  cooking apples (preferably
  Granny Smith)
Finely grated rind of 1 large
  deep-colored orange
½ cup orange juice
3 ounces (¾ stick) unsalted
  butter
¾ cup granulated sugar
2 tablespoons flour
¼ teaspoon vanilla extract
3 large seedless navel oranges,
  sectioned (see page 15)

9 PORTIONS

Biscuit Topping

These are traditional, old-fashioned biscuits made with sweet milk. (If you want to make these separately, to serve as bread, bake them on an unbuttered shiny metal cookie sheet or use any cookie sheet lined with parchment or aluminum foil shiny side up. Bake at 450° for about 12 minutes until lightly browned.)

Adjust a rack to the middle of the oven and preheat oven to 450°.

Into a mixing bowl sift together the flour, salt, and baking powder. Add the butter and with a pastry blender cut it in until the mixture resembles coarse meal; there may be a few pieces the size of small dried split peas. (The recipe may be prepared ahead of time to this point and refrigerated overnight.)

Make a well in the middle of the ingredients. Pour the milk into the well. With a fork quickly stir around and around to incorporate the dry ingredients. Handle as little as possible. If necessary, add a bit more flour or milk, but mix or stir only briefly.

Turn the rough mixture out onto a lightly floured board or work surface and knead it only a few times (only a few seconds—no more) until the mixture is barely smooth.

With a lightly floured rolling pin roll out the dough until it is about 10 inches in diameter and about ½ inch thick.

Use a small, round cookie cutter (the dessert looks fabulous if the cutter is only about 1½ inches wide). Dip the cutter into flour each time before cutting the dough. Start to cut at the outside edge. Cut biscuits as close to one another as possible. Do not twist the cutter. Use a wide metal spatula to transfer the biscuits to the top of the cobbler. Place them only about ½ inch apart (28 to 30 biscuits cut with a 1½-inch cutter will fit the top of an 11 x 8-inch baking dish nicely).

With a pastry brush, brush the tops of the biscuits with heavy or light cream. Then sprinkle granulated sugar generously all over the fruit and the biscuits, using about 2 to 3 tablespoons of sugar. (Do not top the biscuits with cream or sugar if they are to be served as bread.)

Bake for about 20 minutes until the tops of the biscuits are beautifully browned. For the last few minutes, place the baking dish under a broiler to melt the sugar topping; watch it carefully.

Serve plain or with ice cream.

2 cups minus 2 tablespoons sifted all-purpose flour
¼ teaspoon salt
2¾ teaspoons baking powder
3 ounces (¾ stick) unsalted butter, cold and firm, cut into ½-inch pieces (it is best to cut the butter ahead of time and refrigerate it)
⅔ cup cold milk
Heavy or light cream
Granulated sugar

Georgia Peach Cobbler

I have read that possibly the Scottish-Irish brought cobblers with them when they came here in the early 1700s, and that possibly the name came from the phrase to "cobble up," which meant to put together in a hurry.

This has a layer of cake batter covered before baking with a juicy peach mixture. During baking most of the peaches sink to the bottom, most of the batter rises to the top, and as they pass each other going up and down, the peach mixture absorbs some of the batter and thickens to a wonderful consistency.

The fruit mixture can be prepared ahead of time and can wait at room temperature. The dry ingredients for the batter can be sifted ahead of time. Then it takes only a few moments to finish the batter and "cobble up" the dessert.

You will need an ovenproof baking dish with at least a 2-quart capacity.

Peach Mixture

Blanch and peel the peaches (see page 178), cut them in half, remove the pits, and slice them coarse. Place the peaches in a 3-quart heavy saucepan with the sugar, butter, and water. Stir briefly over moderately high heat just until the mixture comes to a boil. Remove from the heat and set aside.

About 2 pounds (6 medium-large) just-ripe freestone peaches
⅔ cup light brown sugar, firmly packed
1 tablespoon unsalted butter
1¼ cups water

Cake Batter

Adjust a rack to the middle of the oven and preheat oven to 375°. Generously butter a shallow ovenproof baking dish with at least a 2-quart capacity (11 x 8 x 1¾ or 2 inches); it can be larger but not smaller.

Sift together the flour, baking powder, and salt and set aside. In the small bowl of an electric mixer beat the butter with the vanilla and almond extracts. Beat in the sugar to mix. On low speed add in half of the milk, then half of the sifted dry ingredients, the balance of the milk, and the balance of the dry ingredients, scraping the sides of the bowl with a rubber spatula as necessary and beating only until mixed.

Pour the batter into the baking dish and spread it smooth. With a large slotted spoon, place the prepared peaches (which may be boiling hot or may be cool) evenly over the batter (reserve the peach syrup for a moment). Place the dish in the oven.

Now, pouring the peach syrup (it will be thin) over the fruit will be easiest if you pour it in two additions into a 2-cup measuring cup, and then reach into the oven and quickly pour it over the top of the fruit in the baking dish. (It is best to do it this way—in the oven—because it will fill the dish almost to the top and might spill if it is moved.)

Place a cookie sheet or a large piece of foil on a rack below the baking dish, or on the floor of the oven, to catch any juice that might bubble over during baking (it probably will if your dish has a 2-quart capacity).

Bake at 375° for 20 minutes. Then lower the temperature to 325° and bake for 25 more minutes (total baking time is 45 minutes).

Serve immediately or within 20 to 30 minutes on large flat plates or in dessert bowls, spooning some of the thickened syrup from the bottom over or alongside each portion.

Serve plain or with ice cream.

1½ cups sifted all-purpose flour
1 tablespoon baking powder
Pinch of salt
2 tablespoons unsalted butter
½ teaspoon vanilla extract
¼ teaspoon almond extract
⅔ cup light brown sugar, firmly packed
¾ cup milk

8 PORTIONS

Peach Pandowdy

This is a very old American recipe. Pandowdies were first made in the 1600s in the Middle Colonies—Pennsylvania, New Jersey, and Delaware. Although they were most often made with apples, there were a few with rhubarb, apricots, or peaches. It was customary for the host or hostess to cut into the top of the dessert with a serving spoon and stir the top and bottom together a bit before serving. Hence "Will you please dowdy the pan and serve the dessert?"

In a shallow baking dish, you will have sweetened and flavored uncooked fresh peaches and their delicious juice on the bottom, and a layer of quite plain but wonderful batter similar to a soft biscuit dough over the top.

The peaches should be just ripe, but for the best flavor and texture they should not be overripe.

When I could not stop eating this and my husband tried to reason with me about it, I quoted Mae West's immortal line, "Too much of a good thing is wonderful."

Peach Mixture

Adjust a rack one-third down from the top of the oven and preheat oven to 400°. Butter a shallow baking dish with a 2-quart capacity (11 x 8 x 2 inches) and set it aside.

Blanch and peel the peaches (see page 178). Cut them in half, remove the pits, and cut each half in three or four lengthwise slices; you should have 6 generous cups of sliced peaches.

Place the sliced peaches in a bowl, add the sugar and lemon juice, and sprinkle the cinnamon all over. With a rubber spatula toss the fruit gently to mix the ingredients evenly. Let stand for about 10 minutes to draw a bit of the juice.

Then place the mixture in the buttered baking dish, including every bit of the juice that has collected. Smooth the top and sprinkle on the raisins. Let stand while you prepare the topping.

3 pounds (9 medium-large) fresh just-ripe peaches, preferably freestone
⅓ cup dark brown sugar, firmly packed
1 tablespoon lemon juice
1 teaspoon cinnamon
⅓ cup light raisins

6 PORTIONS

Topping

Sift together the flour, baking powder, sugar, and salt and set aside.

In the small bowl of an electric mixer beat the eggs with the milk, butter, and vanilla and almond extracts. On low speed add the dry ingredients and beat briefly only until smooth.

The mixture will be thick but fluid. Either pour it slowly to make a thin layer (it will form a wide ribbon when it is poured) or spoon it by small spoonfuls over the fruit. Do not pour or spoon too much in any one spot or there will not be enough to cover the fruit. Actually, the topping might not cover the fruit completely anyhow, but it should almost cover it. Some of the topping will run down into the spaces between the fruit.

Bake for 28 to 30 minutes. The juices will bubble dark around the rim and through any little spots that the topping did not cover. The topping will darken slightly.

Serve warm as is, or with ice cream. However, if it is not possible to serve it warm, then definitely serve the ice cream with it.

1¼ cups sifted all-purpose flour
1 teaspoon baking powder
3 tablespoons granulated sugar
¼ teaspoon salt
2 eggs
⅓ cup milk
2 ounces (½ stick) unsalted butter, melted
1 teaspoon vanilla extract
Few drops almond extract

Pennsylvania Dutch Peach Cobbler

A thick and juicy peach filling with a cookielike topping that is both soft and crisp: irresistible.

You will need a shallow ovenproof baking dish about 13 x 8 x 2 inches with about a 3-quart capacity.

If you wish, this can all be prepared a few hours before it is baked and it can wait at room temperature to go into the oven when you sit down to start dinner.

Topping

Have ready a shallow 3-quart baking dish.

Sift together the flour, sugar, baking powder, and salt and set aside. In the small bowl of an electric mixer beat the butter with the vanilla and almond extracts to mix. Beat in the egg, and then, on low speed, gradually add the sifted dry ingredients. Beat until the mixture holds together.

Remove the bowl from the mixer and transfer the mixture to a piece of wax paper about 15 inches long. Cover with another 15-inch length of wax paper. Sprinkle a few drops of water on a work surface (to keep the wax paper from slipping) and place the wax papers with the dough between them on the damp surface. With a rolling pin roll over the top paper until the dough measures about 11 inches in length by about 8 inches; it may be an oval shape (or approximately an oval)—it should be about ¼ inch thick. Slide a flat-sided cookie sheet under the bottom piece of paper and transfer to the freezer for 45 to 60 minutes, or for a few hours if you wish.

1 cup unsifted *all-purpose flour*
⅔ cup granulated sugar
1 teaspoon baking powder
¼ teaspoon salt
1 ounce (¼ stick) unsalted butter, at room temperature
½ teaspoon vanilla extract
¼ teaspoon almond extract
1 egg

Filling

Blanch and peel the peaches (see page 178). Cut them in half. Remove the pits. Place them on a towel briefly to drain; then cut each peach into quarters and let the quarters continue to drain on the towel.

Place the flour, sugar, and honey in a 3-quart heavy saucepan. Very gradually add the water, stirring well with a rubber spatula or a wire whisk until the mixture is smooth.

Place over moderate heat and cook for a few minutes, scraping the sides and bottom constantly with a rubber spatula until the mixture thickens. Reduce the heat and cook, stirring, for 1 minute.

Then add about one-third of the peaches (reserve the remaining peaches) and cook, stirring, for another minute.

Remove from the heat; stir in the butter and lemon juice.

Place the reserved two-thirds of the peaches in the baking dish and smooth the top. Then pour the cooked mixture over the peaches in the baking dish and smooth the top again. (There must be headroom because the filling will

About 4 pounds (12 medium-large) just-ripe peaches, preferably freestone
¼ cup unsifted *all-purpose flour*
¼ cup light brown sugar, firmly packed
¼ cup honey
½ cup water
1 ounce (¼ stick) unsalted butter
1½ tablespoons lemon juice
Nutmeg, preferably freshly grated

6 TO 8 PORTIONS

bubble during baking.) Grate about half of a nutmeg over the peaches or sprinkle on about ¼ teaspoon of ground nutmeg.

When you are ready to bake, adjust a rack to the middle of the oven and preheat oven to 375°.

Remove the firm topping from the freezer. Peel off the top piece of wax paper just to release it, and then replace it. Turn the rolled-out topping (still between both pieces of wax paper) over. Peel off the other piece of paper but do not replace it. With a round cookie cutter (I use a cutter that is 2 inches in diameter—you could use any size) cut as many rounds as possible from the dough, starting at the outside edge and cutting the rounds just touching each other. Don't discard a speck of this dough—it makes great sugar cookies. (The scraps may be pressed together, chilled, rolled, cut, and baked on a foil-lined cookie sheet in a 350° oven until lightly colored.)

Place the rounds of dough over the peaches, leaving small spaces between them (they will spread a bit during baking). For my 13 x 8-inch baking dish I use 15 rounds of dough (three rows, five in each row).

Bake for 45 minutes, reversing the dish front to back as necessary to ensure even browning. If the top still looks pale after 30 minutes of baking, raise the rack to the highest position for the last 15 minutes.

Serve hot or warm as is, or with ice cream.

Peach Crisp

Quick and easy; it is an old Southern recipe from the area of Colonial Williamsburg. A layer of fresh peaches is covered with a crunchy, crumbly, deliciously crisp topping.

Adjust a rack one-third down from the top of the oven and preheat oven to 400°. You will need a shallow ovenproof baking dish with about a 2-quart capacity (it might measure about 11 x 8 x 1½ or 2 inches). Butter the dish and set it aside.

Blanch and peel the peaches (see page 178). Cut them in half, remove the pits, and cut the halves into rather wide slices (if they are thin, they will overcook and become mushy). You should have about 6 cups of sliced peaches. Place them in a wide bowl. Combine the lemon juice and vanilla, drizzle it over the peaches, and toss gently with a rubber spatula to mix.

Place the peaches in the buttered baking dish.

Sift together into a mixing bowl the flour, sugar, and salt. Stir the almond extract into the egg. Drizzle it and the melted butter over the dry ingredients and stir very well with a fork until the dry ingredients are barely moistened and the mixture is crumbly.

Sprinkle the crumbs loosely all over the peaches.

Bake for 30 to 35 minutes.

If the topping is still pale, place the dish about 12 inches under the broiler to brown a bit; it should not be too close to the broiler or the topping will burn before it browns.

Serve hot or warm, if possible. Serve alone or with ice cream.

3 pounds (about 9 medium-large) just-ripe fresh peaches, preferably free-stone
1½ tablespoons lemon juice
1 teaspoon vanilla extract
1 cup sifted all-purpose flour
¾ cup granulated sugar
¼ teaspoon salt
¼ teaspoon almond extract
1 egg, beaten
3 ounces (¾ stick) unsalted butter, melted

6 PORTIONS

Peach Kuchen

A quick, easy, and delicious coffee cake, wonderful for breakfast or brunch, or as a dessert (with or without ice cream). This is an unusual recipe that uses yeast (but there is no kneading or rising time) and also baking powder; they work their magic together in the oven and you will be surprised and delighted.

Topping

Adjust a rack to the middle of the oven and preheat oven to 350°.

Place the almonds in a shallow pan in the oven to bake for about 5 minutes until hot but not colored. Set aside to cool.

In the small bowl of an electric mixer beat the butter until soft. Add the sugar and cinnamon and beat to mix, then add the flour and beat only until the mixture is crumbly. Stir in the cooled almonds.

Set aside the topping to use later.

½ cup chopped or slivered (julienned) blanched almonds
3 tablespoons unsalted butter
½ cup light or dark brown sugar, firmly packed
1 teaspoon cinnamon
¼ cup unsifted all-purpose flour

Cake

Butter a 9 x 13 x 2-inch cake pan and place it in the freezer (it is easier to press out a thin layer of dough if the pan is frozen).

Place the warm water in a small bowl; add 1 teaspoon of the sugar (reserve the remaining ½ cup of sugar) and the yeast. Stir briefly with a knife just to mix. Set aside.

Sift together the flour, baking powder, and salt and set aside.

In the large bowl of an electric mixer beat the butter until soft. Add the remaining ½ cup of sugar and beat to mix. Add the yeast mixture, the eggs, the vanilla and almond extracts, and the lemon rind and beat to mix. (It is okay if the mixture looks curdled now.) On low speed mix in half of the sifted dry ingredients, then the milk, and finally the remaining dry ingredients. Beat until well mixed.

Spread half of the mixture (about 1¼ cups) over the bottom of the buttered, frozen pan—it will be a very thin layer.

Place the prepared peaches in rows, each slice just barely touching the one before it, or there may be a little room left between the slices. Or, if you wish, the amount of fruit can be increased slightly and the slices can just barely overlap.

Sprinkle the optional raisins over the fruit.

Next, using two teaspoons—one for picking up with and one for pushing off with—place small spoonfuls of the remaining cake mixture over all the fruit and the bottom layer. There will be places where the fruit shows through; it is okay but you do not want much of it uncovered.

Then, with your fingers, carefully sprinkle the prepared topping to cover as much of the cake as possible.

Bake for about 35 to 40 minutes until the top is nicely browned.

2 tablespoons warm water (105° to 115°)
1 teaspoon plus ½ cup granulated sugar
1½ teaspoons active dry yeast
2 cups unsifted all-purpose flour
1 tablespoon baking powder
½ teaspoon salt
4 ounces (1 stick) unsalted butter
2 eggs
½ teaspoon vanilla extract
¼ teaspoon almond extract
Finely grated rind of 1 large lemon
¼ cup milk
4 to 6 cups blanched, peeled, and sliced fresh peaches (see Note)
Optional: ¼ cup raisins

8 GENEROUS PORTIONS

Icing

Prepare this 5 minutes before the cake is done.

In a small bowl stir the ingredients with a rubber spatula to mix. The icing should be smooth and thick, just barely thin enough to flow when some of it is picked up on the spatula.

As soon as the cake is removed from the oven, drizzle

1 cup sifted confectioners sugar
1½ teaspoons lemon juice
1 tablespoon boiling water

thin lines of the icing every which way over the cake. (I drizzle it off the rubber spatula.)

Serve hot, or let stand in the pan until cool. Cut into large squares and use a wide metal spatula to transfer the portions.

NOTE: This is equally good with apples, pears, blueberries, or a combination of fruits. If you are using peaches, see the directions on page 178 for blanching and peeling. Then cut them in half, remove the pits, and slice the peaches into wedges about ½ inch thick at the curved edge. If you use apples or pears they should be peeled, quartered, cored, and cut into wedges about ½ inch thick at the curved edge.

Blueberry and Peach Buckle

A delicious and tantalizing flavor and texture—a coffee cake, of sorts—colorful, beautiful, moist, loaded with fruit (with only enough batter to hold the fruit together).

Buckles are in most very old Southern cookbooks. The name, meaning to crumble up, probably came about because of the crumbly topping.

Make this in the summer when fresh blueberries and peaches are in season.

I thought this had to be served hot, right out of the oven. However, I recently made it early in the day to serve at 10:00 A.M. when I had invited friends for coffee, but when my husband and I had it again 12 hours later it was still very good. (But if it stands even longer than that, the moisture in the peaches and berries soaks into the cake and makes it mushy.)

Topping

In the small bowl of an electric mixer (or in any small bowl) beat the butter until soft, mix in the cinnamon and sugar, and then the flour. Refrigerate.

2 ounces (½ stick) unsalted butter
1 teaspoon cinnamon
⅓ cup dark brown sugar, firmly packed
⅓ cup sifted all-purpose flour

Cake

Adjust a rack one-third down from the top of the oven and preheat oven to 375°. Butter a shallow ovenproof baking dish with a 2-quart capacity (11 x 8 x 1½ or 2 inches) and set it aside.

Wash the berries (see To Wash Blueberries, page 14) and let them drain and dry.

Remove and reserve 2 tablespoons of the flour. Sift together the remaining flour, baking powder, and salt and set aside.

In the small bowl of an electric mixer beat the butter until soft. Beat in the vanilla and almond extracts and ⅔ cup of the sugar (reserve the remaining 2 tablespoons of sugar). Beat in the egg. Then, on low speed, add the sifted dry ingredients in three additions alternately with the milk in two additions. The mixture will be thick and stiff. Set it aside.

Place the blueberries in a large mixing bowl. Add the reserved 2 tablespoons of flour. With a rubber spatula toss gently to coat the berries without squashing them. (If some of the flour settles to the bottom of the bowl, spread out a large piece of wax paper, place a wide colander or strainer over the paper, turn the berries and flour into the colander or strainer, and shake gently. Any flour that lands on the wax paper should be folded into the cake batter.)

Then add the floured blueberries and fold gently just barely to mix without squashing the berries.

Turn half of the mixture into the buttered baking dish and spread to level it a bit; it will be a very thin layer.

Blanch and peel the peaches (see page 178), place them on a towel to drain, and then slice them about ½ inch thick on the outside curve. Place the peaches in a layer over the cake batter. (If your dish is the size mentioned above, you will be able to make three lengthwise rows of overlapping slices.) Sprinkle the peaches with 1 tablespoon of the remaining sugar.

Place the remaining batter by very small spoonfuls over the peaches; it will not be enough to cover the peaches completely, but be patient and work slowly to cover as much of the peaches as possible.

With your fingertips sprinkle the refrigerated topping, a bit at a time, over the cake. It will not completely cover the cake,

12 ounces (3 cups) fresh blueberries
2 cups sifted all-purpose flour
2 teaspoons baking powder
½ teaspoon salt
2 ounces (½ stick) unsalted butter
1 teaspoon vanilla extract
¼ teaspoon almond extract
⅔ cup plus 2 tablespoons granulated sugar
1 egg
½ cup milk
3 fresh just-ripe medium-large peaches

8 PORTIONS

but, again, patience. Sprinkle the remaining 1 tablespoon of sugar over the top.

Bake for 35 minutes until the pale part of the top is medium brown and dry and springs back if pressed lightly with a fingertip.

To serve, cut into squares and remove the squares with a metal spatula. Serve directly from the baking dish either warm or at room temperature.

This is so yummy I do not think it needs anything with it, but Crème Fraîche (see page 255) or whipped cream or ice cream may be passed, or spooned alongside each portion.

Blueberry Crumble

A crisp, nutty, crumbly topping over a thick layer of sweet juicy blueberries. This is easy to make and it is equally good hot or cooled. But if you want it hot (wonderful) it can all be prepared ahead of time, and it can wait in the refrigerator a day, if you wish, before it is baked.

Blueberry Layer

Wash the berries (see To Wash Blueberries, page 14) and let them stand to drain and dry.

Adjust a rack to the middle of the oven and preheat oven to 375°. Butter a wide, shallow 2-quart ovenproof baking dish (for instance, one 11 x 8 x 2 inches) and set aside.

In a large bowl mix the sugar with the flour and cinnamon. Add the washed and dried berries and turn the ingredients gently a few times with a rubber spatula to mix. Pour the mixture into the dish. Sprinkle any sugar and flour mixture remaining in the bottom of the bowl evenly over the top. Smooth the top. Drizzle the lemon juice all over. Set aside.

6 cups (2 pint boxes) fresh
   blueberries
⅓ cup dark brown sugar,
   firmly packed
3 tablespoons sifted all-
   purpose flour
¾ teaspoon cinnamon
2 teaspoons lemon juice

6 TO 8 PORTIONS

Crumble Topping

This will stay crisp long after the dessert is baked, even after it has cooled.

Sift together into a bowl the flour, nutmeg, and granulated sugar. Add the brown sugar and stir to mix. Add the butter and with a pastry blender cut it in until the mixture resembles coarse crumbs (not too fine). Stir in the oats.

Sprinkle the nuts over the berries, and sprinkle the topping over the nuts.

Bake for 25 to 30 minutes until the berries are bubbly around the edge. Then place the baking dish under the broiler for about a minute or so to darken the top a bit—watch it carefully.

Serve warm or cooled, as is or with Top Secret (see page 252), White Custard Cream (see page 254), or with plain sour cream or unwhipped heavy cream. (But it is delicious alone.)

½ cup sifted all-purpose flour
¼ teaspoon nutmeg
¼ cup granulated sugar
½ cup dark brown sugar, firmly packed
4 ounces (1 stick) unsalted butter, cold and firm, cut into pieces (it is best to cut the butter ahead of time and refrigerate it)
½ cup "old-fashioned" Quaker oats (must be the kind labeled "old-fashioned" or the topping will not be as crunchy as it should be)
3½ ounces (1 cup) pecans, toasted (see To Toast Pecans, page 6), cut into medium-size pieces

Colonial Blueberries

Especially easy—and especially delicious. It has a thick, juicy, dark, purple layer of slightly cooked fresh blueberries covered with a wonderfully light cake (only ¾ inch thick), baked together. It may be served hot or at room temperature but the fresher the better. The blueberry part can be made ahead of time, but it hardly pays, since the whole thing can be made quickly. You need a shallow ovenproof baking dish with a 3-quart capacity (for instance, 9 x 13 x 2 inches).

Blueberry Layer

Wash the blueberries (see To Wash Blueberries, page 14), and let them drain and dry. Place 3 cups of the berries (reserving the remaining 2 cups) in a heavy 2½- to 3-quart saucepan with the sugar and butter. Stir occasionally with a wooden spoon over low heat until the mixture comes to a low boil. Let simmer gently for 3 minutes. Remove from the heat, cool for about 10 minutes, and then stir in the remaining 2 cups of berries.

Pour the mixture into a 3-quart baking dish, smooth the top, and sprinkle the cinnamon through a fine strainer over the berries.

Set aside. (If this is made hours ahead, it can wait either at room temperature or in the refrigerator.)

1¼ pounds (5 cups) fresh blueberries
1 cup dark brown sugar, firmly packed
3 ounces (¾ stick) unsalted butter
½ teaspoon cinnamon

Cake Layer

Adjust a rack to the middle of the oven and preheat oven to 350°.

Sift together the flour, baking powder, and salt and set aside.

In the small bowl of an electric mixer beat the butter until soft. Beat in the vanilla and sugar. Then add the eggs one at a time, beating until incorporated after each addition.

Place the orange juice in a 1-cup glass measuring cup and add cognac or bourbon to reach the ¾-cup line (or use ¾ cup of orange juice).

On low speed gradually add the sifted dry ingredients in three additions alternately with the liquids in two additions, beating until smooth after each addition. Remove from the mixer and stir in the grated rind. (The mixture will appear slightly curdled—it is okay.)

Slowly pour the cake mixture over the berries. (The batter will cover all the berries but if there are a few spots uncovered it is okay.)

1½ cups sifted all-purpose flour
2 teaspoons baking powder
¼ teaspoon salt
5⅓ ounces (10⅔ tablespoons) unsalted butter
½ teaspoon vanilla extract
¾ cup granulated sugar
2 eggs
⅔ cup fresh orange juice (grate the rind of 1 orange before squeezing)
Cognac, bourbon, or more orange juice
Finely grated rind of 1 large deep-colored orange

ABOUT 10 PORTIONS

Bake for 45 minutes. The top of the cake will be richly browned and will spring back when pressed gently with a fingertip.

Serve hot or cooled. To serve, use a wide metal pancake turner and a large serving spoon. Serve on flat dessert plates. Serve as is or with ice cream. Or pass a bowl of Crème Fraîche (see page 255) or whipped cream (whip 2 cups whipping cream with ¼ cup confectioners sugar and ⅓ cup cognac, bourbon, or Grand Marnier, until thick but not stiff). Or serve with White Custard Cream (see page 254)—divine.

Rhubarb Crumble

Rhubarb, which is also called pieplant, is, botanically speaking, a vegetable, although we use it as a fruit. Frozen rhubarb is available but use the fresh for this recipe. Generally during April the first young, springtime rhubarb starts to show up in the markets. Watch for it. The season does not last long, and rhubarb is especially delicious when it is young.

This Pennsylvania Dutch recipe is certainly one of the easiest and quickest ever. You can prepare it ahead of time (in just a few minutes), you can bake it immediately or bake it later, you can serve it warm or cooled, plain or with ice cream. (The combination of warm tart rhubarb with cold, sweet ice cream is great.)

This is a shallow baking dish of the tart rhubarb covered with a buttery brown sugar, crunchy, crumb topping.

Adjust a rack one-third up from the bottom of the oven and preheat oven to 350°. You will need a shallow ovenproof baking dish with an 8- to 9-cup capacity (about 11 x 8 x 2 inches); butter it lightly.

Wash the rhubarb with a vegetable brush under cold running water. Cut off any leaves and a thin slice from the top and bottom of each stalk. On a board with a heavy knife cut the rhubarb into 1-inch pieces and place in the baking dish.

Combine the rind, juice, and rum and pour it evenly over the rhubarb. Sprinkle the granulated sugar evenly over the top.

Place the flour, cinnamon, brown sugar, and butter in a wide mixing bowl. With your hands, work the ingredients together, rubbing them between your fingertips and then between your palms, to form crumbs. Sprinkle the crumbs evenly over the rhubarb, covering it all.

Bake immediately or set aside and bake later.

Bake for 40 to 45 minutes only until the rhubarb in the middle of the baking dish just tests tender when tested with a toothpick and the juices are bubbly, thick, and shiny and the crumb topping is nicely browned.

Serve hot, warm, or at room temperature, but don't let it wait more than a few hours after baking; the crumb top starts to soften. Serve plain or with ice cream.

2 pounds fresh rhubarb (to make 8 cups, cut up)
Finely grated rind of 1 large orange
⅓ cup orange juice
3 tablespoons dark rum
⅔ cup granulated sugar
1 cup unsifted *all-purpose flour*
1 teaspoon cinnamon
1 cup dark brown sugar, firmly packed
4 ounces (1 stick) unsalted butter, cut into small pieces

8 PORTIONS

Cranberry Grunt

They say that this name came about because when it comes out of the oven it makes a noise similar to a grunt. In my kitchen it does not grunt, it doesn't make a sound—it just smiles.

The first settlers in America found cranberries here just waiting to be picked; different varieties grow from Newfoundland to the Carolinas and west to Arkansas and Minnesota, and in Oregon and the state of Washington. The berries, which are related to blueberries, are in season in the fall and early winter. But now you can buy them frozen all year, or you can freeze them yourself. (They don't need any preparation; just put them in a freezer bag in the freezer. Do not wash them until you are ready to use them; then rinse quickly in cold water and use them frozen.)

This very old recipe is made in a shallow baking dish. It has a layer of juicy and spicy cranberries and apples which is then covered with light and tender biscuits that resemble slices of jelly roll (they have a filling of strawberry preserves).

It is quick and easy. It is great hot, warm, or at room temperature, but do not bake it more than 2 or 3 hours ahead of time; when it is just baked the biscuits are light and tender and terrific—after a few hours they lose their special tenderness, and the juicy apple and berry mixture becomes less juicy.

Both the fruit and the biscuits can be prepared up to a few hours ahead of time, if you wish. If so, cover the fruit mixture and let it wait at room temperature. Place the biscuits on a tray covered with wax paper, cover the biscuits loosely with plastic wrap or wax paper, and refrigerate. Wait until you are ready to bake before placing the biscuits on the fruit layer.

Fruit Layer

Adjust a rack one-third up from the bottom of the oven and preheat oven to 425°. Generously butter a shallow oven-proof baking dish with at least an 8-cup capacity (11 x 7 x 1½ or 2 inches).

Quickly wash and pick over the berries, drain, and place them in a heavy 4- to 6-cup saucepan. Peel, quarter, and core the apples; then cut them into small chunky pieces about ½ to ¾ inch. Add the apples and the water to the berries. Bring to a boil over moderate heat, cover, reduce the heat slightly to maintain a simmer, and simmer for about 10 minutes. Remove from the heat, stir in the sugar, butter, cloves, nutmeg, and allspice, and let the mixture stand, uncovered.

12 ounces (3 cups) cranberries (fresh or frozen)
2 large apples (see Note), to make a generous 2 cups, cut up
⅔ cup water
½ cup granulated sugar
1 ounce (¼ stick) unsalted butter
Scant ¼ teaspoon ground cloves
½ teaspoon nutmeg
Scant ¼ teaspoon allspice

ABOUT 8 PORTIONS

Jelly-Roll Biscuits

Cut ½ stick of the butter into small pieces and refrigerate. Melt the remaining ¼ stick of butter and set aside.

Sift together into a bowl the flour, baking powder, salt, and sugar. Add the cut-up butter and with a pastry blender cut it in until the mixture resembles coarse crumbs. Make a well in the middle, add the milk all at once to the well, and stir with a fork until the flour is just barely moistened.

Turn the mixture out onto a lightly floured board and knead it very briefly (the less the better) only until the flour is incorporated.

Shape the mixture into an oblong. Place it on a lightly floured pastry cloth and with a lightly floured rolling pin roll out the dough until it measures 8 x 12 inches, keeping the shape as even and as neat as you can.

Brush with the melted butter.

Stir the preserves a bit to soften and spread them over the whole surface of the dough, but staying ½ inch away from one 12-inch side. Then, with your hands, roll up the dough like a jelly roll, starting at the 12-inch side opposite the ½-inch border.

Cut into twelve 1-inch pieces.

Transfer the fruit mixture (which may still be warm) to the baking dish, smooth the top, and place the biscuits cut side up (and down) over the fruit layer (I make three rows, 4 biscuits in each row).

Bake for 20 to 25 minutes until the biscuits are well browned and crusty.

Serve hot, warm, or at room temperature. Serve plain or with ice cream, or with ice-cold Ricotta Cream (see page 253); if you are serving 4 or 5 portions, 1 15-ounce container of ricotta cheese will be enough, but for 6 or more portions use 2 15-ounce containers.

3 ounces (¾ stick) unsalted butter
1½ cups sifted all-purpose flour
1 tablespoon baking powder
¼ teaspoon salt
2 tablespoons granulated sugar
⅓ cup milk
½ cup strawberry preserves (or any other red preserves)

NOTE: I like Golden Delicious apples for this. They are not as sour as Granny Smith apples—the cranberries are sour enough—and they hold their shape and do not fall apart the way some other sweet apples do.

Fruit Desserts

Fresh Strawberries with Sour Cream

This is one of the easiest and also one of the most popular desserts that I know. Years ago, when I told the chef at the Pier House in Key West about this dessert, he made it often and later told me that it was the most requested dessert he served.

Wash the berries by placing them briefly in a large bowl of cold water. Pick them out quickly, one at a time, and as you do, remove the stems and hulls. Place the berries on paper towels to drain; let them stand until they are thoroughly dry.

Place the berries in a wide, shallow serving bowl. Cover with the cream and smooth the top. With your fingers sprinkle the sugar over the cream. Refrigerate for 3 to 6 hours. (If it stands overnight the sugar will melt too much and will lose its dark color and generally be less attractive.) The sugar will melt into a very dark, thin layer of deliciousness resting on the white cream (with the red berries showing through the bowl, if you have used a glass bowl).

The secret of this dessert is to handle the cream as little as possible so it remains thick.

This can be prepared in individual shallow dessert bowls instead of one large serving bowl, in which case you will probably have to use more sugar to cover all of the cream.

2 pint boxes (2 pounds) fresh
   strawberries
2 cups thick sour cream
⅔ cup dark brown sugar,
   firmly packed

4 TO 6 PORTIONS

Strawberries De Luxe

This is quick and easy and terrific! It may be prepared about 3 or 4 hours before serving. It is prepared in individual glasses, and makes a marvelous dinner-party dessert.

Wash the berries quickly in a large bowl of cold water. Hull them and drain well on paper towels. If the berries are very large, cut them in halves or quarters. (Taste the berries; if they are wonderful, leave them alone. But if they are flat, place them in a bowl, sprinkle with 2 tablespoons granulated sugar and 5 tablespoons kirsch or Cointreau. Toss gently, and let stand for about an hour.)

In the small bowl of an electric mixer beat the cream cheese until it is soft and smooth. Beat in the Grand Marnier and honey. Remove from the mixer.

In a small bowl whip the cream until it barely holds a shape.

Fold the whipped cream into the cheese mixture.

Shortly before serving divide the berries among six large wineglasses or champagne glasses. Pour the cheese mixture on top.

OPTIONAL: Top each portion with a small sprig of fresh mint. (Or you could use a chocolate leaf, a bit of candied violet or rose petals, a few seedless grapes, or what-have-you.)

2 pint boxes (2 pounds) fresh strawberries
Optional: 2 tablespoons granulated sugar
Optional: 5 tablespoons kirsch or Cointreau
3 ounces Philadelphia brand cream cheese, at room temperature
3 tablespoons Grand Marnier
3 tablespoons mild honey
1 cup heavy cream
Optional: a few fresh mint leaves

6 PORTIONS

Brandied Strawberries with Cream

This is elegant and easy; the preparation can be done several hours before serving.

In a small chilled bowl with chilled beaters whip the heavy cream until it just holds a shape. In a small bowl stir the kirsch into the sour cream and mix until smooth. Fold both creams together. Cover and refrigerate.

Wash the berries quickly in cold water, hull, and drain thoroughly on paper towels.

Place the berries in a bowl. Add the sugar and brandy. Stir gently with a rubber spatula. Let stand for about an hour, stirring occasionally. Then cover and refrigerate.

To serve: The berries may be at room temperature or cold; the cream should be very cold. Place the berries in wineglasses or individual dessert bowls; pour on any remaining marinade. Stir the cream gently and spoon it generously over the berries.

1 cup heavy cream
3 tablespoons kirsch
1 cup sour cream
2 pint boxes (2 pounds) fresh strawberries
¼ cup dark or light brown sugar, firmly packed
3 ounces brandy or cognac

6 PORTIONS

NOTE: The brandied berries alone, without the cream, are perfectly wonderful over coffee ice cream.

Southampton Strawberries

This is a Long Island version of Strawberries Romanoff; it is very pretty, elegant, and easy. The preparations may be completed about 3 hours before serving, but it must be put together at the last minute; however, that takes only a minute to do.

This should be served at the table from a shallow bowl (preferably crystal or silver, with about a 2-quart capacity). The bowl should be placed in the freezer ahead of time so it will be frosty at serving time.

To wash the berries, place them (1 box at a time) in a large bowl of cold water for only a few moments. Quickly lift them from the water, remove the hulls, and drain on paper towels.

About 3 hours before serving, slice each berry into two or three slices and place them in a bowl with 2 tablespoons of the sugar (reserve the remaining 1 tablespoon of sugar), 3 tablespoons of cognac (reserve the remaining 1 tablespoon cognac), and the Grand Marnier. Mix gently. Cover with plastic wrap or foil and refrigerate.

Whip the heavy cream with the reserved 1 tablespoon sugar, the reserved 1 tablespoon cognac, and the vanilla, whipping only until it holds a soft shape—not stiff. Refrigerate.

About half an hour before serving, place the ice cream in the refrigerator to soften a bit.

Immediately before serving, mix the ice cream and the berries only slightly—they should each retain their own identity—and place in the chilled serving bowl.

Check to see if the whipped cream has separated a bit; if it has, beat it slightly with a small wire whisk. Pour the whipped cream over the berries and ice cream.

Sprinkle with the optional candied leaves or petals.

Serve in shallow dessert bowls (which also may have been chilled in the freezer).

*2 pint boxes (2 pounds) fresh
    strawberries
3 tablespoons granulated
    sugar
4 tablespoons cognac
3 tablespoons Grand Marnier
1 cup heavy cream
½ teaspoon vanilla extract
1 cup vanilla ice cream
Optional: candied violet
    leaves or rose petals*

6 PORTIONS

Fresh Strawberries in Honeyed Raspberry Sauce

This is quick, easy, and elegant. The sauce can be prepared a day ahead, if you wish.

Sauce

Unless the berries really need it, do not wash. But if they do, dip them quickly in and out of a bowl of cold water. Spread on paper towels to drain.

1½ to 2 cups fresh raspberries
¼ cup honey

Press the berries through a food mill or process them in a food processor to purée. Strain to remove the seeds. Stir in the honey.

If you plan to use this within a few hours, it is not necessary to refrigerate it. If you want to keep it for a day or two, refrigerate, and then bring it to room temperature before serving. Or, although many people are positive that it must be served at room temperature, you may serve it cold. I think it is delicious either way.

Strawberries

Quickly rinse the berries, remove the hulls, and drain well on paper towels.

4 to 6 cups strawberries

Place the berries in wine glasses or dessert bowls and spoon or pour the sauce over them.

6 PORTIONS

Serve at room temperature or refrigerated.

NOTE: In a nouvelle cuisine kitchen, the chef might grind a bit of black pepper over the berries and add a bit of raspberry vinegar to the sauce. Both wonderful. Or you can add a very little bit of kirsch to the sauce.

Fresh Strawberries with Raspberry Sauce

This is easy, unusual, and delicious. The sauce may be prepared a day or two ahead of time.

Sauce

Thaw the berries. Drain the juice, but reserve it. In a blender or a food processor purée the berries with the sugar, lemon juice, and kirsch.

Strain the mixture to remove the seeds.

Stir in a bit of the drained juice (you will not use all of it) to thin the sauce slightly. Refrigerate.

1 10-ounce package frozen raspberries, packed in syrup
2 tablespoons granulated sugar
1 tablespoon lemon juice
1 tablespoon kirsch

Strawberries

Wash the berries quickly in cold water, remove the hulls, and drain thoroughly on paper towels.

When they are thoroughly dry, place them in a bowl. Add the kirsch and sugar, stir gently, and let stand, stirring occasionally, for about an hour.

Transfer the berries to individual wine glasses or to a serving bowl. Cover and refrigerate.

Shortly before serving prepare the whipped cream.

4 to 6 cups strawberries
1 tablespoon kirsch
1½ tablespoons granulated sugar

4 TO 6 PORTIONS

Whipped Cream

In a chilled bowl with chilled beaters whip the cream and the vanilla until the cream holds a shape but not until it is really stiff. In a small bowl stir the preserves with a small wire whisk to soften them. Add about one-quarter of the cream and stir to mix. Then add the preserves to the remaining cream and fold together, but do not be too thorough; it does not have to be completely blended. Refrigerate.

1 cup heavy cream
½ teaspoon vanilla extract
⅓ cup raspberry, strawberry, or currant preserves

To serve: Just before serving, pour the sauce over the berries and the whipped cream over the sauce. Or the whipped cream may be passed separately in a pitcher, to be poured over each portion.

Rhubarb Strawberries

The rhubarb and strawberries should both be fresh—it is not as good with frozen fruit. This is very easy, and it is a delicious dessert to serve after a big meal. And it can be made a day ahead. It consists of fresh strawberries mixed with baked rhubarb; it has a slightly tart flavor and a beautiful color. It is very pretty served in small wine glasses. This recipe may be multiplied by any number.

Adjust a rack to the center of the oven and preheat oven to 350°. Wash the berries quickly in a large bowl of cold water; do not let them soak. Remove the hulls and let the berries drain on paper towels. Refrigerate.

1 pint box (1 pound) fresh
  strawberries
1 pound rhubarb
½ cup granulated sugar
2 tablespoons lemon juice

4 PORTIONS

Cut the leaves and the ends off the rhubarb stalks (unless you buy them already trimmed). Brush them with a vegetable brush under cold running water. Do not peel unless they are very tough, and in that case they would probably not be good for this recipe anyhow. Cut the stalks into 1-inch pieces (there should be about 4 cups). Place them in a pot or an ovenproof casserole that has a tight cover. Add the sugar and lemon juice. Cover tightly.

Bake for 25 to 30 minutes, stirring occasionally, until the rhubarb is tender. Test it with a toothpick. As it becomes tender it will fall apart somewhat as you stir it; that is to be expected.

As soon as the rhubarb is done, pour it into a bowl and add the cold berries; stir gently with a rubber spatula. Don't worry about the rhubarb losing its shape and falling apart.

Cover and refrigerate.

Spoon into small wine glasses or dessert bowls.

NOTE: This can also be served as a sauce over vanilla ice cream. It is a perfect combination, tart and sweet. It is tantalizing.

Saidie Heatter's Apple Fritters

This was one of my mother's specialties. She made them for breakfast, brunch, lunch, or supper, either as an entrée or as dessert. Whatever and whenever, they were always a special treat.

These fritters are fried in deep fat and then they are glazed under the broiler. They should be served as soon as they are done, but they don't take long to prepare.

I have made these fritters, all ready to fry, an hour or so ahead of time. When you add the apple slices be sure they are all coated with the batter (it is best to add them one at a time); that way they will not discolor. Cover and refrigerate. Or, if you want to start it hours ahead, or the night before, prepare the egg yolk mixture, cover, and refrigerate it; cover the whites and let them stand at room temperature for a few hours, or refrigerate them for longer. Then complete the mixing and add the apples shortly before frying.

Pour the fat about 1 inch deep in a wide, deep frying pan (or you can use two pans if you wish). Heat the fat to 375° on a frying thermometer. Adjust the heat to maintain the correct temperature. (Do not fry at a lower temperature or the fritters will be greasy.)

Adjust a rack about 10 inches below the broiler and preheat the broiler.

Butter a large jelly-roll pan and set aside.

Resift the flour with the baking powder and salt, and set aside.

In a small bowl beat the egg yolks until thick and pale. Gradually mix in the milk, brandy, and butter. Add the sifted dry ingredients and beat only until the mixture is smooth. Set aside.

Peel and core the apples (with an apple corer) and slice them crossways into rings about ⅓ inch thick.

Beat the egg whites until they hold a shape but not until they are stiff or dry, and fold them into the yolk mixture.

Add several slices of the apples to the batter, thoroughly coating the slices with the batter.

Use a fork with two or three long prongs or a wooden or metal skewer, place it through the hole in an apple ring, raise the ring and hold it briefly so that a bit of (but not too much) excess batter runs off, and then slip it gently into the 375° fat. Add as many slices as there is room for.

Fry on one side until golden brown, then turn the rings without piercing them and brown the other sides. As the rings finish frying, drain them briefly on brown paper and then transfer them to the buttered jelly-roll pan. Do not let them cool off any

Fat for deep frying (Crisco in a can, or Crisco, Mazola, or Wesson oil)
1 cup sifted all-purpose flour
2 teaspoons baking powder
½ teaspoon salt
2 eggs, separated
⅔ cup milk
1 tablespoon brandy
2 tablespoons unsalted butter, melted
4 large, tart, crisp apples
Granulated sugar (to be used after the fritters are fried)

more than necessary—work quickly. With your fingers sprinkle the slices generously with granulated sugar (there is no sugar in the batter) and place the pan under the broiler.

Watch them very carefully!!! Broil until the sugar melts; it may begin to caramelize (delicious), but do not let the sugar turn black anywhere.

As soon as the rings are done, place them on warm plates and serve immediately.

VARIATION: If the broiled sugar topping seems to be more than you want to bother with, you can eliminate it and simply sprinkle the fried and drained rings generously with confectioners sugar, sprinkling it through a strainer held over the slices.

Banana Fritters

Follow the preceding recipe, using bananas instead of apples. Use bananas that are not overripe; they must not be too soft. Peel and cut them crossways into 1½-inch pieces. Use a wide fork, a flat wire whisk, or a slotted metal spoon for turning and transferring the banana fritters.

Saidie often served a combination of apple and banana fritters; since the bananas fry more quickly, they were fried after the apples.

Vermont Baked Apples

I had heard about the Phoenix in Sugarbush Village, Warren, Vermont. A friend had told me, "Next time you leave Florida, if you go north, don't miss their chocolate desserts. They have dozens of them—all wonderful."

So when we next went north, I remembered the Phoenix. We drove to a perfectly gorgeous area in the mountains of Vermont, to a ski village. The chocolate desserts were everything I had heard. We had some of each—literally dozens. All carefully and beautifully made by Peter Sussman, the owner. We had a wonderful and deliciously good time.

When we left, we took away gallons of maple syrup and a small, prized collection of local maple syrup recipes. This is one.

The apples will be mildly spiced, shiny, dark, crunchy, and chewy; made with both honey and maple syrup. Serve these with Honey Ricotta Cream (see page 253). Divine! Wonderful for a brunch or for any casual meal.

Adjust a rack one-third up from the bottom of the oven and preheat oven to 400°. Have ready a shallow baking dish that measures about 11 x 8 inches.

With scissors cut the dates into small pieces (¼ to ½ inch). In a small bowl combine the dates with the honey, pecans, and grated lemon rind. Set aside.

In a small bowl combine the crumbs with the cinnamon, nutmeg, and ginger and set aside.

Wash the apples. With a vegetable parer peel the top third of each apple. With an apple corer remove the cores from the stem end to about three-quarters of the way down; do not cut through the bottoms.

With a pastry brush, brush the peeled part of the apples with the melted butter and, after you brush each one, roll it in the crumbs to coat the buttered part. You will have some leftover butter and leftover crumbs; reserve them.

Place the apples in the baking dish. Then, with a small spoon, fill the apples with the date mixture. Using your fingertips, press it firmly down into the holes in the apples; then mound some of the mixture on top of the apples. All the remaining crumb mixture should be sprinkled over the apples and/or placed in the baking dish. Pour the reserved butter into the dish over the crumbs.

Pour the maple syrup and boiling water in the baking dish around the apples over the crumbs and butter.

Bake for about 30 minutes. Baste several times with the maple syrup mixture, or spoon it slowly over the apples. Whichever, basting or spooning, it should be done slowly

⅓ cup pitted dates, firmly packed
¼ cup light honey
¼ cup pecans, cut into small pieces
Finely grated rind of 1 large lemon
¼ cup graham cracker crumbs
1 teaspoon cinnamon
¼ teaspoon nutmeg
¼ teaspoon ground ginger
6 large baking apples (preferably Rome Beauty)
2 ounces (½ stick) unsalted butter, melted
⅔ cup maple syrup
⅓ cup boiling water

6 PORTIONS

and gently with a light touch in order not to dislodge the crumb mixture from the apples.

Test the apples with a cake tester and bake only until they are just barely tender. By the time the apples are done, the sauce should be thick and darkly caramelized.

Set aside and serve warm (warm, these are luscious) or at room temperature or refrigerated (refrigerated, the filling and sauce will thicken and become caramel-candylike and fabulous).

Serve with ice-cold Honey Ricotta Cream (see page 253).

It is best to serve the apples and any of the date and nut mixture on flat dessert plates (preferably rather wide plates) with a small sharp knife and a fork and spoon for each serving. And pass the Honey Ricotta Cream with a large spoon or a ladle; you will be surprised at how fast this cream disappears.

American Beauty Apples

These apples are basted while they bake, with puréed frozen raspberries flavored with honey and cassis. The apples become the color of American Beauty roses.

The apples will be slightly tart; if you do not enjoy slightly tart desserts, add another 1 to 2 spoons of honey or add 1 to 2 spoons of sugar.

This is best during the winter, when Rome Beauty apples are available.

Adjust a rack to the middle of the oven and preheat oven to 350°. You will need a baking dish about 8 x 11 x 2 inches, or any shallow baking dish that will hold the apples comfortably, with a bit of room around each one. Do not butter the dish.

In a food processor, a blender, or a food mill purée the raspberries with their syrup and work the mixture through a fine strainer resting over a bowl (do not use a narrow fine strainer—it will take too long). Stir the honey and cassis into the purée and set aside.

Wash the apples and remove the cores with an apple corer, but do not cut all the way down; leave the bottoms of the apples intact. Then,

2 10-ounce packages frozen red raspberries in syrup, thawed
3 tablespoons honey
2 tablespoons crème de cassis
6 large baking apples (preferably Rome Beauty)

6 PORTIONS

with a vegetable parer, remove the peel from the top halves of the apples. Place the apples in the baking dish.

Pour the raspberry mixture into and over and around the apples. Bake uncovered. With a bulb baster, or with a spoon, baste or spoon the raspberry mixture over the apples about every 10 minutes. Bake until a toothpick inserted into the apples lets you know they are just barely tender; it should take about 1 hour.

Remove from the oven and set aside to cool, still basting or spooning the raspberry mixture frequently over the apples while they cool. By the time they are cool there will be only a few spoonfuls of the raspberry mixture (it thickens and evaporates).

Refrigerate.

Serve the apples on chilled flat dessert plates with a knife and fork, pouring whatever bit of raspberry syrup remains over the apples.

These are perfect just as they are, but they are even more so with a bit of Crème Fraîche (see page 255) or Honey Ricotta Cream (see page 253) alongside or over each apple.

Brandied Apples

This must be served immediately, but it takes 5 minutes to make, is very pretty—and delicious. Serve this after a luncheon or a dinner.

You need a large nonstick frying pan (preferably about 12 inches in diameter), and a plain or scalloped 2½-inch round cookie cutter, as well as a plain or scalloped ¾-inch round cutter or an apple corer.

Two apples makes 2 to 4 portions depending on whether you serve them plain or with ice cream or sour cream. To double the recipe, see Notes.

Place an unpeeled apple on its side. Cut it into slices about ⅜ inch wide, discarding the two ends. You should get five or six slices from an average large apple. Slice the other apple.

With a plain or scalloped round cookie cutter about 2½ inches wide cut the apple slices, cutting away the peel. Then, with a plain or scalloped round cutter about ¾ inch wide, cut out the cores. If you do not have a small enough round cutter, you can core the apples with an apple corer before slicing them.

Melt the butter over high heat in a 12-inch nonstick frying pan, add the apple slices in a single layer, sprinkle on the sugar, and sauté, turning the slices frequently (with two wide metal spatulas) for about 2 minutes. The apples should be just barely tender when tested with a toothpick.

Add the Calvados and, holding a match at arm's length, light the brandy (it will make a high flame). Twirl the pan briefly until the flame subsides. Add the cream, and twirl the pan a bit more, then shake it back and forth for about a minute to allow the sauce to thicken slightly.

Transfer the apples to individual flat plates, placing the slices in an overlapping row. Raise the heat and boil the sauce for a few seconds longer until it turns a light caramel color, then divide the sauce over the apples.

Serve as is or with a scoop of ice cream or a large spoonful of sour cream alongside the apple slices. Serve quickly while the apples are hot.

2 large tart apples (preferably Granny Smith)
1 large tablespoon unsalted butter
¼ cup granulated sugar
2 ounces Calvados (apple brandy—see Notes)
⅓ cup whipping cream
Optional: ice cream or sour cream

2 TO 4 PORTIONS

NOTES: Applejack or any other brandy or cognac or dark or light rum can be used in place of the Calvados, but Calvados is wonderful.

To double the recipe use two large frying pans. If you double the amount of Calvados in one pan the flame will be dangerously high.

Ginger-Honey Baked Apples

These are especially gorgeous. Try to get large and beautiful apples: Rome Beauties are generally recommended for baking because they hold their shape better than some others. Spy, Jonathan, Cortland are among others that are good for baking. These baked apples will have a richly colored, shiny glaze. And although there are several flavors in the recipe, you will only taste delicious baked apples. These are a perfect dessert for almost any meal.

Adjust a rack to the center of the oven and preheat oven to 350°. Have a shallow ovenproof baking dish ready; there should be a little room around the apples—it is best if they are not touching.

Wash the apples and remove the cores with an apple corer, but do not cut all the way down; leave the bottoms of the apples intact. With a vegetable parer remove the peel from the top halves of the apples. Now score the peeled part of the apples to make a design on them. Here's how: Place an apple on the counter top. Use a four-pronged fork. Gently insert the tips of the prongs slightly into the apple and rotate the apple slowly, so the fork makes a spiral pattern on all of the peeled section.

My mother always decorated baked apples this way, but I remember times when she crosshatched the lines, making them go around and then up and down. And I remember times when each apple had a different design. Fun!

Place the apples in the baking dish. Place the ginger in the cavities of the apples and then fill the cavities with honey. There will be some remaining honey.

Pour the water and the remaining honey into the bottom of the dish. Mix the cinnamon and sugar and sprinkle over the tops of the apples.

Place in the oven and bake uncovered. Use a bulb baster to baste the apples about every 10 minutes. Total baking time may be about 45 minutes to 1 hour. However, after about 30 minutes start testing the apples with a cake tester and bake until they are almost but not completely tender.

Now use the bulb baster to transfer all of the liquid, including what is in the cavities of the apples, to a 1-quart saucepan. Allow the apples to continue to bake without the liquid. Place the saucepan of liquid over high heat and boil uncovered until the liquid reduces to about half its amount; it will take about 7 to 10 minutes. Then add the preserves, stir well, and boil for 2 minutes.

Pour the hot glaze over the tops of the apples. The apples should be completely tender now; be careful not to overbake or they will squash and lose their shape. The liquid should be slightly thickened and very shiny.

Place the apples under the broiler for a few minutes to caramelize the glaze on top slightly.

Set aside to cool. When cool, the liquid will thicken to a soft jelly.

Serve at room temperature or refrigerated. It is best to serve these on flat dessert plates with a knife and fork for each person. Serve some of the jellied liquid over or alongside each portion.

NOTE: The preserves can be almost any kind; the apples will look quite different depending on the preserves. Apricot preserves or sweet orange marmalade (do not strain) will give a nice shine. But if you use red currant or some other red berry jam or jelly, it will also color the apples beautifully. I have made these often, and have varied the preserves depending on what was on hand. Today I used a mixture of half marmalade and half strawberry, and I wish you could see them.

---

6 *large baking apples*
3 *tablespoons finely chopped candied ginger*
½ *cup honey*
1 *cup water*
1 *teaspoon cinnamon*
3 *tablespoons granulated sugar*
¼ *cup preserves (see Note; to be used when the apples are almost finished baking)*

6 PORTIONS

Apple Bread Pudding

This is a great dessert for a buffet party. Bread pudding can be served, as it often is, tepid, cooled, or chilled. But for it to be really super-duper, serve it very hot, right out of the oven. Here's how: Prepare the entire recipe but do not bake it. Cover and refrigerate for several hours or overnight. Remove it from the refrigerator about 2¼ hours before serving. Place it in the oven to bake about 1¼ hours before you plan to serve it.

You will need a 13 x 9 x 2-inch ovenproof casserole, or any shallow casserole with a 12-cup capacity. Butter it well.

To make it easier to handle the bread, cut each loaf so it is only half as long. With a sharp knife remove the crusts. Slice the bread a generous ½ inch thick (do not slice too thin). If the bread is very fresh, place it right on an oven rack in a very low oven (about 200°) for a little while to dry out a bit, but it should not become hard. Meanwhile, prepare the apples and the custard.

Peel, quarter, and core the apples. Cut each quarter into three wedges.

Place 2 ounces (½ stick) of the butter, reserving the remaining 2 ounces, in a very large frying pan to melt. Add the apples and 2 tablespoons of the sugar, reserving the remaining ¾ cup. Cover and cook over moderate heat for about 2 minutes. Then remove the cover, stir gently and carefully, and continue to cook for about 6 minutes more (8 minutes altogether) until the apples are just barely tender; test them with a toothpick. They should not be cooked until they fall apart or get mushy.

Sprinkle the cinnamon all over the apples; stir gently (turning the apples with a wide metal spatula helps) until the cinnamon is absorbed. Set aside uncovered.

Place one layer of the bread slices in the buttered baking dish, packing them close together. Sprinkle with half of the raisins. Spread the apples and all of their juice over the top. Sprinkle with the remaining raisins. Make another layer of bread. (Use only enough bread to make the two layers—you will probably have a few slices left over, depending on how thick or thin you sliced it.) Set aside.

In a mixing bowl beat or whisk the eggs and yolks lightly just to mix. Add the milk, vanilla, nutmeg, salt, and ½ cup of the remaining sugar, reserving the remaining ¼ cup. Mix thoroughly. Pour into a pitcher.

Pour the custard slowly and evenly all over the top layer of bread, being careful to

1 pound Italian or French bread (the commercial loaves are generally ½ pound each)

4 to 5 medium-large tart and crisp apples (1½ to 2 pounds; Granny Smith are good)

4 ounces (1 stick) unsalted butter

¾ cup plus 2 tablespoons granulated sugar

1 teaspoon cinnamon

½ cup raisins

4 eggs plus 2 yolks

4½ cups milk

2 teaspoons vanilla extract

⅛ teaspoon nutmeg

⅛ teaspoon salt

8 TO 12 PORTIONS

wet it all thoroughly. While pouring the custard over the bread, stir the custard occasionally from the bottom—the sugar settles.

Cover the top with a large piece of wax paper and, with the palms of both hands, press down on the paper gently to push the bread down into the custard. You can use a weight (or a few small ones) if you wish, but be careful that it is not so heavy that it makes the custard run over the sides of the dish. Or you can just do it with your hands—about 10 minutes is long enough.

Set aside, or refrigerate, or bake (see introduction).

When you are ready to bake, adjust a rack to the center of the oven and preheat oven to 350°.

Melt the reserved 2 ounces of butter and drizzle it all over the bread. Then, carefully sprinkle the reserved ¼ cup of sugar over the top.

Place the dish of pudding in a larger, shallow baking pan. Pour about 1 inch of hot water into the larger pan. Carefully transfer to the oven and bake uncovered for 60 to 70 minutes. To test for doneness, insert the tip of a small sharp knife into the middle of the pudding; it is done just as soon as the knife comes out clean. Do not overbake.

The bread will have puffed up and started to brown slightly on top. Place it under the broiler briefly (watch it every second because the butter and sugar on top will brown very quickly) until the top becomes gorgeous—crisp and golden honey-colored.

Remove from the hot water.

Serve immediately or let stand.

TO SERVE: Use a small sharp knife to cut the pudding into portions, and use a wide metal spatula to transfer each portion to an individual flat dessert plate.

NOTE: Bread pudding is often served with a sauce. If this one is served piping hot, it is so good as it is that it does not need a sauce. However, after it has cooled or been refrigerated, it becomes more firm and compact and then you will probably like a sauce with it. The following is very quick and easy.

Apricot Sauce

In a small saucepan stir the preserves and water over moderate heat until the mixture comes to a low boil.

Strain the mixture and then stir in the liquor or orange juice.

Serve warm or at room temperature.

12 ounces (1 cup) apricot preserves
1 tablespoon water
3 tablespoons rum, kirsch, brandy, bourbon, or orange juice

GENEROUS 1 CUP

Almond-Apple Pudding

This is a wonderful old Swedish dessert. It consists of sliced apples that are barely cooked on top of the stove, placed in a shallow casserole, and topped with a buttery, macaroonlike mixture made with ground almonds. It is baked and served slightly warm or at room temperature, but it is best while it is very fresh. If you wish, the apples can be prepared, including their preliminary cooking, the day before. Then the rest is quick and easy.

P eel, quarter, and core the apples. Cut each quarter into three or four lengthwise slices. Place the sugar and water in a wide frying pan that has a cover, and stir over moderate heat until the sugar is melted. Add the apples and the lemon juice. Cover for 1 minute. Then un-cover, raise the heat to high, and cook, agitating con-stantly—use something like a wide metal or wooden spatula to move and turn the apples without breaking them—until the apples are barely tender and the juice is just evaporated. If there is still much liquid left when the apples are tender, remove the apples and boil down the juice until it thickens slightly, then pour it back over the apples; if they are almost dry it is not necessary to boil down the juice.

This can now be cooled, covered, and refrigerated if you plan to bake it the next day. Or it can be baked now.

Before baking, adjust a rack one-third up from the bot-tom of the oven and preheat oven to 350°. You will need a shallow casserole with an 8-cup capacity (mine measures 8 x 11 x 2 inches). Butter the casserole.

Place the cooked apples (which may be warm or chilled) any which way in the casserole; press on the top slightly to level it a bit.

Grate a bit of whole nutmeg over the apples, or sprinkle with the powdered nutmeg.

6 medium-large, tart apples (2½ pounds; Granny Smith apples are delicious for this recipe)
3 tablespoons granulated sugar
⅓ cup water
2 tablespoons fresh lemon juice
Freshly grated nutmeg, or about ¼ teaspoon powdered nutmeg

8 PORTIONS

Almond Topping

The almonds must be finely ground. This can be done in a processor, a blender, or a nut grinder—they should be powdery. If you use a processor or blender, add a bit of the sugar to prevent lumping. Set aside.

In the small bowl of an electric mixer cream the butter. Add the almond extract and then ½ cup of the sugar, reserving the remaining 3 tablespoons of sugar, and beat for a minute or two until well mixed. Add the 2 egg yolks and beat well. Add the ground almonds and beat only to mix.

In a clean small bowl with clean beaters beat the 3 egg whites and the salt until the whites hold a soft shape. Reduce the speed slightly and gradually add the reserved 3 tablespoons of sugar, increase the speed to high, and continue to beat until the whites hold a definite shape but not until they are stiff or dry.

Stir about one-quarter of the whites into the yolk mixture. Then, in two additions, fold in the remaining whites.

Pour the mixture in a thick ribbon over the apples and then spread it to cover the apples completely.

Bake for 40 minutes until the top is a rich golden color.

Serve while still slightly warm or at room temperature. Serve as is or with ice cream.

2 ounces (½ cup) blanched almonds
3½ ounces (1 stick minus 1 tablespoon) unsalted butter
Scant ¼ tablespoon almond extract
½ cup plus 3 tablespoons granulated sugar
2 eggs, separated, plus 1 additional white (it may be a white that was left over from another recipe, frozen and then thawed)
Pinch of salt

Connecticut Apple Betty

This is the way my mother made it on our farm, Valley Ridge, in Brookfield Center, Connecticut. She used apples from our own trees; I don't know what kind they were but I have been using Granny Smith apples and the Betty is too good.

The big difference in this recipe from others is that this calls for small squares of bread, not crumbs. The crumbs turn to mush but the squares don't.

Adjust a rack to the center of the oven and preheat oven to 375°. You will need a 2- to 2½-quart ovenproof casserole; mine is round, 8 inches in diameter and 3½ inches deep. Butter the casserole well.

Cut the bread (it is not necessary to remove the crusts) into ¼- to ⅓-inch strips. Then cut it crossways making ¼- to ⅓-inch squares. You will need 4 to 4½ cups of squares. Place them in a large, shallow pan in the heated oven. Shake or stir occasionally only until the bread is dry; do not bake until it browns.

Melt the butter. Place the bread in a mixing bowl. Add the butter, drizzling it over as much of the bread as possible instead of pouring it all on one spot, stirring the bread with a spatula or a fork as you add the butter.

Place the sugar, cinnamon, and mace in a bowl and stir to mix. Mix in the lemon rind and set aside.

Mix the orange juice with the lemon juice and set aside.

Peel, quarter, and core the apples. Cut each quarter into four or five slices. You should have about 6 cups of loosely packed sliced apples.

In a large bowl thoroughly mix the apples with the sugar mixture, raisins, and optional nuts.

Place about one-third of the buttered bread squares over the bottom of the casserole. Cover with one-half of the apple mixture. Then another third of the bread, and then the remaining apple mixture. Now pour the orange juice mixture over the apples, and cover with the remaining bread. If any raisins are exposed place them under some of the apple slices or they will burn.

Cover tightly with aluminum foil, sealing the edges well—it should be airtight.

Bake for 30 minutes.

Remove the foil. If the apples gave off much juice use a bulb baster to baste the top of the Betty. Then bake uncovered for about 30 minutes (total baking time is about 1 hour) until the apples are tender when tested with a cake tester and the top is golden brown. If the top becomes too brown before the apples are done, replace the foil on top.

If it still seems too juicy by the time the apples are tender, don't worry about it. Most of the juice will be absorbed as it stands, and it is best if it is juicy—not dry.

Traditionally, Apple Betty is served warm with a plate of cold heavy cream or with whipped cream or ice cream. Or with the following Old-Fashioned Lemon Sauce. I try to serve it warm with very cold sauce. But it is good at any temperature.

NOTE: If you wish, the raisins may be marinated in rum, brandy, Grand Marnier, or any orange liqueur for several hours or overnight. Any of the marinade not absorbed by the raisins may be used as part of the orange juice.

Firm, thin-sliced, white or whole-wheat bread (Pepperidge Farm, Arnold, or any similar firm sandwich loaf; you will need enough to make 4 to 4½ cups of ¼-inch squares)

2⅔ ounces (5⅓ tablespoons) unsalted butter

1 cup light brown sugar, firmly packed

1 teaspoon cinnamon

½ teaspoon mace

Finely grated rind of 1 lemon

½ cup orange juice

2 tablespoons lemon juice

5 medium-size apples (about 2 pounds)

½ cup raisins (see Note)

Optional: ½ cup walnuts, cut into medium-size pieces

4 TO 6 PORTIONS

Old-Fashioned Lemon Sauce

This is from my first dessert book.

Mix the sugar, cornstarch, and salt in a heavy 1-quart saucepan. Gradually stir in the water. Cook over moderate heat, stirring gently and constantly with a rubber spatula, for about 5 minutes until the mixture comes to a boil and becomes thick and clear. Reduce the heat and boil very slowly, stirring gently, for 2 minutes.

Remove from the heat. Add the butter and stir gently until melted. Stir in the rind and juice.

Serve warm, at room temperature, or refrigerated. This can be refrigerated for about a week. It can be reheated in the top of a small double boiler over hot water.

⅓ cup granulated sugar
1 tablespoon plus 1 teaspoon cornstarch
⅛ teaspoon salt
1 cup hot water
2 tablespoons unsalted butter, at room temperature
Finely grated rind of 1 large lemon
2 to 3 tablespoons lemon juice (to taste)

1⅓ CUPS

Sugarbush Mountain Peaches

Pure, sweet, and simple. Peaches baked in maple syrup—that's it. Make this when peaches are at the height of their season and when you can get large ones that are just ripe but not overripe. Or buy them underripe and let them stand in a single layer at room temperature for a day or two until they just barely give when pressed lightly in your hand. Then, if you wish, they can be refrigerated for a few days before you use them.

Use 1 large freestone peach for each portion. Add 2 tablespoons of maple syrup for each peach (that's ¾ cup for 6 peaches). Blanch and peel the peaches (see below), then cut them in half. Place them cut side down in a lightly buttered shallow baking dish. Pour the maple syrup over the peaches.

Bake in the middle of a preheated 350° oven for about 20 to 22 minutes, basting the syrup with a bulb baster frequently over the peaches. Fresh peaches are best if they are baked only until they are not quite done. Test them with a toothpick. When they are ready, remove them from the oven and use the bulb baster to transfer all of the syrup to a small saucepan.

Place the saucepan over high heat and let the syrup boil hard, uncovered, for about 3 minutes or until it registers 230° on a candy thermometer.

Pour the boiled syrup over the peaches. Let stand, basting occasionally, until cool. Then refrigerate and serve cold.

Serve the chilled peaches on chilled flat dessert plates with a bit of the thick syrup spooned over them. It is easier to eat these with a knife and fork than with a spoon.

Or cut the baked peaches into bite-size pieces and serve them over vanilla ice cream, in dessert bowls.

Or, my favorite: a cold peach and a mound of cold Top Secret (see page 252) on a flat plate. I could swim in it.

Stewed Peaches

During peach season, when they are large and juicy and full of flavor, plain, whole (pit-in) stewed peaches are as delicious as any dessert I know. (This recipe is from my first book.)

To peel the peaches: Have ready a large bowl of ice-cold water, a slotted spoon, and a saucepan of boiling water deep enough to cover the peaches. With the slotted spoon place the peaches in the boiling water, two or three at a time. If the peaches are fully ripe they will need only about 15 seconds in the boiling water; if not quite ripe they will need more. With the slotted spoon raise a peach from the water and move your thumb firmly over the skin. If the skin has loosened enough it will wrinkle and feel loose. At that point transfer it to the ice water.

6 large ripe but firm freestone peaches
1½ cups water
1 cup granulated sugar
1 6- to 8-inch vanilla bean

Peel with your fingers, starting at the stem end, and return the peeled fruit to the ice water. Partially peeled peaches may be returned to the boiling water for additional blanching if necessary. Continue to blanch and peel all of the peaches.

In a saucepan large enough to hold the peaches in a single layer place the water and sugar. Slit the vanilla bean and scrape the seeds into the water; add the pod also. Bring to a boil, stirring, and let boil for about 5 minutes to make a syrup. With the slotted spoon add the peaches and adjust the heat so that the syrup simmers gently. Cook, partially covered, turning the peaches a few times with two rubber spatulas in order not to mar them. Baste occasionally with the syrup.

Test for doneness with a cake tester or a toothpick. Do not overcook. When they are just barely tender, transfer the peaches with the slotted spoon to a wide bowl.

Raise the heat and boil the syrup, uncovered, for a few minutes to reduce slightly. Taste the syrup and continue to boil until it tastes right—sweet enough and not watery. Pour the hot syrup over the stewed peaches. Do not remove the vanilla bean. Set aside to cool, basting occasionally with the syrup.

Cover and refrigerate. Serve cold.

Serve in shallow dessert bowls with a spoon and a fork (sometimes you need the fork to hold the fruit in place while you cut it with the spoon). Serve with a generous amount of the syrup or with a scoop of ice cream.

VARIATION: Stewed Pears—follow the above recipe, substituting firm but ripe pears for the peaches; pears to be stewed should be a little more firm than those for serving raw. Instead of blanching the pears to peel them, peel with a swivel-bladed vegetable parer, leaving the stems on. As you peel the pears, place them in a bowl of cold water that contains the juice of a lemon, to keep them from discoloring. If necessary, cut the bottoms a bit to allow the pears to stand upright.

Stewed Peaches with Brandy

Prepare the preceding plain Stewed Peaches. After the peaches have been removed from the syrup, boil the syrup down about 10 minutes longer to reduce it more. Then add ½ cup brandy, or ¼ cup brandy and ¼ cup kirsch, and simmer gently for only 1 or 2 minutes. Pour the hot syrup over the peaches, and spoon the syrup over the peaches occasionally as they cool.

Brandied Fresh Peaches

These are not the stewed peaches usually found under this name; these are raw. Brandy and honey with almost any delicious fresh fruit is heavenly; especially so with peaches. They may be prepared a few hours before serving.

Blanch and peel the peaches (see page 178) and slice each peach into about eight wedges. For three large peaches mix about ¼ cup honey and ¼ cup brandy or cognac. Stir the peaches gently in the mixture, cover with plastic wrap directly on the peaches, and refrigerate for an hour or two. Stir them gently a few times.

Serve as is or with vanilla ice cream. If the peaches are being served alone as dessert, allow one large peach for each portion. If they are being served with ice cream, one peach will serve two.

Stewed Apricots with Brandy

Follow the previous recipe, substituting about 1½ to 2 dozen fresh apricots for the peaches. Do not peel the apricots—poach them briefly, and follow the previous directions.

Cassis Raspberries

Raspberries do not have to be washed, and they are best at room temperature.

Place the berries in a wide, shallow bowl. Sprinkle the sugar over them and then the cassis. Stir gently with a rubber spatula and let stand for about an hour. If you prepare this hours ahead of time, refrigerate it and then remove it to room temperature for about an hour before serving.

Serve in wineglasses or shallow dessert bowls with an optional spoonful of Crème Fraîche over each portion.

1 quart raspberries
2 tablespoons granulated
   sugar
¼ cup crème de cassis
Optional: Crème Fraîche (see
   page 255)

6 PORTIONS

Cassis Grapefruit

This is a simple and delicious way with grapefruit. Do not make it unless the fruit is wonderful.

Use 1 large grapefruit for 2 portions. Peel and section the grapefruit (see page 15). For each grapefruit add 1 tablespoon honey and 2 tablespoons cassis (black currant syrup) or crème de cassis (black currant brandy). Stir gently to mix without breaking the fruit. Taste, and add a bit more honey and/or cassis if necessary, but it is best if the flavoring is mild. Cover and refrigerate for at least several hours or overnight, stirring occasionally.

Serve in wine glasses or shallow dessert bowls, dividing all of the liquid over the fruit.

Raspberry Pears

*Brilliant, shiny, deep-raspberry-colored pears; poached in a purée of frozen raspberries.
Sensational looks and a fantastic flavor. A spectacular dessert—along with a variety of
cookies—for a Christmas dinner. Or for any night of the week.*

1 10-ounce package frozen
   red raspberries in syrup,
   thawed
2 tablespoons honey
2 tablespoons plus 1 teaspoon
   framboise or kirsch
Juice of ½ lemon
4 large ripe but firm pears (see
   Note)

4 PORTIONS

Place the berries and their liquid in a food processor
or a blender and process or blend until puréed. Force
through a rather fine but wide strainer set over a
bowl, to remove the seeds. Or just mash the berries and
strain them. Stir in the honey and 2 tablespoons of the
framboise or kirsch (reserve the remaining 1 teaspoon) and
set aside.

Stir the lemon juice into a bowl of cold water that is
large enough to hold the pears (to prevent discoloring).
Peel the pears with a vegetable parer; do not remove the
stems or the cores. Place the pears in the lemon water until
they are all ready.

Use a deep, heavy saucepan with a tight cover, one that
the pears will just fit in, either standing up or lying on their sides. Remove the pears
from the water, place them in the saucepan, pour the raspberry mixture over the top,
cover, and place on moderate heat until the mixture comes to a boil. Then reduce the
heat so the syrup just simmers, and cook, basting a few times with a bulb baster.

(If the pears are lying down, turn them around very gently occasionally; use two
rubber spatulas or, if the pears have stems, you can lift the stems with your fingers or
with tongs to turn the pears over gently.)

To test for doneness, pierce the pears carefully with a toothpick at the widest
part. When they begin to feel tender, but before they are done (probably after about
20 to 30 minutes or less), let them continue to cook, only partially covered now (for
the sauce to thicken a bit), and cook only until tender (probably 35 to 45 minutes or
less in all, depending on the pears' ripeness—do not overcook).

Remove from the heat, transfer the pears gently to a wide
bowl, stir the remaining 1 teaspoon of framboise or kirsch into
the syrup, and pour it over the pears.

Let stand to reach room temperature. Then refrigerate,
uncovered (if they are covered they sweat and the wonderfully thick syrup becomes thin).

Serve the pears cold on chilled flat dessert plates with a
knife and fork. There will not be much syrup, but pour or
spoon whatever there is over and around the pears—even just a
bit of the syrup is a real treat.

Serve plain or with White Custard Cream (see page 254) or Crème Fraîche (see page 255) or Top Secret (see page 252).

NOTE: Winter pears, grown in Oregon, Washington, and northern California, are available from September into the spring. The best varieties for cooking are Anjou, light green or yellow green, almost egg-shaped; Bosc, golden brown, with a long tapering neck; and Comice, green to greenish yellow, with a chubby shape and a short neck. Bosc is most frequently recommended for poaching, but I have used others with equally good results. The pears must not be overripe, but if they are underripe they will not have any flavor. The flesh should barely give when pressed firmly with a fingertip.

Broiled Peppered Pears

Quick, easy, light, peppery, sweet, and hot; served right from the broiler. This is unusual and wonderful. The pears should be almost but not completely ripe when you use them. Pears are one of the few fruits that do not ripen well on the tree; they are picked when fully grown but still firm. The Bosc variety is excellent for cooking, but there are others equally good. Generally, I buy pears about a week ahead and let them stand at room temperature. If they begin to ripen before you are ready to use them, refrigerate to slow down the ripening process.

For each portion serve one large half or two smaller halves. This recipe can easily be divided for just two people.

First prepare a bowl of acidulated water to keep the pears from darkening: Stir the juice of 1 lemon into a bowl of 1 to 2 quarts cold tap water. With a vegetable parer peel the pears. Halve them lengthwise. With the tip of a small sharp knife cut a shallow groove to remove the stem from each pear. Remove the core and seeds with a melon ball scoop or with a serrated grapefruit spoon. Place the prepared pears in the acidulated water (this can be done hours ahead, if you wish, in which case, refrigerate).

Before broiling, adjust a rack 3 to 4 inches below the broiler and preheat the broiler. Lightly butter a shallow baking dish that the pear halves will fit in. Drain the pears and place them curved side up close together in the dish. Drizzle the honey over the tops. Cut the butter into tiny pieces and distribute over the pears. Grind on the pepper (or sprinkle if you ground in a mortar and pestle). Pour the cognac or rum into the bottom of the baking dish.

Place under the broiler and baste a few times with a bulb baster. Test the pears for doneness with a cake tester or a toothpick. When they are just barely tender and slightly golden on the tops, sprinkle sugar generously over them. Replace under the broiler. Now, do not baste any more, but just broil to caramelize the sugar. Watch carefully.

The total broiling takes from 10 to 15 minutes, depending on the ripeness of the pears. The sugar on top should melt and caramelize to a golden color.

Serve on warm, flat dessert plates. Each person should have a fork and a spoon.

If you wish, pass sour cream with this, and/or any dessert cheese.

Juice of 1 lemon
Cold tap water
3 large or 6 medium pears
3 tablespoons mild honey
Scant 1 tablespoon unsalted butter
⅜ teaspoon pepper (see Note)
6 tablespoons cognac or dark rum
Granulated sugar

6 PORTIONS

NOTE: The pepper should be finely ground and preferably freshly ground. It may be black, white, or dried green peppercorns (the green ones should be ground with a mortar and pestle).

Ginger Pears

These are whole pears poached in a ginger syrup. Unusual and light, they are a good dessert after chili or curry. They are a snap to make and can be made a day or two before serving. It is important to use pears that are not soft; they get mushy when they are poached. Comice and Bartlett are two good choices; but whichever, they must be firm and not overripe.

Use a saucepan that has a cover and is large enough to hold the pears upright in a single layer. Place the water, sugar, rind, and juice in the saucepan and stir over moderate heat until the sugar dissolves and the mixture comes to a boil. Stir in the ginger and set aside.

With a vegetable parer peel the pears. If necessary, trim the bottoms a bit so they will stand upright. Place the pears in the syrup, cover, and cook over moderate heat.

Baste the pears frequently (a ladle is handy for this since the ginger might get stuck in a bulb baster). Do not over-cook. Test with a cake tester or a toothpick. When they pierce easily they are done. Start testing after 20 minutes.

When the pears are just tender, transfer them with a slotted spoon to a shallow bowl.

Add the marmalade to the syrup and let boil for 5 min-utes. Then add the cognac, rum, or bourbon, and pour the hot sauce over the pears.

With a ladle or a large spoon baste occasionally until cool. Cover and refrigerate.

Serve each pear standing upright in a compote or dessert bowl, with several spoonfuls of the syrup.

1 cup water
1½ cups granulated sugar
Finely grated rind of 2 lemons
3 tablespoons lemon juice
Generous 2 to 3 tablespoons finely diced candied or preserved ginger
6 medium-size firm pears
⅓ cup orange marmalade
2 tablespoons cognac, rum, or bourbon

6 PORTIONS

Ginger-Pear Crisp

This can be made without the ginger and it is very good, but ginger and pears are a special combination—each complements the other. This can be served hot, warm, cooled, or chilled; but if you love it hot, and everyone seems to, try the following procedure: Prepare the topping as much ahead of time as you wish and refrigerate it. Cut up the ginger, mix the lemon juice and water, butter the casserole, and have the spices ready. Then, the last thing before dinner (it can be about 2 hours before), peel and cut the pears, put it all together, and bake. After it is baked it will keep warm for about an hour, but if necessary you can put it back in the oven for 5 or 10 minutes just before serving.

Crumb Topping

This can be made in a food processor or by hand with a pastry blender. In a processor (fitted with the steel blade), place the flour, sugar, and butter in the bowl and process on/off quickly, six or seven times. Then let the machine run for only a few seconds until the mixture resembles coarse meal; it should not hold together.

If you do it with a pastry blender, place the ingredients in a mixing bowl and cut with a pastry blender until the mixture resembles coarse meal.

Then, whichever way you have arrived at this stage, now you must work it slightly with your hands. If you have used a processor, transfer the mixture to a roomy bowl. Use both hands and work (squeeze) the ingredients through your fingers to form it into a lumpy, crumbly mixture—not powdery and not smooth. Set aside.

Adjust an oven rack to the center of the oven and preheat oven to 375°. Butter a shallow ovenproof casserole with an 8-cup capacity (8 x 11 x 2 inches) and set aside. Cut the ginger into dice about ⅛ inch, and set aside. Mix the lemon juice and water, and set aside.

With a vegetable parer peel the pears, cut them into quarters, cut out the cores, and then cut each piece in half the long way. If the pears are small, leave them in quarters—the pieces should not be too small. Work quickly before the pears discolor. Place them in a large bowl, add the cinnamon and nutmeg, toss well to thoroughly coat the pieces with the spices, turn them into the casserole, and press down or rearrange to flatten the top. Drizzle the lemon juice and water all over them. Sprinkle the ginger over the top.

If the topping was refrigerated, work it with your hands a bit to make it crumbly. Sprinkle the topping all over; it should just cover all the fruit. Do not press it down or flatten it.

Bake for 1 hour or until the fruit is barely tender (not mushy) when tested with a cake tester or a toothpick, and the topping is a rich color—is should not be pale. If the fruit is tender and the topping is still pale, place the casserole about 6 inches below the broiler and broil, watching it constantly, only until nicely browned.

Serve this as is or with vanilla ice cream or with sweetened and vanilla-flavored whipped cream.

¾ cup unsifted *all-purpose flour*

1 cup granulated sugar

4 ounces (1 stick) unsalted butter, cold and firm, cut into small pieces

¼ cup candied ginger

¼ cup lemon juice

¼ cup water

3 to 3½ pounds firm, fresh pears (about 8; Anjou, Comice, or Bartlett—they must not be overripe or the least bit soft)

2 teaspoons cinnamon

½ teaspoon nutmeg

6 TO 8 PORTIONS

Blueberries and Cream

Quick, easy, classy, extra-delicious; made with fresh or frozen berries.

Place the 2 tablespoons of water, lemon juice, sugar, and salt in a 2-quart heavy saucepan. Stir over moderate heat until the mixture boils and the sugar dissolves.

Add the berries, reduce the heat a bit (if the berries are frozen wait until the liquid comes to a boil again before reducing the heat), and simmer for 5 minutes.

Place the ¼ cup of cold tap water in a small cup, add the cornstarch, stir to dissolve, stir into the berry mixture, and reduce the heat still a bit more. This should cook slowly, uncovered, without coming to a boil for 4 to 5 minutes, during which time the mixture should be stirred gently and occasionally with a rubber spatula. The mixture will thicken soon after the cornstarch is added, but do not remove it from the heat too soon; it needs these few extra minutes of gentle cooking to remove the raw taste of cornstarch. (Cooking over too-high heat, cooking too long, or stirring too hard would prevent the cornstarch from thickening the mixture properly.)

Remove from the heat. Stir or fold gently with a rubber spatula occasionally until cool. Transfer to a covered container and refrigerate until very cold, or overnight.

To serve, spoon the berry mixture into four to six wineglasses or dessert bowls and spoon the sauce gently over the tops.

2 tablespoons water
3 tablespoons lemon juice
½ cup granulated sugar
Pinch of salt
4 cups fresh blueberries (washed and dried) or 1 1-pound package of frozen dry-packed blueberries (not thawed)
¼ cup cold tap water
2 tablespoons cornstarch
Sweet Sour Cream (see page 255) or The Governor's Crème Fraîche (see page 256), very cold

4 TO 6 PORTIONS

Oranges à la Grecque

One of the most popular desserts to serve after a big meal. Or any time. You must have large, juicy, seedless oranges. You can make this a day or two ahead.

With a vegetable parer peel the thin colored rind from 4 or 5 of the oranges, removing it in long strips rather than short ones. Pile two or three of the strips one on top of the other on a cutting board and with a very sharp knife cut the rind into thin slivers; make them as long as you can and about ⅛ inch wide.

10 large, deep-colored, thick-
    skinned seedless oranges
1½ cups granulated sugar
¼ cup red currant jelly
¾ cup water

6 TO 8 PORTIONS

Place the slivered rind in a saucepan over high heat, cover with boiling water, boil for 10 minutes, and then drain. Return the rind to the saucepan, cover with boiling water again, and boil again for 10 minutes. Repeat for three boilings in all. Drain in a strainer.

While the rind is boiling, prepare the oranges. Peel and cut them into sections (see page 15). Pour over the oranges any juice that remains.

Place the sugar, jelly, and water in a 6-cup saucepan. Stir over moderate heat until the sugar is melted and the syrup comes to a boil. Raise the heat and let boil without stirring for 5 minutes.

Pour the hot syrup over the oranges and let stand for 10 to 15 minutes. Then pour through a large strainer set over the saucepan. Transfer the orange sections to a bowl. Boil the syrup again for 10 minutes more. Add the drained rind to the hot syrup, and pour rind and syrup over the orange sections. Stir gently with a rubber spatula. Cool and then refrigerate.

This must be as cold as possible when it is served. (If possible, place it in the freezer for 20 to 30 minutes just before serving.)

Serve in shallow glasses or dessert bowls, spooning the rind and sauce generously over each portion.

VARIATION: Before pouring the hot syrup over the oranges, drain the juice off the oranges (do not use it for this variation). Sprinkle ¼ to ⅓ cup Grand Marnier, Curaçao, rum, cognac, or whatever over the oranges. Then proceed with the directions. Or follow the above recipe and just before serving pour a little Grand Marnier (or whatever) over each portion.

Raspberry Oranges

This is unusual, exotic, fresh, easy, and light. Use wonderful oranges, or the dessert will not be all that wonderful. This should be prepared at least a few hours ahead or a day ahead.

Peel the oranges (see page 15) and cut them crossways into rounds ⅓ inch thick. Set aside. In a food processor or a food mill purée the berries and, to remove the seeds, strain them through a wide but fine strainer set over a bowl.

Stir in the honey and framboise or kirsch. Add the orange slices, thoroughly moistening each slice on both sides with the raspberry syrup.

Cover and refrigerate for several hours or overnight.

A few hours before serving, remove the orange slices from the raspberry syrup. Transfer the syrup to a saucepan over moderate heat and let boil for a few minutes, stirring occasionally, until the mixture is well thickened; you should have ⅓ to ½ cup of the reduced syrup.

Let cool, and then pour the syrup over, under, and around the slices again. Refrigerate.

To serve, place the slices overlapping one another on chilled flat dessert plates. Divide the sauce over or around the oranges.

Pass The Governor's Crème Fraîche at the table and let the guests spoon it onto their plates.

When I serve this, I serve a knife, fork, and spoon with it, and I find that most guests use them all.

4 seedless oranges
2 10-ounce packages frozen
   raspberries in syrup,
   thawed
⅓ cup mild honey
¼ cup framboise or kirsch
1 cup The Governor's Crème
   Fraîche (see page 256),
   which may be prepared
   several days ahead (the
   Crème Fraîche itself, see
   page 255, may be prepared
   as much as 3 or 4 weeks
   ahead)

4 PORTIONS

Broiled Grapefruit

This is wonderful either as dessert or as a first course. It may be prepared ahead of time but must be broiled immediately before serving and must be served without delay.

It is best to use large, juicy fruit. The combination of flavors—honey, butter, rum, and grapefruit—is delicious. Although this is usually made without the butter, the first time we had it this way was at Chalet Suzanne, a restaurant in Lake Wales, Florida (they are famous for their wonderful soups, which are distributed all over the world), and we were immediately converted.

Grapefruit (pink or white—
 preferably large and
 seedless)
Unsalted butter, melted
Honey (either liquid, or thick
 and butterlike)
Optional: rum

Use half a grapefruit for each portion, but before halving the fruit, trim the ends very slightly if they are uneven, so that the halves will stand upright without tilting. Then cut them in half crossways and, with a curved and serrated grapefruit knife, cut around each section to loosen it completely (but do not remove it); remove any seeds.

Brush each half with a generous teaspoon of melted butter, or simply drizzle the melted butter on. Then, if you are using liquid honey, drizzle a generous tablespoonful over each half; if you are using honey as thick as a spread, smooth a generous tablespoonful over each half. (Some thick honeys are sticky and difficult to spread on wet grapefruit; it does not have to be spread evenly or all over—the heat will melt it and it will run.)

These may be broiled immediately, or refrigerated and broiled later on.

Before broiling, adjust a rack to the top position under the broiler and preheat the broiler until red hot.

Place the fruit in a shallow metal pan, pour water about ½ inch deep in the pan, and broil for about 7 or 8 minutes until the top is well colored (it will not brown evenly, it will be spotty) and the fruit is very hot.

Meanwhile, if you have large, round fresh green leaves, place one on each dessert plate.

Then transfer each grapefruit half to a plate, and sprinkle with the optional rum (I use Myers's dark rum—about 1 to 2 tablespoons per portion).

Serve immediately.

Honeyed Grapes

Helen McCully was one of the country's leading cookbook authors and food editors for many years when she was associated with Ladies' Home Journal and then with House Beautiful. I had the greatest respect for her knowledge of food and for her recipes. I was thrilled when she invited me and my husband to her apartment in New York City for dinner. She served poached striped bass at room temperature with homemade mayonnaise, cucumber salad, sourdough rolls, and several wonderful desserts. This was one.

It is the easiest thing to make. Helen said it should be put together a day ahead, but it is also delicious as soon as it is mixed.

Remove the grapes from the stems (there should be about 2½ cups of grapes), wash and drain them, then spread them on a towel to dry thoroughly.

In a bowl mix the honey, rum or cognac, and the lemon juice. Add the grapes. Turn carefully with a rubber spatula. Refrigerate overnight, stirring occasionally. Or serve sooner.

Divide the grapes among four wine glasses or dessert bowls and spoon a bit of the crème fraîche, sour cream, or yogurt over the tops.

NOTE: Helen used sour cream; I have since tried yogurt and also crème fraîche—they are equally delicious.

1 pound seedless green grapes
¼ cup honey
2 tablespoons rum or cognac
1 teaspoon lemon juice
½ cup Crème Fraîche (see page 255), sour cream, or unflavored yogurt (see Note)

4 PORTIONS

Brandied Prunes

Dried prunes soaked in flavored cognac for at least a week or two, served over vanilla ice cream. The prunes absorb so much of the cognac they remind me of a line in one of Mildred Knopf's wonderful cookbooks. She had made a dessert with a huge amount of liquor. When she served it, a guest said the dessert stood up and announced, "I can lick any man in the house."

*P*lace the prunes in a jar with a tight-fitting cover. Slit the vanilla bean the long way and then crossways, and add it to the prunes. Chop the ginger rather fine and add to the prunes. Add the cognac, honey, and coffee, tea, or water. Cover the jar tightly. Turn the jar from top to bottom and from side to side once or twice a day, and let the prunes marinate for at least a week or two. But this will keep for a month.

After the vanilla bean has softened, the seeds seem to float out into the syrup. However, if you think they need some help, you can scrape the seeds out into the syrup. But leave the bean itself in the jar also.

If this stands for a long time and if the prunes absorb most of the liquids, add a little more of either or all of them; it should have some juice and should not be dry.

This is sensational by itself but it is really best over vanilla ice cream. Or serve the prunes with fresh grapefruit sections—it is an exotic and wonderful combination.

NOTES: If the prunes are very large, they may be cut in half either before or after marinating to make them easier to eat.

This same recipe can be made with a combination of prunes and dried apricots.

12 ounces pitted dried (but soft) prunes
A 2-inch piece of vanilla bean
1 large slice of candied ginger or 1 whole piece preserved ginger
½ cup cognac
¼ cup honey
7 tablespoons strong black coffee, tea, or water

ABOUT 8 PORTIONS

California Fresh Figs

Fresh figs are very scarce. If you are among the lucky ones who can get them, here's an easy, delicious, and unusual way of serving them.

*C*ut the figs in half the long way through the stems. Place them cut side up on a large plate or tray. Sprinkle with the sugar and then with the cognac or rum. Cover and refrigerate for at least half an hour or longer.

Mix the Crème Fraîche and the Curaçao and refrigerate.

At serving time, place the figs and their liquid in shallow dessert bowls, and pour the cream over the tops.

12 fresh figs
3 tablespoons granulated sugar
3 tablespoons cognac or rum
1 cup Crème Fraîche (see page 255)
⅓ cup Curaçao

6 PORTIONS

Mangoes, Key West Style

Mangoes taste like peaches/pears/apricots/pineapple. This way of serving them, which I learned in Key West, is so gorgeous that I would be a mangophile even if it did not taste like all the delicious fruits rolled into one.

As far as I know, the only mangoes that are grown commercially in this country are in an area just south of Miami. They come in all sizes from plum size to large ones that weigh two to three pounds. The larger the mango is, the more dramatic and impressive this presentation will be. There are many varieties of mangoes; the Hayden is the best known and probably the most delicious.

M
angoes must be thoroughly ripe in order to have the most and the best flavor. (Green mangoes are used like green apples, for pie.) To ripen, just let the fruit stand at room temperature. To test ripeness, gently press the fruit—it should "give" slightly more than a ripe peach does. As it ripens, it might develop black spots on the skin the way bananas do. Some varieties might be green when ripe, and others might be green, gold, and red.

When you are quite sure that the fruit is ripe, refrigerate it either long enough to chill, or for a few days.

Before serving, rinse the fruit under running water to wash it.

Mangoes are not freestone. On the contrary, the fruit clings tenaciously. To such a degree that Floridians who are quite familiar with mangoes (and adore them) are divided into two groups. Those who say the only way to eat a mango is leaning over the kitchen sink, and those who opt for a bathtub.

The seed is long and flat (it reaches the top and the bottom of the fruit and almost two sides). Hold a mango upright, resting it on a work surface. Use a long, sharp knife and, cutting parallel with a long, flat side of the fruit, cut from the top to the bottom (a straight cut, not curved), cutting off a piece that is a scant half of the fruit (you should be cutting right next to—and barely touching—the seed). Then do the same on the other side of the fruit, starting the cut about ¾ inch (which is the width of the seed) from the first cut.

You now have two halves of the fruit and the seed with a bit of fruit clinging to it, which is not part of this recipe. (Incidentally, for some other time, the two halves may be peeled and sliced or diced, or you can eat the fruit from the halves with a spoon like melon.)

Cut each half as follows: Rest it, cut side up, on the work surface. With the tip of a small sharp paring knife, cut completely through the fruit but not through the skin. Cut straight down into the flat side of the fruit, making cuts from the top to the bottom ¾ inch apart. Then repeat, making cuts ¾ inch apart at right angles to the lengthwise cuts. It is a checkerboard effect.

Now, for the fun. Hold the fruits cut side (flat side) up. Hold the fingers of both hands (except the thumbs) underneath, touching the skin. Gently, with both hands, push the skin up to make it convex. This will cause the fruit to open up in a bold, dramatic pattern of ¾-inch squares.

Serve the mango on a flat dessert plate (which may first be covered with a large fresh green leaf, or a few lemon leaves) either just as it is or with a wedge or a half of a lime, an optional sprinkling of rum, and a shaker or a bowl of confectioners sugar. And with a fork and a sharp knife for each portion.

If the mangoes are large, one will make two portions. If they are small, serve two halves to a portion.

NOTE: You can prepare the fruit before dinner, but do not press the bottoms up to open the squares until right before serving. Wrap the prepared halves in plastic wrap; they will not discolor.

By the way, about that center slice that has the seed in it: Peel it, hold it with both hands, bend over the sink, and eat around the seed, pulling the fruit through your teeth.

Island Pineapple

Try to get Hawaiian pineapple for this scrumptious combination. It is delicious. I could eat it all day. The green peppercorns do not taste too peppery or spicy; they just give it a tang.

Both the pineapple and the sauce can be prepared a day before serving. Or they can be served as soon as an hour after they are prepared.

Place the pineapple in a bowl. In a small cup mash the peppercorns with the back of a spoon to purée (they are soft); they do not have to be mashed until smooth. Stir in the honey and kirsch. Pour over the pineapple. Stir occasionally until thoroughly marinated.

Refrigerate for an hour or more.

2 to 3 cups diced fresh pineapple
1 teaspoon (about 20) green peppercorns, packed in wine vinegar or brine (available in specialty food stores)
¼ cup honey
¼ cup kirsch

4 PORTIONS

Island Sauce

When you taste this, you might want to double the recipe.

In a small bowl stir the yogurt to soften. Mix in the remaining ingredients. Cover and refrigerate. To serve: Divide the pineapple and any juice among six wine glasses or small dessert bowls.

Immediately before serving, spoon the sauce over each serving of the pineapple.

This may be served just as it is, although in Hawaii it was originally decorated with a slice of fresh mango and one strawberry on each portion. Aloha.

1 cup plain yogurt
¼ cup honey
2 tablespoons light or dark
  rum
¼ cup Grand Marnier

Portuguese Pineapple

Everybody should have a recipe like this up their sleeve for the times they want something very fancy and elegant, but easy. You can prepare the ingredients from 1 to 10 hours before serving; then put it together in just a few minutes right before serving.

I am not giving amounts, since they are flexible. But 1 pineapple, 4 cups of berries, and 1 pint of ice make 6 generous portions.

Peel the pineapple, removing all the eyes. With a long, thin, very sharp knife cut the pineapple into very thin rings (⅛ to ¼ inch). Place the rings on a large shallow platter; sprinkle lightly with a bit of sugar and kirsch. Let stand at room temperature for about half an hour, turning the rings over occasionally to flavor them all. If necessary, add a little more sugar and kirsch after the rings have been turned.

Wash the berries quickly in a large bowl of cold water, remove the hulls, and drain thoroughly on paper towels. Place the berries in a wide, shallow bowl and sprinkle them lightly with sugar and Grand Marnier or Curaçao. Let the

Fresh pineapple
Granulated sugar
Kirsch
Fresh strawberries
Grand Marnier or Curaçao
Strawberry Sorbet, Lemon or
  Orange Ice (bought or
  homemade, see pages
  240–242)
Optional: candied violets or
  rose petals

berries stand at room temperature, turning occasionally, for about half an hour.

With an ice cream scoop, form the ice into balls, place them on a shallow tray, cover, and place in the freezer.

Cover the pineapple and the berries and refrigerate.

Choose large, flat plates for serving this. If you have room, place the plates in the freezer to chill well.

Immediately before serving, arrange two or three rings of the pineapple overlapping on each plate. Place a mound of the berries on one side and a scoop of the ices on the other side. Place a few of the optional violets or rose petals into the top of the ices.

Serve with a knife and fork.

Mousses, Puddings, Custards, etc.

French Baked Custard

This is a classic. It is simple and wonderful. It is baked and served in individual cups, which should be pottery (it bakes even better).

Adjust a rack one-third up from the bottom of the oven and preheat oven to 325°. You will need six 6-ounce (measured to the very tops) custard cups or individual soufflé dishes. Place the cups or dishes in a shallow baking pan that must not be deeper than the cups or dishes. Set aside.

Place the milk in a saucepan, uncovered, over moderate heat. Let stand until you see a slightly wrinkled skin on top or tiny bubbles around the edge.

Meanwhile, place the eggs and yolks in a large mixing bowl. Beat or whisk briefly only to mix, not until they are foamy or light. Gradually mix in the sugar, vanilla and almond extracts, and the salt, beating only to mix.

Very gradually at first, add the hot milk to the egg mixture, stirring or whisking gently only to mix.

Strain the mixture into a wide-mouthed pitcher.

Check the flavoring; sometimes it is necessary to add a bit more salt, which brings out the vanilla and almond flavors.

Pour into the cups or soufflé dishes. Do not fill all the way to the tops; there should be a bit of headroom left. There should not be any foam on the tops; if there is, remove it with a teaspoon.

Carefully pour hot water into the pan up to one-half the depth of the cups. Carefully transfer to the oven and then cover the tops of the cups or soufflé dishes with a cookie sheet.

Bake for 40 to 50 minutes until a small sharp knife gently inserted about 1 inch into the middle of a custard comes out clean. Testing the custards leaves scars, which become larger as they cool. So test as little as possible with a knife. It is also possible to test without the knife; just tap the side of a cup gently with a knife or spoon—if the custard is not done you will be able to see that it is still liquid, but when it is done you will see that it is no longer runny, and is set. Do not overbake.

Remove the pan from the oven and remove the

2½ cups milk
3 eggs plus 3 egg yolks
⅓ cup granulated sugar
1 teaspoon vanilla extract
Scant ¼ teaspoon almond extract (a small amount of almond flavoring is delicious in custard, but the least bit too much can ruin it)
Pinch of salt

6 PORTIONS

cups from the water. (Some people use a bulb baster to remove most of the water first. And/or use a wide metal spatula to transfer the cups.)

Let stand until the cups reach room temperature. Then refrigerate for several hours. The custards may be placed in the freezer for about 15 minutes before serving.

These may be served perfectly plain, or they may be topped with a rosette or a spoonful of whipped cream and, if you wish, a candied violet or rose petal, or a very thinly sliced fresh strawberry.

VARIATION: A cook I know from Kingston, Jamaica, makes this same custard with the following changes: Omit the almond extract and add 1 teaspoon powdered ginger—it is delicious.

Grape-Nut Custard

The Inn at Saranac Lake in upper New York State was a luxurious resort (and probably it still is), famous for the view, the lake, the climate, fishing and boating, and buffets a mile long. This simple dessert was a specialty, and was always one of the first desserts they ran out of. I have never seen it any other place.

Follow the preceding recipe for French Baked Custard but before pouring the mixture into the custard cups, place 2½ to 3 teaspoons of Grape-Nuts in each cup; pour the custard over the Grape-Nuts. Bake as directed. Some of the cereal will rise to the top and some will remain in the bottom, where it will form a thicker texture somewhat like bread pudding. It is delicious. Serve it very cold. If you have time and space, place it in the freezer for about 15 minutes before serving.

Orange Custard

Extremely light, delicate, tender, creamy—with a refreshing orange flavor; baked in individual cups and served in the cups. This is a wonderful dessert to serve after a sharp and spicy main course.

Adjust a rack one-third up from the bottom of the oven and preheat oven to 325°. Place the eggs and yolks in a large mixing bowl and beat or whisk until they are mixed but not foamy or light. Add the remaining ingredients one at a time, beating or whisking lightly only until everything is well mixed.

Pour through a strainer set over a pitcher with a wide mouth.

Pour into eight 4-ounce custard cups (preferably pottery cups). Place the cups in a large, shallow pan that must not be deeper than the cups. Pour hot water into the pan up to half the depth of the cups.

Place in the oven and cover with a cookie sheet.

Bake for 50 to 60 minutes until the custards just test done. To test, uncover and insert about an inch of a small sharp knife into the middle of one of the cups. If the knife comes out clean, the custard is done. Or tap on the side of a cup with a knife; you will be able to see when the custard is no longer runny. Do not overbake.

These should be refrigerated for at least a few hours, but if they are refrigerated for more than 24 hours they begin to shrink and will not be attractive. These should be very cold when they are served. (The cups may be placed in the freezer for about 15 minutes before serving.)

These do not need any topping. But, if you wish, top with a spoonful of whipped cream and/or a fresh strawberry.

5 eggs plus 3 egg yolks
¾ cup granulated sugar
Finely grated rind of 2 deep-colored oranges
Pinch of salt
1⅓ cups orange juice
1 cup heavy cream

8 PORTIONS

NOTE: During baking these might separate into two barely visible layers—a heavier, creamier layer on top and a lighter, juicier layer on the bottom. Yummy.

Crème Renversée

This is the elegant, classic French caramelized baked custard. It is made in a ring mold and is served either with or without fresh or stewed fruit, and either with or without whipped cream. The custard is silky smooth and is indescribably delicious. You will need a 5- to 6-cup metal ring mold, and since the mold must be placed in water during baking, you will need something large enough to hold it (it can be deeper than the mold if necessary, although it only needs to be deep enough for 1½ to 2 inches of water). This has to be refrigerated for at least 3 or 4 hours before serving, or it may stand overnight.

To Caramelize the Mold

Place the sugar, water, and cream of tartar in a heavy 1-quart saucepan over moderate heat. Stir with a small wooden spoon until the sugar is dissolved and the mixture comes to a boil. Wash down the sides with a pastry brush dipped in water to remove any undissolved crystals. Let boil

¾ cup granulated sugar
3 tablespoons water
⅛ teaspoon cream of tartar

without stirring until the mixture barely begins to caramelize. (It takes about 8 minutes.) If it starts to darken in one spot, twirl the pan gently. Then stir with the wooden spoon briefly until the mixture becomes a lovely caramel color. (If it is too pale, it will not have any flavor; if it is too dark, it will taste bitter.)

Immediately pour the boiling syrup into the mold. Hold the mold carefully with pot holders and tilt it gently in all directions to make the caramel run all over the bottom and up the sides to about ½ inch from the top of the mold. Continue to tilt and turn the dish until the caramel stops running. You will not be able to make the caramel run up on the center tube—that's okay.

When the caramel stops running and is cool, butter the center tube to make it easier to unmold the custard.

French Custard

Adjust a rack one-third up from the bottom of the oven and preheat oven to 325°.

Scald the milk and cream in an uncovered saucepan over moderate heat just until a slight skin forms on top or tiny bubbles form around the edge.

Meanwhile, in a large mixing bowl, stir the eggs, yolks, sugar, vanilla and almond extracts, and the salt with a wire whisk to mix thoroughly; do not beat until light or foamy.

When the milk and cream are ready, pour them very gradually at first into the egg mixture, stirring steadily to mix.

Pour through a rather fine strainer into a large, wide-mouthed pitcher.

Check the flavoring; sometimes it is necessary to add a bit more salt, which brings out the vanilla and almond flavors.

Place the caramelized mold in a larger pan (see introduction). Carefully pour the custard into the mold. Then carefully pour hot water into the larger pan until it comes halfway up the sides of the mold.

Transfer the pan to the oven.

Bake uncovered for 35 to 40 minutes until a small sharp knife gently inserted into the custard comes out clean.

Remove from the oven and let stand for 5 or 10 minutes. Then carefully remove the mold from the water and let stand uncovered at room temperature to cool.

Refrigerate for 3 to 4 hours or overnight, but no longer.

Do not unmold the custard any earlier than necessary. (The beautiful, shiny caramel will become dull if it stands too long—about 1 hour is not too long.) To unmold: With a small sharp knife carefully cut around the outside edge of the custard to loosen. Then cut around the tube to be sure it is not stuck. Cover the mold with a large, flat dessert platter that has a small rim; be sure the platter is centered. Hold the platter and the mold together and carefully turn them over. Don't rush—be patient—the custard will slip out of the mold. The caramel will have melted into a sauce and will coat the top of the custard and run onto the plate.

Return to the refrigerator.

2½ cups milk
1 cup light cream
4 eggs plus 4 egg yolks
½ cup granulated sugar
¾ teaspoon vanilla extract
Scant ½ teaspoon almond
  extract
Pinch of salt

8 PORTIONS

Whipped Cream

If you serve whipped cream, the amount to use depends on the number of people you are serving. For four, 1 cup is enough; for six or eight use 2 cups. Use 2 tablespoons of granulated or confectioners sugar for each cup of cream, and about 2 tablespoons of kirsch, rum, or cognac, or ½ teaspoon vanilla extract for each cup of cream. Whip the cream, sugar, and flavoring in a chilled bowl with chilled beaters only until the cream holds a soft, not stiff, shape. If you whip the cream ahead of time, refrigerate it and then stir it a bit with a wire whisk just before serving (to blend it if it has separated slightly).

It is best to serve the cream separately and spoon or pour it alongside each portion.

OPTIONAL: It is not necessarily traditional to serve fruit with this, but it is good; it goes wonderfully with the custard and with the caramel, and you will like it. It may be served separately and spooned alongside each portion, or it may be placed around the rim of the mold or piled up in the center. This has been one of my favorite desserts for many years and I have always served it with fruit. Many guests prefer a generous amount of the fruit, and just a small serving of the custard. It is wonderful with fresh strawberries or raspberries, or with stewed pears, or with any brandied fruits.

Use a wide cake server or spatula for serving the custard.

Lemon Mousse

This is food for angels; it is like eating a sweet lemon-flavored cloud, like a glass of delicious nothingness. Plan it for any luncheon or dinner; you will love it! Make it at least 4 hours ahead or the day before. It is prepared in individual glasses that should have at least a 10-ounce capacity, although they can be larger if you wish.

Sprinkle the gelatin over the water in a small cup and let stand for a few minutes. Meanwhile, place the rind, juice, and ¾ cup (reserve the remaining ¼ cup) of the sugar in a small saucepan and stir with a wooden spatula until the sugar is dissolved and the mixture just comes to a boil. Add the softened gelatin, stir to melt, remove from the heat, and pour the mixture into a rather large mixing bowl (preferably metal—it will chill faster).

Partially fill a larger bowl with ice and water and place the bowl of lemon mixture into it; stir constantly until the mixture is cool (test it on the inside of your wrist) but not until it starts to thicken. Remove the bowl from the ice water temporarily (but reserve the ice water) and set aside.

Place the whites in the large bowl of an electric mixer. Add the salt and the cream of tartar and beat until the whites hold a soft shape. Reduce the speed to moderate and gradually add the reserved ¼ cup of sugar. Then, on high speed again, beat only until the whites barely hold a definite shape; they should not be stiff or dry. Set aside.

1 envelope unflavored gelatin
2 tablespoons cold water
Finely grated rind of 2 large lemons
½ cup plus 1 tablespoon fresh lemon juice
1 cup granulated sugar
1 cup egg whites (about 8 whites; they may be whites that were left over from other recipes, frozen and then thawed)
⅛ teaspoon salt
⅛ teaspoon cream of tartar
1 cup heavy cream

8 PORTIONS

In a small chilled bowl with chilled beaters whip the cream until it just barely holds a definite shape; it should not be stiff or dry. (If the cream or whites are beaten too much the finished dessert will not be as good.) Set aside.

Replace the bowl with the lemon mixture over the bowl of ice water and scrape the bowl constantly with a rubber spatula until the mixture thickens to a syrupy consistency. Remove from the ice immediately before it really stiffens and quickly fold about one-quarter of it into the whipped cream. Then fold in a second quarter. And then a third. If you have a large-size rubber spatula, use it now. Then, in either bowl, briefly fold the cream and the remaining lemon mixture together. Next, fold about a cupful of the beaten whites into the cream—do not be too thorough. Then another cupful. Finally, in either bowl, fold the cream and the remaining whites only until barely blended. Do not handle any more than necessary.

With a large spoon, spoon the mixture into eight wine glasses or straight-sided old-fashioned glasses (that is, the drink "old-fashioned"). If you can cover the glasses with plastic wrap without having it touch the mousse, do so.

Refrigerate for 4 hours or overnight. These do not need any decoration. I like them plain. Or with a tiny sprinkling of crumbled candied violet or rose petals sprinkled on top, or a few very thin slices of fresh strawberries.

It is nice if you can get some large, flat green leaves to place under the glasses on the dessert plates. (Here in Florida, I pick sea grape leaves outside of either door. In other areas it might be necessary to get them from a florist. I have also used a few lemon leaves from a florist on each plate.)

Tangerine Mousse

This Florida mousse is as light as air, as delicate as a soft breeze, and as fresh and delicious as if you just picked the tangerines yourself. Tangerines are in season during the winter; remember this recipe when you see them. It is prepared in individual glasses, and should be made at least 4 hours before serving or it may stand overnight.

Sprinkle the gelatin over the 2 tablespoons water (or other substitute liquid) in a small cup and let stand. Place the egg yolks in the top of a large double boiler off the heat. With a wire whisk, stir to mix well. Measure out the sugar. Remove and reserve 3 tablespoons; add the remaining sugar to the yolks and beat briskly with the whisk until foamy. Mix in the tangerine juice and the lemon juice.

Place over the bottom of the double boiler partly filled with hot water on moderate heat. Stir and scrape the bottom and sides almost constantly with a rubber spatula until the mixture thickens enough to coat a metal or wooden spoon. When it is just right it will register 170° on a candy thermometer, and will look like soft, fluffy mayonnaise. Do not overcook.

Remove the top of the double boiler, add the gelatin, and stir to dissolve; stir in the grated rind and transfer the mixture to a large mixing bowl. Stir occasionally until cool.

Then, in a chilled bowl with chilled beaters, whip the cream only until it holds a soft, not stiff, shape and set aside.

In the large bowl of an electric mixer (or in a large copper bowl with a wire whisk) add the salt to the egg whites and beat only until the whites hold a soft shape. Reduce the speed to moderate, gradually add the reserved 3 tablespoons of sugar, then increase the speed to high again and continue to beat until the whites barely hold a definite shape, not until they are stiff and dry.

Fold about one-third of the whites into the yolks. Then add the remaining whites and the whipped cream and fold gently and carefully only until the mixtures are barely blended; do not fold until they are completely blended or you will lose some of the air. It is all right if you still see a few slight streaks of whipped cream or egg whites and a few streaks of the tangerine mixture.

With a large spoon gently transfer the mousse to dessert bowls or wineglasses or straight-sided old-fashioned glasses. Cover airtight with plastic wrap and refrigerate for at least 4 hours.

These do not need any topping; they may be served quite plain, or each one may be topped with a thin slice or wedge of kiwi fruit and/or a thinly sliced strawberry, or a few blueberries, or a bit of candied violet or rose petal, or a fresh mint leaf. Whatever, it should be delicate.

*1½ teaspoons unflavored
  gelatin*
*2 tablespoons water, Grand
  Marnier, kirsch, or
  additional tangerine juice*
6 eggs, separated
⅔ cup granulated sugar
*⅓ cup tangerine juice (grate
  the rind to use later before
  squeezing the juice)*
2½ tablespoons lemon juice
*Finely grated rind of 2 or 3
  large, deep-colored
  tangerines*
1 cup heavy cream
Pinch of salt

8 PORTIONS

Orange Mousse with Blueberries

This is a very pretty molded mousse—light, creamy, tender, delicate, and delicious.
You will need a metal mold with an 8-cup capacity; it can be a round-bottomed bowl, a charlotte mold, or a loaf pan. (If the pan has a design, it must not be a small, detailed design.) The prepared mousse should be refrigerated 4 to 10 hours before serving.

Wash, drain, and dry the berries. Place them in a plastic bag in the freezer for about 30 minutes; it is best if they are very cold or almost but not quite frozen when you use them.

Sprinkle the gelatin over the cold water in a small bowl. Let stand for 5 minutes. Then add the boiling water and stir with a metal spoon to dissolve. (Examine it carefully; if it is not completely dissolved, place it in a little hot water over low heat and stir to dissolve.)

Transfer the gelatin to a large mixing bowl. Add ¾ cup of the sugar (reserve the remaining ¼ cup), the lemon juice, and the orange juice. Stir until the sugar is dissolved.

Place the bowl in a large bowl of ice and water. Stir occasionally until the gelatin mixture thickens slightly.

While the gelatin mixture is chilling, prepare the egg whites and the heavy cream. In a small bowl beat the whites with the salt until they hold a soft shape. On low speed gradually add the reserved ¼ cup of sugar, then beat on high speed again until the whites hold a firm shape but not until they are stiff and dry. Set aside. In a small, chilled bowl with chilled beaters whip the cream until it holds a shape; it should be rather firm but not stiff. Set aside.

When the gelatin mixture thickens enough so that it does not completely flatten out if some of it is dropped back onto itself, whip it briskly with a large wire whisk or with a beater.

Gradually fold in the beaten whites and then the whipped cream. If the mixture appears to separate slightly (the gelatin part is heavier and it might sink) pour the entire mixture gently back and forth from one large bowl to another. If it still separates, place it in the freezer briefly, and then fold again.

Fold in the very cold blueberries. (The very cold berries will help to set the mousse.)

Quickly rinse an 8-cup plain (not fancy) metal mold with ice water. Shake it out; do not dry it. Pour the mousse into the wet mold.

Refrigerate for at least 4 hours or all day.

When you are ready to unmold the dessert, which should be as close to serving

1 cup fresh blueberries
  (approximately)
1 envelope plus 1½ teaspoons
  unflavored gelatin
⅓ cup cold water
⅓ cup boiling water
1 cup granulated sugar
3 tablespoons lemon juice
1 cup orange juice
3 egg whites
Pinch of salt
1 cup heavy cream

6 TO 8 PORTIONS

time as possible (1 to 1½ hours is all right), lightly oil (with tasteless vegetable oil) an area the size of the mold on a flat serving platter—the oil will make it possible for you to move the mousse if necessary.

Cut around the top of the mousse with a small sharp knife to release the edges. Quickly dip the mold for only a moment or so (actually, count slowly to three if the mold is thin metal; count to six if it is heavy metal) in hot (not boiling) water at least as deep as the mold. Then quickly place the mold on a towel to dry it, place the dessert platter over it, and holding the mold and the platter firmly together, turn them both over. If the mousse does not slip out easily, bang both the platter and the mold against the counter top. If it still does not slip out easily, it may be necessary to dip it in hot water again. (If so, be careful while turning the mold upright again. It has happened that a dessert was ready to come out, had actually started to come out, when the mold was raised to be turned upright for another hot-water dip. And it did indeed come out, but not on the platter. Therefore, to turn the mold upright again, keep the platter over it and invert both together.)

If the mousse is not in the center of the plate, use your hands to move it very slowly and gently.

VARIATIONS: This does not want whipped cream; it is perfect just as it is. However, fresh strawberries are terrific with it. Either place a ring of washed and drained, but unhulled, berries around the mousse; or hull the berries, slice them thick, sprinkle with a bit of sugar and some Grand Marnier, let stand for about an hour or more and then serve the berries separately, spooning them alongside each portion.

Here's another way I have made this—a sort of fruit cup mousse; it was wonderful. I mixed the blueberries into the mousse and poured about two-thirds of it into the mold. Then I added a layer of strawberries (not too many). And I folded some orange sections into the remaining mousse before pouring it on top of the strawberries.

If you wish, either of the versions of this mousse can be prepared individually in large wine glasses; it is easier and equally nice.

Grapefruit Mousse

This recipe comes from a fishing guide in the Florida Keys who used to take my father tarpon fishing. My father supplied roast chickens, vegetable salad, and the makings for martinis; the lady guide supplied dessert, the fishing bait, and the boat.

This is light, creamy, sweet-and-sour, deliciously refreshing. Prepare in individual glasses.

Peel and section the grapefruits (see page 15). They should be puréed in a food processor or a blender (or, as was told to me, cut up and then mashed with a potato masher in a large bowl). You should have 1¾ cups of purée.

Place the cold water in a small cup and sprinkle the gelatin over the top. Let stand.

Place the egg yolks in the top of a large double boiler off the heat. Measure out the sugar and remove and reserve 2 tablespoons; add the remaining sugar to the yolks. Stir briskly with a small wire whisk. Then, with a wooden spoon or rubber spatula, gradually stir in the grapefruit purée.

Place over boiling water on moderate heat and cook, stirring frequently, until the mixture thickens slightly. It will not thicken as much as most custard sauces do. It will take about 5 to 7 minutes. A candy thermometer inserted into the mixture should register 180°.

Add the softened gelatin and stir to dissolve.

Remove from the hot water. Stir in the orange rind. Transfer to a wide mixing bowl. Place the bowl in a larger bowl partly filled with ice and water. Stir occasionally until the mixture barely starts to thicken. Remove it from the ice water and set aside.

In a chilled bowl with chilled beaters whip the cream until it holds a shape, but not until it is really stiff. Set aside.

In the small bowl of the electric mixer beat the egg whites with the salt until the whites hold a soft shape when the beaters are raised. Add the reserved 2 tablespoons of sugar and continue to beat the mixture until the whites barely hold a definite shape, but do not beat them until they are stiff or dry.

The grapefruit mixture should be thick enough to mound slightly when some of it is dropped back into the bowl; if necessary, stir it a bit more over the ice. (The ideal condition for

2 large, sweet grapefruits
¼ cup cold water
1 envelope unflavored gelatin
3 eggs, separated
¾ cup granulated sugar (see Note)
Finely grated rind of 2 deep-colored oranges
1 cup heavy cream
Generous pinch of salt

6 PORTIONS

incorporating these three mixtures is to have them all the same consistency.) With a whisk or a beater, beat the grapefruit mixture briefly.

Fold one-quarter of the grapefruit mixture into the whipped cream. Fold in another quarter without being too thorough. Then fold the cream into the remaining grapefruit mixture. If some of this seems heavier than the rest and sinks to the bottom of the bowl, pour it all gently back and forth from one large bowl to another to blend the mixtures.

Then fold one-quarter of the grapefruit-cream mixture into the whites. Now fold the whites into the remaining grapefruit-cream. Again, if some of the mixture sinks to the bottom, pour it all gently from one large bowl to another to blend. Whatever you do, try not to lose the air that was beaten into the whites and the cream.

Gently transfer the mousse to a wide pitcher and pour it into six 8-ounce wine glasses. Cover them with plastic wrap. Refrigerate for at least 4 hours or overnight.

Serve these plain. Or, if you want to top them with something, it should be fruit: a few thinly sliced strawberries, a few raspberries, a slice of kiwi fruit, or a few canned black Bing cherries. Or a sliced preserved kumquat.

NOTE: If the grapefruits are extra sour, add an additional 1 to 2 tablespoons of sugar.

Sour Lime Mousse with Strawberries

This is light and airy, tender and delicate, and it is sour. Which makes it a perfect hot-weather dessert, or serve it after a big meal in any weather. Make it at least a few hours before serving or as long as a day ahead. It is served in individual glasses.

Combine the egg yolks, ½ cup of the sugar (reserving the remaining ¼ cup of sugar), lime rind, ½ cup of the lime juice (reserve the remaining ¼ cup of juice), and the butter in the top of a large double boiler. Place over hot water on moderate heat. While the mixture cooks, continuously scrape the bottom and sides with a rubber spatula.

Meanwhile, sprinkle the gelatin over the reserved ¼ cup of lime juice in a small cup, and let it stand.

Cook the egg yolk mixture until it thickens slightly, or until it registers about 180° on a candy thermometer.

Remove the top of the double boiler, add the softened gelatin, stir to melt the gelatin, and set aside to cool to room temperature.

Stir in the vanilla.

In the large bowl of an electric mixer (or in a large bowl with a balloon-type wire whisk) beat the egg whites and the salt until the whites hold a soft shape. Gradually add the reserved ¼ cup of sugar and continue to beat until the whites hold a definite shape but not until they are stiff or dry.

Fold about one-quarter of the yolk mixture into the whites. Then fold in another quarter. And then fold the remaining yolk mixture and the whites together only until they are barely blended.

Gently pour the mixture into a wide-mouthed pitcher and pour it into six wine glasses that have a 10-ounce capacity. Do not fill the glasses all the way; leave room for the berries.

Cover the glasses with foil or plastic wrap and refrigerate for at least a few hours or overnight.

This may be served with a topping of just barely thawed and partially drained frozen strawberries. Or with the following fresh strawberries.

6 eggs, separated
¾ cup granulated sugar
Finely grated rind of 1 large
    lime
¾ cup fresh lime juice
1½ tablespoons unsalted
    butter
1½ teaspoons unflavored
    gelatin
½ teaspoon vanilla extract
Pinch of salt

6 PORTIONS

Strawberries

Wash the berries quickly, hull, drain thoroughly, and then cut each berry into three or four slices.

In a bowl toss the berries gently with the sugar and liquor. Let stand at room temperature, stirring occasionally, for about half an hour. Then cover and refrigerate until serving time.

Just before serving, spoon the berries over the mousse.

About 4 cups fresh
    strawberries
3 tablespoons granulated
    sugar
3 tablespoons Curaçao,
    kirsch, Grand Marnier, or
    dark rum

Zabaglione Freddo

Mama mia! That's amore! It is a sweetened egg yolk and wine mixture with cognac and lemon, and a small amount of gelatin (just barely enough—the way it should be) and a generous amount of whipped cream folded in, and it is a bit of Italian heaven served in individual wine glasses. If you are serving an Italian dinner, serve this for dessert. Or if it is any other dinner—French, Chinese, seafood, what-have-you—serve this for dessert. It is the fluffiest, lightest, airiest mixture of sweetness ever.

To be serious for a moment, if I can come back to earth after the zabaglione cloud I have been flying on, zabaglione is traditionally served hot (without gelatin) the moment it has cooked and risen to beautiful proportions (timed like a hot soufflé). It is a headwaiter's show-stopper in the finest Italian restaurants. This version is different. "Freddo" or "cold" is the difference—this should chill for at least 4 hours.

As fabulous as this is—and it is—it is easy. The most important thing is a double boiler in which the top has more than a 9-cup capacity (9 cups is exactly the capacity of my largest one and it is not quite large enough). Unless yours is larger, find a bowl or saucepan, preferably with a round bottom, that you can set over a saucepan of shallow hot water to make your own double boiler. A capacity of 10 or 11 cups should be large enough, but even larger is okay.

*M*ix the rind and juice in a small cup and set aside. Place the cold water in a small custard cup and sprinkle the gelatin over the top; set aside to soften.

In the small bowl of an electric mixer beat the yolks and sugar at high speed for 5 minutes until very pale and thick. On lowest speed slowly add the Marsala, scraping the bowl with a rubber spatula and beating only until incorporated.

Transfer the mixture to the top of a large double boiler or any bowl with at least a 10-cup capacity. Place over a little hot water on *low* heat. Beat with a portable electric mixer for about 10 minutes or until the mixture has risen and holds a soft shape when the beaters are raised.

Immediately (to stop the cooking) transfer to the large bowl of an electric mixer.

Finley grated rind of 1 small lemon
1 tablespoon lemon juice
1 tablespoon cold tap water
1 teaspoon unflavored gelatin
8 egg yolks
½ cup granulated sugar
1 cup dry Marsala
2 tablespoons boiling water
¼ cup cognac or other brandy
2 cups heavy cream

8 PORTIONS

Add the boiling water to the softened gelatin and stir until dissolved. Then, while beating on low speed, gradually add the gelatin to the yolk mixture; beat only to mix. Remove from the mixer. Add the lemon juice and rind mixture and gradually add the cognac, while folding gently and lightly with a large rubber spatula. Set aside until cool.

Meanwhile, in a chilled bowl with chilled beaters whip the cream until it holds a shape but not until it is stiff or dry. Fold about half of the egg yolk mixture into the whipped cream and then fold the cream into the remaining egg yolk mixture.

Transfer to a wide-mouthed pitcher and pour into eight 8- or 10-ounce wine glasses or straight-sided old-fashioned glasses. If the zabaglione is below the tops of the glasses, cover them with foil or plastic wrap; if not, just leave them uncovered.

Refrigerate for 4 to 8 hours.

Do not add anything to decorate this; it is too classic and simple and wonderful just as it is.

Raspberry Bavarian

There are some parties that must be pink for one reason or another; this is the dessert to make—it is a gorgeous color. (But unless you have one planned soon, don't wait for a pink party to make this.) It is wondrously smooth, creamy, and refreshing, with an intense and irresistible raspberry flavor. And it is so easy you will be tickled pink.

It can be made in a mold or in wine glasses. You will need a blender. Make it at least 4 or 5 hours before serving or the day before. To double the recipe, see Notes at the end of the recipe.

Place the frozen berries and the lemon juice in a bowl and let stand until the berries have thawed. (Or, if you are in a hurry, place the plastic bag or water-proof package of berries in warm water for about 10 to 15 minutes to thaw, then turn it into a bowl and add the lemon juice.) As the berries start to thaw, you can help them along by breaking the frozen block into small pieces with a fork. When it is completely thawed, pour it into a strainer set over a bowl. Let the juice drain. You should have 2/3 cup or a little more.

Sprinkle the gelatin over the milk in a small custard cup, stir with a fork, and let stand for 5 minutes.

Meanwhile, place the drained juice in a small, uncovered saucepan over moderate heat and bring it to a boil. Then add the softened gelatin, stir to dissolve (the mixture might not look smooth but

1 10-ounce box frozen
    raspberries in syrup
3 tablespoons fresh lemon
    juice
1 envelope unflavored gelatin
1/4 cup milk
2 egg yolks
Pinch of salt
1 cup heavy cream
1 cup crushed ice (see Notes)

6 PORTIONS

it is okay), transfer to the container of a blender, and blend at high speed for 1 minute.

Remove the cover of the blender, add the raspberries, egg yolks, and salt, and blend at high speed for 5 seconds. Then add the cream and crushed ice and continue to blend for 10 to 15 seconds until perfectly smooth. (Easy?)

Now, to remove the seeds, strain the mixture through a wide strainer set over a bowl or a wide pitcher (a small strainer will take forever, and it might seem slow even in a wide strainer—work the mixture through with a rubber spatula).

If you have strained the mixture into a bowl, and if you are going to prepare it in individual glasses, transfer it to a pitcher and pour it into six 6- or 8-ounce wine glasses. Cover airtight and refrigerate for at least 4 hours.

If you are preparing this in a mold, use a thin metal mold (it is easier to unmold than a heavy pottery one) with a 4-cup capacity and not too much detail in the mold; you might like a plain round bowl or ring mold best. Rinse the mold with ice water, shake it out but do not dry it, and pour the mixture into the mold. Refrigerate until set, then cover with plastic wrap and refrigerate for at least 5 hours or overnight.

To unmold, lightly oil a large, flat dessert platter with tasteless vegetable oil. This will make it easy to move the unmolded dessert if necessary to center it on the platter. (It also makes it easier to serve; the dessert doesn't cling to the plate. No one will see or taste the oil.) Cut around the top of the mold with a small sharp knife. Then dip the mold into a large bowl or dishpan of hot tap water up to ½ inch from the top, hold the mold in the water for 8 to 9 seconds, remove from the water, dry the mold quickly, place the oiled platter over the mold, center it carefully, and, holding the mold and the platter firmly together, turn them both over. Bang the mold and the platter a few times on a heavy folded towel on the counter top. The dessert should slide out after a few seconds. If not, raise the mold slightly and bang it against the plate a few more times. Or, as a last resort, tilt the mold on a slight angle—sometimes it will slip out more easily on an angle than it will drop straight down. If it is still in the mold, carefully turn it upright and dip it again in hot water but only for a few seconds.

Dry the platter around the mold and immediately place the Bavarian in the refrigerator.

Whipped Cream

In a chilled bowl with chilled beaters whip the ingredients until they just hold a shape. If the Bavarian is in glasses, place a large spoonful of the cream on each portion. If it has been molded, the cream may be served separately or, better yet, place it in a pastry bag fitted with a medium-size star-shaped tube and form a border of whipped cream rosettes around the base of the mold. And maybe a few on top also. Or use it on the top only.

1 cup heavy cream
2 tablespoons confectioners or granulated sugar
2 tablespoons kirsch or framboise (raspberry brandy)

If, by some good luck, fresh raspberries are available, of course it is lovely to serve some with the Bavarian; but if not, don't worry—this is great as it is.

NOTES: To double this recipe: If you are making it in a mold, prepare it once, set it aside, prepare it again, mix the two batches and pour it into a wet 8-cup bowl or simple mold. If possible, refrigerate this larger amount overnight. If you are making it in glasses, prepare it once, pour into six glasses, prepare it again, and pour into six more glasses. In other words, blenders are not large enough to handle double the amount in one load.

If you do not have an ice crusher, crush the ice in a processor, or put ice cubes in a canvas or heavy plastic bag. Work on a board or outdoors. Pound the ice with a hammer to crush it. Place the bag in the freezer until you are ready for it.

Cold Orange Soufflé

Cool and refreshing, extremely light, creamy, and delicate.

Gelatin desserts should be just barely stiff enough to hold their shapes. They are best as soon as they become firm, they toughen slightly if they stand overnight, and they become rubbery if they stand longer. It is best to make this during the day for that night; it should be refrigerated for at least 4 hours before serving.

This is a festive dessert; make it for a party.

*Y*ou will need a straight-sided soufflé dish with a 5-cup capacity; the classic white china French one with that capacity measures 6¾ inches in diameter and 3 inches in depth.

To prepare a wax paper collar: Tear off a piece of wax paper long enough to wrap around the dish and overlap itself by a few inches (for a 6¾-inch dish you need 24 inches of paper). Fold the paper in half the long way and wrap it around the dish, placing the folded edge even with the bottom of the dish. Wrap string around the collar about ½ inch below the top of the dish and tie it securely. Fasten the top overlapping ends with a straight pin or a paper clip. Set aside.

Place both grated rinds and the lemon juice in a small cup and set aside.

Place the gelatin and ¾ cup plus 2 tablespoons of the sugar (reserve the remaining ¼ cup) in the top of a large double boiler off the heat. Stir to mix and set aside.

In a bowl beat the yolks just to mix them well. Gradually mix in the orange juice, beating to mix well, and pour this mixture over the gelatin and sugar, and stir to mix. Let stand for about 3 minutes to soften the gelatin.

Place the top of the double boiler over hot water on moderate heat and stir almost constantly with a rubber spatula until the gelatin and sugar are dissolved (it takes about 5 minutes—test by dipping a metal spoon in and out; undissolved granules show up against the metal).

Remove the top of the double boiler and stir in the grated rinds and lemon juice.

Place the top of the double boiler in a large bowl of ice and water. With a rubber spatula scrape the bottom and stir frequently until the mixture cools and begins to thicken.

Meanwhile, in a chilled bowl with chilled beaters whip the cream until it holds a soft shape (it should not be stiff or it will make the soufflé heavy). Set aside.

Also meanwhile, in the small bowl of an electric mixer (or in a large copper bowl with a large wire whisk), beat the egg whites with the salt until they barely hold a soft shape. Reduce the speed to moderate and gradually add the reserved ¼ cup of sugar. Then increase the speed to high again and continue to beat briefly only until the whites resemble a thick marshmallowlike fluff, not stiff or dry.

When the orange mixture thickens to the consistency of a soft mayonnaise, transfer it immediately to a mixing bowl (if you leave it in the cold top of the double boiler, it will continue to set and will quickly become too firm).

With a rubber spatula, gradually (not all at once) fold about half of the orange mixture into the whites and then gradually fold the other half into the whipped cream. Then, in a large bowl with a rubber spatula, fold the two mixtures together. Handle as little as possible. If necessary, pour gently from one bowl to another to ensure thorough blending.

Pour the mixture into the prepared soufflé dish (it will come about 1½ inches above the top), smooth the top, and refrigerate for at least 4 hours.

Finely grated rind of 2 large, deep-colored oranges
Finely grated rind of 1 large lemon
⅓ cup lemon juice
1 envelope plus 1 teaspoon unflavored gelatin
1 cup plus 2 tablespoons granulated sugar
4 eggs, separated
1½ cups orange juice
1½ cups heavy cream
⅛ teaspoon salt

8 PORTIONS

Optional Accompaniments

In a small saucepan over moderate heat stir the preserves occasionally until melted. Mix in the Grand Marnier, press through a strainer set over a bowl, and set aside.

Coarsely break up the macaroons and then process them in a food processor, or grind them in a blender, to make fine crumbs. Set aside.

Before serving (as close to serving time as is comfort-

⅓ cup apricot preserves
1½ tablespoon Grand Marnier, cognac, rum, or water
2 or 3 dry almond macaroons (I use Amaretti)

able) remove the string and pin or paper clip, and slowly and carefully peel away the wax paper collar; have a small sharp knife handy in case the paper needs a little encouragement.

Place the crumbled macaroons on a large piece of wax paper. Support the soufflé dish on the palm of your left hand, hold it over the crumbs, pick up a generous amount of the crumbs in the palm of your right hand, turn your hand toward the soufflé and place the crumbs on the side of the soufflé, allowing excess crumbs to fall back onto the others. Repeat, coating the sides all around with the macaroon crumbs. Wipe the side of the dish clean.

With a pastry brush, gently and lightly brush the thinned and strained preserves over the top of the soufflé to make a beautifully shiny layer.

This may be served just as it is, or with almost any delicious fresh, stewed, or frozen fruit on the side. Following are two suggestions.

Frozen Raspberries (sauce)

Strain 1 box of the berries; set the berries aside—you will not use the drained syrup for this recipe.

Purée the other box of berries with their syrup in a food processor, a blender, or a food mill. Pour it through a wide but fine strainer set over a bowl to remove the seeds.

Mix the puréed and strained berries with the whole berries and the honey and kirsch or framboise. Refrigerate.

2 10-ounce boxes frozen raspberries in syrup, thawed
1 tablespoon honey
2 tablespoons kirsch or framboise (raspberry brandy)

Fresh Strawberries

Wash, hull, and drain the berries. Slice them thin, mix with the sugar and kirsch or brandy, and refrigerate for at least an hour.

NOTE: If you wish, whip ½ cup heavy cream and use it to decorate the top of the soufflé. Fit a pastry bag with a medium-small star-shaped tube, place the whipped cream in the bag, and press out either a border of rosettes or a lattice design.

About 4 cups (1 pound) strawberries (generally called a 1-pint box)
2 to 3 tablespoons granulated sugar
2 to 3 tablespoons kirsch or brandy

Hot Lemon Soufflé

This is one of the recipes that I often taught in cooking courses because it is quick and quite easy, very delicious, and because it rises into a dramatically high, photogenic, picturesque, show-off dessert. Many of the people in the classes told me that they had been afraid of soufflés, but that they had made this right after seeing it in class, and it was wonderful and they were thrilled.

Part of this can be made a few hours ahead of time; the mixture can stand at room temperature until about 40 minutes before serving, when you beat the whites and fold them in. But I have a theory about soufflés. I do not think you should be concerned about rushing breathlessly into the kitchen at some point to finish the soufflé, timing it carefully so you will be able to serve it without keeping your guests waiting. I think it is better to announce, "We are having a soufflé for dessert; I am going in to finish it now, then we will have a little wait, during which I wish you would all pray for the soufflé to rise." It adds to the fun and the excitement and makes it all more dramatic.

This does not have the usual flour-and-butter base; the ingredients are few and simple.

Adjust a rack to the lowest position in the oven and preheat oven to 375°. Butter a 2-quart soufflé dish (7½ x 3¼ inches). Tear off a piece of aluminum foil long enough to wrap around the dish and overlap itself a few inches. Fold the foil in half the long way. Butter one-half of the length (along the open end, not along the fold). Wrap the foil tightly around the dish, open end up, with the fold lined up with the bottom of the dish. Fasten it securely by wrapping string about ½ inch below the top of the dish and tying it tightly. Shake granulated sugar (additional to that called for in the ingredients) around in the dish to sugar both the dish and the foil. Shake out excess sugar, and set the dish aside.

Place the yolks in the small bowl of an electric mixer. Add ¼ cup of sugar (reserve the remaining ¼ cup) and beat at high speed for about 5 minutes until the mixture is pale and thick and forms a wide ribbon when the beaters are raised. On low speed gradually mix in the juice. Remove from the mixer, stir in the grated rind, and set aside. (The recipe may be prepared up to this point a few hours ahead of time. If you want to do this ahead, cover tightly and let this mixture and the egg whites stand at room temperature.)

To finish the soufflé: In the large bowl of the mixer, with clean beaters, or in a large copper bowl with a large wire whisk, beat the 7 egg whites and the salt until the

6 eggs separated, plus 1 additional egg white, (the additional white may be one that was left over, frozen, and then thawed)
½ cup granulated sugar
⅓ cup lemon juice (grate the rind before you squeeze the juice to use below)
Finely grated rind of 2 large or 3 small lemons
Generous pinch of salt
Optional: confectioners sugar (to sprinkle on before serving)

4 TO 6 PORTIONS

whites hold a soft shape. Reduce the speed to moderate and gradually add the reserved ¼ cup of sugar. Increase the speed to high again and continue to beat only until the whites hold a shape but not until they are stiff or dry.

In three additions carefully fold the egg yolk mixture into the whites, folding only until the mixtures are barely incorporated—do not handle any more than necessary.

Turn the mixture into the prepared dish. (It will reach to the top of the dish.) Smooth the top. Place the dish in a large pan that must be wider than the dish but must not be deeper. Pour about 1 inch of hot water into the large pan. Place in the oven immediately.

Bake for 30 minutes until the soufflé is well risen and browned on the top. Quickly sprinkle the top with the optional confectioners sugar through a strainer.

Now, I have another theory about soufflés. You can quickly and carefully remove the string and the collar in the kitchen and then quickly and carefully carry the soufflé to the table. But my theory is that it is more fun and more exciting to take the dish right to the table and remove the string and the foil at the table.

Have a plate or tray ready to put the soufflé on, have scissors ready for cutting the string, have flat dessert plates ready to serve on (they should be warm), and don't waste any time.

Serve with one of the following sauces, which you should either pass and let the guests help themselves to (so you can quickly get on with serving), or have someone else spoon out while you serve the soufflé. It is best to serve the sauce alongside, rather than on top of the soufflé.

Marmalade Sauce

This is the easiest. Simply stir some marmalade to soften, and add a few spoonfuls of Grand Marnier, cointreau, or orange juice. Serve at room temperature.

Strawberry and Raspberry Sauce

Slice about a cup of fresh strawberries rather thin. Sprinkle with 2 tablespoons of granulated sugar and 2 tablespoons of kirsch or framboise (raspberry brandy). Let stand at room temperature, stirring occasionally. Meanwhile, thaw and drain a 10-ounce box of frozen raspberries (they should be whole raspberries packed in syrup, although you will not use the drained syrup for this recipe). Purée them in a processor or a blender, or force them through a food mill. Strain to remove the seeds. Stir the strained raspberries with the sliced strawberries. Serve at room temperature.

Ginger-Marmalade Yogurt

This has a tantalizing and fascinating flavor. The texture—a smooth, jellied yogurt studded with tiny chunks of chewy ginger—is sensational! Serve this any time, anywhere, any way; it is probably most appropriate as a summer dessert, but I could eat it for breakfast, lunch, and dinner; as appetizer, entrée, and/or dessert. The recipe can be multiplied by any number. It is prepared in individual glasses or individual soufflé dishes.

P lace the orange juice and lemon juice in a custard cup. Sprinkle the gelatin over the top. Let stand for 5 minutes to soften.

Meanwhile, place the marmalade, ginger, and brown sugar in a bowl and stir to mix. Set aside.

Place the yogurt in another bowl and stir until it is softened and smooth. Set aside.

Now place the cup of gelatin mixture in a little hot water in a pan over low heat. Stir occasionally with a metal spoon until the gelatin is dissolved.

Then add the gelatin to the marmalade mixture and stir until thoroughly mixed. Gradually add the gelatin mixture to the yogurt, stirring well after each addition until well mixed.

Place the mixture (preferably in a metal bowl because it chills faster) into a larger bowl of ice and water. Stir constantly and gently with a rubber spatula until the mixture thickens enough to keep the ginger and the marmalade from sinking.

Transfer to a wide-mouthed pitcher and pour into four 6-ounce glasses or dessert cups.

Refrigerate for 2 to 3 hours or all day.

This does not need any topping; it can be served as is. But if you want to make it more colorful and festive, top each portion with a very thinly sliced strawberry, or with a thin slice of peeled kiwi fruit cut into four or six pie-shaped wedges.

These may also be unmolded. Prepare them in custard cups. When they are firm, cut around the sides to release. Then dip the cup in hot water and hold it for 2 or 3 seconds, cover with a flat plate, turn the plate and cup over; the molded yogurt should slip right out. It is pretty surrounded by a border of very thinly sliced strawberries.

⅓ cup orange juice
2 teaspoons lemon juice
1 envelope unflavored gelatin
⅓ cup sweet orange
   marmalade
3 to 4 tablespoons finely
   chopped crystallized ginger,
   firmly packed (see Note)
3 tablespoons light or dark
   brown sugar, firmly packed
1 pint (2 cups) unflavored
   yogurt

4 PORTIONS

NOTE: This will have a good gingery flavor with 3 tablespoons of chopped ginger—but if you love ginger as I do, you will want to use 4 tablespoons.

Yogurt Cheese

This might be as old as recorded history. The Bulgarians and Turks and Armenians et al. have probably made it for as long as they have been making yogurt. But it is new to me. And so good! If you like yogurt, you will be wild about this. It is simply unflavored regular or low-fat yogurt that has drained and is like cream cheese with a yogurt flavor. Serve it with crackers as an hors d'oeuvre, serve it as a dessert cheese with fresh fruit, or spread it on sliced apples or pears. It is delicious and unusual.

This must drain for 6 to 24 hours, but then it can be refrigerated for 2 weeks.

You will need a large strainer, a large bowl, cheesecloth, and yogurt—as much or as little as you want. I use Dannon low-fat yogurt.

Here goes: Place a large, wide strainer over a large bowl. Line the strainer with a double thickness of wet cheesecloth (if the cheesecloth is tubular, it should be split down one side to make it wide enough).

Empty the yogurt into the lined strainer. You might like to try this first with only ½ pint (1 cup) of yogurt. If so, you can use a smaller strainer, although it doesn't hurt if the strainer is too large. I use 6 half-pints (6 cups) in a 9-inch strainer. Cover with an inverted bowl or a flat plate and let stand at room temperature or in the refrigerator if there is room for 6 to 24 hours. After 3 or 4 hours stir the yogurt very lightly to encourage all of the whey to drain off. Occasionally, as the whey collects in the large bowl, it may be emptied out (it should be emptied if it is touching the strainer). The longer the yogurt drains, the drier the cheese and the sharper the taste.

When drained, transfer the cheese to any container and refrigerate.

You will have about 2 cups of cheese from 6 half-pints (6 cups) of yogurt if it has drained the full time; more if it has drained less time.

Two cups of yogurt cheese should serve 6 to 8 people, if I am not one of them.

NOTE: A technicality—the older the yogurt is, the more tart the cheese will be. Good either way, but I use the freshest I can get.

Apricot Bread Pudding

Serve this as dessert, or serve it as the main course at a breakfast or brunch party. Serve it hot/hot, right from the oven, or only warm, up to an hour after baking. This can be prepared hours ahead of time and can stand in the kitchen until you are ready to bake it. It is a rich, bland, creamy custard combined with the delicious tartness of dried apricots. It tastes wonderful, and looks beautiful; plan to serve it at the table or at a buffet so everyone can see it.

The bread should be stale, or as dry as stale bread (not as dry as melba toast). If it is necessary to dry it, place it in a single layer on a cookie sheet in a 250° oven for 10 to 15 minutes, or as necessary. Do not remove the crusts.

You will need a large, shallow ovenproof baking dish with a 2½- to 3-quart capacity (13 x 8 x 2 inches). Butter the dish lightly and set aside.

With scissors cut the apricots into slices that measure about ¼ to ½ inch in width. Then steam the apricots as follows: Place the apricots in a vegetable steamer or in a wide strainer over shallow hot water on moderate heat, covered. Bring the water to a boil, then lower the heat to let simmer for about 30 minutes, during which time it will probably be necessary to add additional water. During the last 5 or 10 minutes of steaming add the raisins to the apricots. Then uncover and let stand off the heat.

Meanwhile, butter the bread, stack it in two or three piles, and cut the slices in half into rectangles.

Place about one-third of the bread strips, buttered side up, in the dish, leaving spaces between the strips. Sprinkle with one-half of the softened apricots and raisins. Place another one-third of the bread on top, forming a layer of strips going in the opposite direction from the first layer. Sprinkle with the remaining fruit and top with the remaining strips (in the same direction as the first layer). The design of the strips of bread will show, so plan accordingly.

To scald the cream and milk, place them in the top of a large double boiler over hot water on moderate heat and let cook, uncovered, until a slightly wrinkled skin forms on the surface.

Place the eggs and the yolks in a large bowl. Mix with a wire whisk or a mixer only to mix (the eggs should not become foamy or bubbly). Add the vanilla and al-

10 slices firm white bread, such as Pepperidge Farm or Arnold
6 ounces (½ to ⅔ cup, packed) dried apricots
⅓ cup dark or light raisins
3 ounces (¾ stick) unsalted butter, at room temperature
2 cups whipping cream
2 cups milk
5 eggs plus 4 egg yolks
2 teaspoons vanilla extract
Scant ½ teaspoon almond extract
¼ teaspoon salt
½ cup plus 2 tablespoons granulated sugar

8 GENEROUS PORTIONS

mond extracts, the salt, and ½ cup of the sugar (reserve the remaining 2 tablespoons of sugar), then very gradually stir in the hot cream and the milk.

Gradually ladle or pour the mixture over the bread. There should not be many of the apricot strips or raisins floating on top; if there are, move them under some of the bread slices.

Place a piece of wax paper or plastic wrap over the top, and press down on the paper with both hands to encourage the bread to absorb as much of the liquid as possible. Let stand for 30 minutes, or longer, if you wish.

Before baking, adjust a rack one-third down from the top of the oven (baking this high helps to brown the top) and preheat oven to 325°.

Remove the wax paper or plastic wrap from the top of the pudding and sprinkle the remaining 2 tablespoons of sugar over the top (this also helps the top brown nicely).

Place the baking dish in a large, shallow pan that must not be deeper than the dish. Put both pans into the oven, then reach in and pour hot water into the large pan about 1 inch deep.

Bake for about 40 minutes or longer (see Note) until a small sharp knife inserted gently into the middle comes out just barely dry. During baking carefully reverse the pans front to back to ensure even browning. If the top is still too pale when the pudding tests done, place it under the broiler for a few moments to help it brown; it should be a rich golden color.

I think this is most delicious served right away. Or any time during the next hour. After that it is still wonderful, but it would be a second choice.

This does not actually need a sauce, but here's a quick and easy one that is very good: Simply mix some apricot preserves with a tiny bit of rum, bourbon, or water, and heat just before serving. It is not necessary to strain the preserves.

NOTE: If the pudding waits a long time before it is baked the ingredients will cool off and might therefore need a little longer baking time.

Fried Bread Pudding

This is sensational! We had some leftover Apricot Bread Pudding in the refrigerator, and I used it for lunch for unexpected guests. If I had thought about and planned the meal weeks ahead, it could not have been more of a hit. We had just this, with maple syrup, and bowls of fresh strawberries.

This will remind you somewhat of French toast, but better. The inside of the fried slices is unbelievably light/moist/custardy; the outside is divinely crisp/crunchy.

This is made with Apricot Bread Pudding (preceding recipe) that has cooled and been refrigerated overnight. The remaining preparation can be done hours before serving or immediately before serving.

For each two or three people you plan to serve, beat 1 egg with ¼ cup milk lightly just to mix. Place the egg and milk mixture in a wide, shallow soup plate or serving dish. Place a generous amount of dry bread crumbs on a large piece of wax paper or foil.

In the baking dish cut the cold pudding into slices 1 inch thick. Cut each slice into pieces 3 or 4 inches long. Carefully cut around the sides of the dish to loosen the slices. Then, with a wide metal spatula, transfer the slices one at a time to the egg and milk mixture.

Handle the slices of pudding very carefully—they are delicate. It is safer to handle the slices while they are very cold than if they have been standing at room temperature for a while. Turn each slice over gently in the egg mixture and then in the bread crumbs to coat it thoroughly.

Place the prepared slices on wax paper. They can now stand for a short time at room temperature or they can be refrigerated for a few hours.

To sauté the slices it is best to use clarified butter (see next page). Refrigerated butter burns and the slices will not be the gorgeous color they become with clarified butter.

Use a larger frying pan than you think you will need (preferably nonstick) so that you will have room for turning the slices easily. Place the pan over moderate heat. Add a generous spoonful of clarified butter. When the butter is melted and hot, carefully place the slices in the pan. Fry on each side until golden brown and crisp. Turn the slices gently and carefully with two wide metal spatulas, one in each hand.

Drain the fried slices briefly on a brown paper bag.

Serve quickly on warmed plates. You may sprinkle a bit of confectioners sugar through a fine strainer over the slices, if you wish, or serve with maple syrup or preserves or marmalade.

If you are making this for more than three people, I suggest that you use two large frying pans at the same time.

I served three generous slices as an entrée portion; one or two could be enough for a dessert portion.

Clarified Butter

Since this keeps indefinitely, and since I use it whenever I fry eggs or potatoes, calves liver, or blintzes, et cetera, I make several pounds of it at a time. (I often give a jar of it as a gift.)

Use unsalted butter. Place it in a saucepan, uncovered, over moderate heat. When the butter has melted and starts to bubble, use a large serving spoon to skim off every bit of foam from the top—and discard it. Boil gently for a few minutes, skimming the top as the foam rises.

Then pour the clear, hot butter slowly and carefully into a container; do not include the milky sediment that remains in the bottom of the pan—discard it.

This may be stored in the freezer or refrigerator.

Bread Pudding with Peaches

This is a real peachy, peaches-and-cream, country-style pudding that is superdelicious and "as pretty as a picture." It can be prepared hours before baking and the baking can be timed so the pudding is served HOT—when it is at its best. Serve this as a dinner dessert or as a main course for a breakfast or brunch party. Or serve it at a coffee party. But get it while it's hot!

You will need a shallow ovenproof baking dish with at least a 2-quart capacity (about 11 x 8 x 1¾ or 2 inches). Butter the dish and set it aside. The bread should be stale, or you can dry it a bit. If necessary, place the slices in a single layer on a cookie sheet in a 250° oven for about 15 minutes. Do not remove the crusts from the bread. Butter one side of each slice of bread. Stack three or four slices of bread at a time and cut through the pile, cutting the slices into three fingers. Place the fingers, buttered side up, touching one another, to cover the bottom of the baking dish, fitting the bread slices tightly together. If necessary, trim the slices to fit the dish. This first layer of bread should use about half of the total amount of bread.

Sprinkle the raisins over the bread.

Blanch and peel the peaches (see page 178). Cut the peaches in half, remove the pits, cut each half into about four lengthwise slices. Place the slices neatly overlapping in rows to cover the bread and raisins, fitting the slices close together.

Stir the apricot preserves in a small bowl with a small wire whisk just to soften, and then drizzle over the peaches.

Cover with the remaining bread fingers buttered side up, fitting them closely together. If necessary, trim the slices.

In a bowl beat the eggs just to mix. Add the brown sugar, salt, milk, cream, rum, and the vanilla and almond extracts, beating after each addition just to mix.

With a ladle, gradually ladle the egg-milk mixture over the bread.

Cover the bread with a long piece of wax paper or plastic wrap. With your hands gently press down on the paper to encourage the bread to absorb the egg-milk mixture, but watch the edges of the dish and do not allow the liquids to run over. Then, to encourage the top layer to absorb still more of the liquids, place small items as weights on the paper or plastic wrap. (I use boxes and bars of chocolate; they are the right size and shape and weight and they are always at hand. One-pound boxes of brown sugar are good too.) Gradually, as the bread absorbs the liquids, you will be able to apply more pressure without having it run over.

The pudding can wait this way at room temperature for an hour or two or in the refrigerator for several hours.

Before baking, adjust a rack to the middle of the oven and preheat oven to 325°. Remove the wax paper or plastic wrap.

Drizzle the ⅓ cup whipping cream over the bread (it will not become absorbed and it will not be an even or smooth layer—okay—leave it as it is) and sprinkle the granulated sugar over the top. (The cream and sugar on top make a crisp, crunchy, candylike topping that is wonderful.)

Wipe the rim of the baking dish and place it in a wide, shallow baking pan. Put the pans in the oven, then reach in and pour hot water about 1 inch deep in the large pan.

Bake for about 1 hour and 10 or 15 minutes until a small sharp knife inserted gently between bread fingers in the middle of the baking dish comes out clean. (If the pudding was refrigerated before baking it will probably need more baking time; test it carefully to be sure it is done.)

Then, if the top is pale (and it probably will be) place the baking dish under the broiler briefly, watching it closely, until the top is a lovely golden brown all over.

Remove the baking dish from the hot water and let stand for about 10 minutes before serving.

9 to 10 slices firm white bread, preferably a square-sliced sandwich loaf such as Pepperidge Farm or Arnold

Unsalted butter, at room temperature

⅓ cup light raisins

2 pounds (6 or 7 medium-size) just-ripe freestone peaches

½ cup apricot preserves

4 eggs

½ cup light brown sugar, firmly packed

¼ teaspoon salt

1 cup milk

1 cup whipping cream

3 tablespoons dark or light rum

1 teaspoon vanilla extract

¼ teaspoon almond extract

Additional ⅓ cup whipping cream to be used just before baking

⅓ cup granulated sugar to be used just before baking

10 PORTIONS

Mother's Spanish Cream

It is not Spanish and it does not have cream (although whipped cream is usually served alongside). When my mother and father were married, Spanish Cream was a popular dessert of the time. It was in all the American cookbooks and it appeared often in newspapers and magazines (so my mother told me). She served it regularly for many, many years; we never got tired of it, we could never get enough of it.

One hundred years ago they called this Quaking Custard—it has custard ingredients plus gelatin. But in this recipe the yolks and the whites are beaten separately and folded together. It is then poured into a mold and refrigerated. When it is turned out of the mold there will be a layer of a smooth and shiny mixture on top with a light, airy, spongy layer on the bottom—and a thin brown line of macaroon crumbs between the two layers.

This may be served with or without whipped cream and with or without fresh berries, fresh peaches, or any stewed fruit. Mother always surrounded it with a generous amount of strawberries and passed a bowl of softly whipped cream. For a party she doubled the recipe, poured it into two melon molds, unmolded them end-to-end on a huge platter, formed mounds of whipped cream at both ends, and piled strawberries along the long sides. Spectacular!

You will need a mold with a 7-cup capacity; it should preferably be thin metal (the dessert comes out more easily than if it is heavy pottery), and it should be a simple shape: a round bowl will do, a ring mold is nice (put the berries around the outside and the whipped cream in the middle). Years ago everyone who cooked had a melon mold. Then, for years, manufacturers stopped making them. Now, happily, they seem to be available again. I have also used an 8 x 3-inch one-piece cheesecake pan and it looked wonderful.

Coarsely break up the macaroons and crumb them in a food processor or a blender, or put them in a plastic bag, wrap them in a towel, and pound with a hammer. It is best if they are not all powdery; there should be some slightly coarser pieces. Set aside.

Place the milk in a heavy saucepan over moderate heat and let cook, uncovered, until you see heavy steam coming off the top and a few tiny bubbles on the surface.

Meanwhile, sprinkle the gelatin over the water and let stand.

In a medium-size bowl beat the yolks a bit with a wire whisk. Remove and reserve 2 tablespoons of the sugar; gradually add the remaining sugar to the yolks and whisk briskly for a minute or two until it is slightly pale in color.

(It helps with this next step if you place the bowl of

Dry almond macaroons (see Note), to make ⅔ cup crumbs
3 cups milk
2 envelopes unflavored gelatin
½ cup cold water
3 eggs, separated
½ cup granulated sugar
½ teaspoon vanilla extract
¼ teaspoon almond extract
Generous pinch of salt
Optional: fresh or stewed fruit

6 TO 8 PORTIONS

yolks on a folded towel to prevent slipping.) Very gradually at first add the hot milk to the yolks, whisking constantly. Then return the yolk mixture to the saucepan and cook over medium-low heat, scraping the bottom and the sides constantly with a rubber spatula, until the mixture thickens enough to coat a spoon (in this case that will be 180° on a candy thermometer).

Remove from the heat. Add the softened gelatin and whisk or stir gently until the gelatin is completely melted and incorporated. Stir in the macaroon crumbs and the vanilla and almond extracts. Set aside briefly.

In the small bowl of an electric mixer add the salt to the egg whites and beat until the whites barely hold a firm shape. Reduce the speed to moderate, gradually add the reserved 2 tablespoons of sugar, increase the speed to high again, and beat briefly only until the whites hold a straight peak when the beaters are raised. Remove from the mixer.

The yolk-milk mixture should still be very hot. It is going to be folded gradually into the whites; it is most convenient to use a ladle to add the hot yolk-milk mixture, about ½ cup at a time, and fold it in with a rubber spatula. After adding about half of the hot mixture the remainder will not want to blend well. Don't fight it—it is all right. When necessary transfer to a large bowl and add the final third or quarter of the hot mixture all at once. Fold briefly.

Pour ice water into a mold with at least a 7-cup capacity, shake it out (leaving the mold cold and wet), pour the dessert into the mold, and refrigerate for at least 3 hours, or all day if you wish.

To unmold: Before unmolding onto a large platter, rub the platter lightly with a bit of oil (to make it easy to move the dessert a bit if necessary—and it usually is).

Fill a large bowl or dishpan with hot tap water; with a small sharp knife cut around the top of the mold to release the edge, and place the mold in the hot water to the depth of the dessert—hold it there for about 15 seconds. Remove the mold, quickly dry it, cover with the oiled platter, and, holding the mold and platter together, turn them over. This dessert always comes out easily for me, but if you have any trouble, dip it in the hot water again for a few seconds.

Refrigerate.

Before serving, surround the mold any way you wish with optional fresh or stewed fruit.

Cut with a sharp knife and serve with a pie server.

Whipped Cream

If you are going to serve 4 to 6 portions, 1 cup of cream is enough; for 8 portions use 2 cups of cream. For each cup of cream add 2 tablespoons of confectioners or granulated sugar and ½ teaspoon vanilla extract. In a chilled bowl with chilled beaters whip the ingredients until the cream holds a soft shape.

If you prepare this ahead of time, refrigerate it. Then whisk it a bit before serving.

NOTE: I use Amaretti di Saronno crisp Italian almond macaroons. They are available at most fine food stores around the country.

Banana Pudding

Banana Pudding is an old Southern recipe; my husband was brought up on it as a child in Texas, and it seems that many of his happiest memories involve this Banana Pudding. It is a luscious combination of cold, smooth, and creamy vanilla custard pudding (made with cornstarch), sliced bananas, and bought vanilla wafers, all layered in a serving bowl. The wafers absorb some of the moisture from the pudding and they become deliciously soft and chewy instead of crisp. (I had to try it to believe it. Soggy, I thought. Well, soggy it is— delightfully and deliciously soggy, you will agree.)

This is best 4 to 8 hours after it is made.

⅓ cup unsifted cornstarch
½ cup granulated sugar
¼ teaspoon salt
4 cups milk
2 eggs
2 tablespoons butter, cold and firm, cut into small pieces (it is best to cut the butter ahead of time and refrigerate it)
1 teaspoon vanilla extract
About 8 ounces bought vanilla wafers
4 large just-ripe bananas (not the least overripe)

6 TO 8 PORTIONS

You will need a wide serving bowl similar to a spaghetti bowl, or a shallow baking dish (for instance 8 x 11 x 1¾ or 2 inches) with an 8- to 10-cup capacity.

In the top of a large double boiler off the heat stir the cornstarch, sugar, and salt to mix thoroughly (it is important that these ingredients be completely mixed). Then, very gradually at first, add the milk, stirring well to make sure there are no lumps; use a wire whisk if necessary.

Place over shallow hot water on moderate heat; stir gently and scrape the pan slowly and constantly with a rubber spatula for 12 to 15 minutes until the mixture thickens and reaches 185° on a candy thermometer.

Remove the top of the double boiler and set aside temporarily.

In the small bowl of an electric mixer (or in any other bowl and using a wire whisk) beat the eggs to mix. Very gradually at first, on low speed, beat about half of the thickened milk mixture into the eggs. Then stir the eggs into the remaining milk mixture.

Replace over the hot water on moderate heat and stir slowly and extremely gently for only 2 minutes.

Remove the top of the double boiler. Add the cold butter and stir gently until melted.

Stir in the vanilla.

Do not let the pudding stand now; without waiting complete the dessert. Place about one-third of the vanilla wafers over the bottom of the baking dish, placing them about 1 inch apart.

Peel the bananas and cut them into round slices ¼ to ⅓ inch thick. Place half of the slices over and between the wafers.

Pour half of the custard pudding over the banana layer.

Then make a second layer of cookies, place the remaining banana slices over the wafers, and the remaining pudding over the bananas. Be sure the banana slices are all covered. Place the remaining one-third of the cookies over the top.

Cover with wax paper or plastic wrap, letting it touch the top (to prevent a skin from forming on the exposed pudding).

Refrigerate.

Serve this at the table; it should be very cold and is best on chilled plates or in chilled dessert bowls.

Cream Cheese Flan (Flan de Queso Crema)

This is a Miami-Cuban custard, but that simple statement doesn't begin to tell it. This deserves a special name, and a special award; it is thick and dense, smooth as honey, creamy, a taste thrill. (The Cubans have brought some wonderful cooking to this country.) It is an exciting and extraordinary dessert. It is both simple and elegant, appropriate for a casual meal or for a fancy party. Make it a day before serving or early in the day for that night.

You will need a 2-quart straight-sided ovenproof soufflé dish (7 inches wide and 3 inches deep) and a large baking pan that is wider but not deeper than the soufflé dish (for hot water).

djust a rack one-third up from the bottom of the oven and preheat oven to 350°. Place a large kettle of water on to boil and then just keep it hot until you are ready for it.

First, caramelize the sugar, as follows, to coat a soufflé dish: Place the sugar in a wide frying pan (an 11-inch non-stick pan is best). Place over high heat and stir constantly with a wooden spoon. When the sugar begins to melt, gradually reduce the heat. The sugar will form lumps before it all melts; just continue to cook and stir. When the lumps begin to melt and the sugar begins to caramelize, reduce the heat even more (it should be about medium-low by now) and cook until it is all smoothly melted and is a rich butterscotch color. If it is too pale it will not have any flavor; if it is too dark it will taste burnt.

Pour the caramelized sugar into the soufflé dish. Immediately, holding the dish on both sides with pot holders, tilt the pan from side to side to coat the bottom of the dish and about an inch (more or less) up the sides. Continue to tilt the pan until the caramel stops running. Set the dish aside. (The caramel might crack while it stands—don't worry.)

When the dish has cooled, spread butter on the sides above the caramelized part. You can use a brush and melted butter, or spread soft butter with your fingertips.

In the small bowl of an electric mixer beat the cheese until soft. Beat in the eggs one at a time and then the yolks in several additions, scraping the bowl with a rubber spatula and beating until smooth after each addition. Gradually beat in the condensed milk. Transfer the mixture to the large bowl of the electric mixer. Beat on rather low speed while you add the evaporated milk, salt, vanilla, and lime juice. When the ingredients are mixed and smooth remove the bowl from the mixer and stir in the grated lime rind.

Pour the mixture into the caramelized dish.

Place in the wider but not deeper pan. Place in the oven and then reach in and pour hot water from the kettle 1 to 1½ inches deep in the larger pan. Cover the soufflé dish with a cookie sheet.

Bake, covered, for 1½ hours until a small sharp knife inserted gently in the middle just comes out clean. (If you tap the dish to wiggle it, the flan will shake and look as though it is not set enough, but if the knife comes out clean it is done.)

Uncover, remove from the water, and let stand until completely cool. Refrigerate for 6 to 8 hours or overnight.

Do not unmold until only moments before serving; this is glorious-looking—smooth liquid gold and shiny the moment it is unmolded. It loses the shine and becomes dull as it stands. To unmold, you will need a dish at least as wide as but preferably wider than the soufflé dish, with a slight rim to catch the caramel, which

¾ cup granulated sugar

8 ounces Philadelphia brand cream cheese, at room temperature

3 eggs plus 6 egg yolks

1 14-ounce can sweetened condensed milk

1 13-ounce can evaporated milk

Generous pinch of salt

1 teaspoon vanilla extract

3 tablespoons lime juice (before squeezing the juice, grate the rind of 1 lime to use below)

Finely grated rind of 1 large lime

Optional(but highly recommended): several packages Birds Eye Quick Thaw Raspberries frozen in syrup (see Note)

10 TO 12 PORTIONS

will run like a sauce. With a small sharp knife cut around the rim of the flan to loosen it, and then cut all the way down around the sides. Cover with the serving dish, hold them together firmly and carefully, turn them both over, wait a few seconds for the flan to slip out of the dish, remove the soufflé dish, and serve immediately.

Cut the portions with a knife and serve as though it were cheesecake, on flat dessert plates (preferably chilled).

NOTE: Serve with a generous spoonful of the optional frozen raspberries. Plan on 1 package of the berries for each 2 or 3 portions. The berries should not be thawed ahead of time; they should be barely thawed when served. About 5 minutes before you unmold the flan, place the bag of berries in a bowl of warm water. Separate the berries with your fingers. When they are just barely thawed, pour the berries and a bit of their syrup (not all of it) into a serving bowl.

Now, unmold the flan.

California Lemon Pudding

A light, delicate, smooth pudding that separates while baking into a soft cake layer on top and a softer sauce on the bottom. All lemony and creamy.

This is a very old recipe that has been popular all around the country for a long time. It has stood the test of time, not only because it is quick and easy but because it is so good. It is baked in individual pottery custard cups and is inverted onto flat plates (see Note).

This is best about 3 hours after it is baked. The longer it stands the more dense it becomes. But if necessary it can wait all day.

Adjust a rack to the middle of the oven and preheat oven to 400°. Butter five 6-ounce or six 5-ounce pottery custard cups (with additional butter than called for). Place the buttered cups in a shallow baking pan that must not be deeper than the cups. Set aside.

In the small bowl of an electric mixer beat the butter with ½ cup of the sugar (reserve the remaining ¼ cup of the sugar) to mix.

Beat in the egg yolks (reserve the whites). Then beat in the lemon juice, the flour (scraping the sides of the bowl as necessary with a rubber spatula), and add the milk gradually at first. When the mixture is smooth remove the bowl from the mixer. Stir in the grated rind. It will be a thin mixture.

If you do not have an additional small bowl for the mixture transfer the mixture to any other bowl and wash the bowl.

In the small bowl with clean beaters beat the whites until they hold a soft shape. On moderate speed gradually add the remaining ¼ cup of sugar. Then increase the speed again and beat briefly until the whites hold a straight shape when the beaters are slowly raised. The beaten whites will resemble a thick marshmallow fluff; do not beat until they are stiff or dry.

Very gradually at first, in many small additions, fold about half of the lemon mixture into the whites, and then fold the whites into the remaining lemon mixture.

Transfer to a pitcher or use a ladle and pour or ladle the mixture into the buttered cups, dividing the mixture evenly and filling the cups almost to the top.

Pour hot water about 1 inch deep into the larger pan.

Bake for about 25 minutes until the tops are golden and spring back when gently pressed with a fingertip.

Remove the cups from the water and let cool. While cooling, the puddings will sink down to their original level and they will look wrinkled and cracked. They are supposed to look that way. Refrigerate. These should be served very cold.

Immediately before serving, cut around the pudding with a table knife, cover with a plate, turn the plate and the cup over, if necessary tap the cup and plate together against the work surface to release the pudding, remove the cup, and use a spoon or a rubber spatula to scrape out every bit of the sauce that remains in the cup.

This is wonderful just as it is, or with a few fresh strawberries or raspberries.

NOTE: It is more casual, not as fancy, to serve these directly from the cups they were baked in. If you do serve these in the custard cups you might want to top each portion with a bit of whipped cream and/or a few berries.

1 tablespoon unsalted butter
¾ cup granulated sugar
2 eggs, separated
¼ cup lemon juice (before squeezing the juice, grate the rind of 1 lemon to use below)
2 tablespoons sifted all-purpose flour
1 cup milk
Finely grated rind of 1 large lemon

5 OR 6 PORTIONS

Raspberry Pâté

It's in the pink—it's the berries—it's gorgeous, creamy, a dessert pâté. It may be prepared a day ahead. It has a brilliant shocking-pink sauce and also white whipped cream; when it is served the sauce will go on one side of the portion, the cream on the other. It is appropriate for a fancy party or a simple meal.

You need a loaf pan with a 6-cup capacity.

P repare a loaf pan with a 6-cup capacity as follows: Turn the pan over. Fold one long piece of aluminum foil the long way shiny side out to fit the length of the pan including the two small sides of the pan (it may extend a bit above the sides). Also, fold a length of aluminum foil the long way to fit the width including the two large sides (this may extend a bit above the sides also). The pieces of foil should not be the least bit too wide or they will wrinkle and the pâté will not be smooth. Carefully place one piece over the pan and fold down the two sides to fit. Remove and set aside. Then place the other piece over the pan and fold down the two sides to fit. Remove. Turn the pan right side up. Carefully place one piece of foil in place in the pan, and then do likewise with the second piece of foil (there will be a double thickness on the bottom). If the foil is longer than necessary, fold the ends out over the rim of the pan. Set the pan aside. (Do not butter or oil the foil.)

3 10-ounces packages frozen red raspberries in syrup, thawed (see Notes)
1 envelope unflavored gelatin
¼ cup cold tap water
1 cup whipping cream
8 ounces Philadephia Brand cream cheese, at room temperature
½ cup granulated sugar
Pinch of salt
3 tablespoons lemon juice

ABOUT 8 PORTIONS

Place the thawed berries in a wide strainer over a wide bowl to drain. Reserve ¼ cup of the drained syrup; you will not need the remaining syrup for this recipe.

Place the drained berries in the bowl of a food processor fitted with the metal chopping blade and process for about 20 seconds until puréed. (Or, in a blender, purée a small amount at a time. Or work the berries though a food mill.)

Now, to strain the seeds out of the berries, place a wide but fine strainer (if it is not fine enough the seeds will go through—and you really do not want them) over a wide bowl and push the berries though the strainer. (I use a rather firm rubber spatula or a wooden spoon for pushing the berries through, but many professionals use the back of the bowl of a ladle.) You should have 1¼ cups of strained purée. Let stand.

Sprinkle the gelatin over the water in a 1-cup glass measuring cup or in a Pyrex custard cup. Let stand for about 5 minutes.

Meanwhile, in the small bowl of an electric mixer whip the cream only until it is softly whipped; it should just hold a shape but it should not be firm. Refrigerate.

In the large bowl of the mixer beat the cheese until it is soft and smooth. Beat in the sugar, salt, and the lemon juice. Then beat in the puréed raspberries. Let stand.

To melt the gelatin, place the cup in a pan of warm water only as deep as the gelatin mixture over low heat. Let stand for a few minutes until the granules are dissolved. Remove from the water. Quickly and briefly stir in the reserved ¼ cup of the drained raspberry syrup and, with the mixer at medium speed, beat the gelatin, which may be warm, into the raspberry and cheese mixture. Beat for a few moments, scraping the bowl with a rubber spatula. Be sure it is all thoroughly mixed.

The raspberry and cheese mixture should thicken slightly before the whipped cream is folded in. Place the bowl into a large bowl of ice and water and stir frequently until the mixture thickens slightly. (Actually, this mixture should become almost as thick as the softly whipped cream.)

In three additions, fold about three-quarters of the berry mixture into the cream, and then fold the cream into the remaining raspberry mixture. If the mixtures resist blending into each other, pour back and forth gently from one bowl to another once or twice until smooth.

Pour into the lined pan (it will not fill the pan to the top). Cover the pan with plastic wrap or aluminum foil.

Refrigerate for 6 hours or overnight.

Raspberry Sauce

This can be prepared ahead of time.

The amount of sauce to prepare depends on how many people you plan to serve. (With enough sauce, the pâté will serve ten people.) For each three or four people, use one 10-ounce package of red raspberries frozen in syrup (see Notes). Thaw the berries. Drain in a strainer over a bowl; reserve the drained syrup. Purée the berries in a food processor or a blender or a food mill. Force through a fine strainer to remove the seeds. Add 1 teaspoon of kirsch, framboise, cassis, or lemon juice for each package of berries. And then stir in enough of the drained syrup to make a sauce that is not too thick. I use about three-quarters of the syrup. Refrigerate.

Whipped Cream

For each three or four people use 1 cup of whipping cream, 1 tablespoon of granulated or confectioners sugar, and ½ teaspoon of vanilla extract.

In a chilled bowl with chilled beaters whip the ingredients until the cream is softly whipped; it should hold a soft shape, not firm. Think "sauce." Refrigerate.

If the cream is whipped ahead of time, it will separate slightly and should be whisked a bit with a wire whisk just before serving.

To serve: Remove the covering from the pan. Fill a dishpan with hot tap water. Place the pan of pâté in the hot water for only 3 to 4 seconds (see Notes). Dry the pan quickly. The pâté will slip out of the pan quickly when it is turned over; you'd better be ready. First, wet the serving platter with cold water (which will make it possible for you to move the pâté if necessary). And second, be sure to center the serving platter over the pâté. Hold the pan and platter together firmly and turn them over. Remove the pan. Peel off the foil. If the surface of the pâté needs to be smoothed (which I doubt), dip a small metal spatula into very hot water, shake it off lightly, and with the hot and wet spatula smooth the surface.

If you serve this at the table, the sauce and whipped cream should be in pitchers, or in bowls with ladles.

Serve on wide (luncheon-size) flat plates (chilled). The pâté slices perfectly. Use a sharp knife and cut slices about 1 inch wide. With a pie or cake server place a slice of the pâté on a plate. Pour or ladle the Raspberry Sauce generously on the plate next to one long side of the pâté, and the whipped cream next to the other long side. (The Raspberry Sauce and the whipped cream should just run into each other at the top and bottom sides of the slice.)

Notes: Birds Eye red raspberries frozen in light syrup (less sugar) make a dessert that might not be quite sweet enough for many people; the original frozen berries in regular syrup are probably better here.

The only reason for dipping the pan into the hot water is to help to loosen the pâté in the corners of the pan, because the pan is probably flared and, if so, the foil does not fill in the corners.

Strawberry Yogurt Cream

This is typical of new American desserts; it is made with fresh fruit and yogurt, it is made quickly, it can be made weeks ahead and frozen (although it is served at refrigerator temperature), and it is pink and pretty. Delicious.

This is prepared in individual dishes, glasses, or molds and is served either in the dishes or glasses or unmolded onto individual flat plates.

ash and hull the berries. Remove six large berries for decoration and refrigerate them. Drain the remaining berries.

Sprinkle the gelatin over the water in a small cup and let stand.

Place the drained berries in a food processor fitted with the metal chopping blade and process until smoothly puréed or liquefied. Or purée them in batches in a blender. Or mash them on a plate with a fork. You should have 1 cup of purée.

Stir the purée and sugar in a small saucepan over moderate heat until the mixture comes to a boil. Add the gelatin, stir to dissolve, remove from the heat, stir in a bit of the optional red food coloring to give the dessert a nice rich color, and set aside briefly.

In a bowl with a wire whisk beat the yogurt until it is soft and smooth. Gradually whisk in the warm strawberry mixture.

To remove the tiny strawberry seeds, press the mixture through a wide but fine strainer set over a bowl.

Stir in the lemon juice, rum or brandy, salt, and vanilla.

Place the bowl into a larger bowl of ice and water and stir and scrape the bowl frequently with a rubber spatula until the mixture just begins to thicken slightly.

Meanwhile, in a small chilled bowl with chilled beaters whip the cream until it just holds a shape.

Gradually, a little bit at a time, fold the berry mixture into the cream.

If you would like to prepare this in portions to be unmolded, use small cups (preferably metal or Pyrex—oval tin *oeuf en gelée* molds are wonderful) with a 5- to 6-ounce capacity. Rinse the containers with ice water just before filling them; they should be cold and wet when they are filled. Or prepare this in individual soufflé dishes or stemmed wineglasses to serve without unmolding.

Cover individually with foil and refrigerate from 4 hours to overnight. Or freeze them (see Note).

To unmold, cut around the tops of the desserts with a small sharp knife to release, hold the container in a bowl of hot tap water as deep as the dessert itself for 10 to 20 seconds (the time depends on the material of the container), dry quickly, then, holding the container at about a 45° angle, bang it sharply against the side of your left hand a few times. It will force the dessert away from the container and will make it easy to unmold (wiggle the container a bit and you will see that the dessert is no longer clinging to the container—if it is, bang it again). Cover with a flat plate—center the plate carefully—and turn the plate and container over. (The dessert will probably slip out when you least expect it to. It cannot be moved once it is out, so always be sure to hold the container in the middle of the plate.)

---

1 1-pound box washed fresh strawberries (see To Wash Strawberries, page 14)
1 envelope unflavored gelatin
2 tablespoons plus 2 teaspoons cold tap water
¼ cup granulated sugar
Optional: red food coloring
¾ cup unflavored yogurt
1 tablespoon lemon juice
2 tablespoons dark rum or brandy
Pinch of salt
1 teaspoon vanilla extract
½ cup whipping cream

6 PORTIONS

Use the reserved six strawberries to decorate the desserts either in cups or glasses or on plates. The berries may be left whole or sliced. And if the desserts have been unmolded onto plates and if you have plenty of room and if you have more berries, use them, if you wish.

NOTE: To freeze, just place the dishes, glasses, or molds in the freezer for up to 2 weeks. Thaw several hours or overnight in the refrigerator. Do not serve frozen.

Grand Marnier Strawberry Soufflé

You need six 5-ounce individual soufflé dishes, fresh strawberries, egg whites, and someone special to share this happiness with. It is fluffy, gorgeous—it must be served immediately.

Butter six 5-ounce soufflé dishes. To make collars for them tear off six 6-inch lengths of aluminum foil (keep the foil smooth and neat). Fold each piece in half the long way, shiny side out. Butter about half of the length of one long side of the pieces of foil (buttered part should be 12 x 1½ or 2 inches). Carefully wrap the pieces of foil, buttered side up and in, around the dishes; wrap a piece of string around each dish and tie it carefully and tightly to make the foil secure. Sprinkle about a teaspoonful or more of sugar (additional to that called for) in each dish. Working over wax paper or foil, turn and tap each dish to coat the dish and its collar with the sugar. Then turn the dishes over and tap to shake out excess sugar. Place the prepared dishes on a jelly-roll pan and set aside.

Adjust a rack to the bottom position in the oven and preheat oven to 400°.

Wash, hull, and drain the berries (see page 14); you will not use them all.

Coarsely slice or cut up six to eight large berries. Place them in a small bowl. Add 1 tablespoon of the sugar (reserve the remaining ½ cup of sugar) and 2 tablespoons of Grand Marnier. Let stand at room temperature, stirring occasionally.

2 1-pound boxes fresh strawberries
½ cup plus 1 tablespoon granulated sugar
Grand Marnier
1½ teaspoons lemon juice
A few ladyfingers or a small piece of any sponge cake, pound cake, or a sweet bun (you can even use white bread)
7 egg whites (they may be whites that were frozen and then thawed; they should measure 7 liquid ounces)
⅛ teaspoon salt

6 PORTIONS

Measure about 1½ cups of the remaining berries. Purée or liquefy them in a food processor fitted with the metal chopping blade or mash them finely on a plate with a fork.

Place a wide but fine strainer over a wide bowl. Press the puréed berries through the strainer to remove the seeds.

Measure the strained berries. You need 1 cup; if necessary purée or mash more. Stir in the lemon juice and set aside.

You need six small pieces, one for each dish, of the ladyfingers, pound cake, or whatever (to absorb the Grand Marnier, which will perfume the whole soufflé). The pieces should be about the size of lump sugar, or almost as large as a domino. Place one piece in each prepared dish. Then divide the sliced berries and all their juice among the dishes. If you wish, drizzle an additional ½ teaspoon of Grand Marnier into each dish.

All of the above (except lighting the oven) can be done early in the day, if you wish; if so, let the dishes stand at room temperature.

Place the egg whites in the large bowl of an electric mixer, add the salt, and beat until the whites hold a soft shape. Reduce the speed to moderate, gradually add the remaining ½ cup of sugar, then increase the speed to high again and continue to beat until the whites hold a peak when they are lifted with a rubber spatula but not until they are stiff or dry. Remove from the mixer.

Gradually, in small additions at first, with a rubber spatula fold the strained berries into the beaten whites. Do not fold or handle any more than necessary; if the mixtures are just barely blended that is fine.

With a large spoon divide the mixture among the dishes. Then, with a teaspoon, smooth the tops just a bit and immediately place the soufflés in the oven.

Bake for 18 to 20 minutes. Remove from the oven and quickly cut the strings with scissors (if you have someone to help right now, you will be glad), remove the foil collars, and with a wide metal spatula or pancake turner quickly place each soufflé on a plate and serve IMMEDIATELY. A bit of the soufflé might have run down the sides of the dishes and might have caramelized on the jelly-roll pan. Do not pay any attention to it; do not take one second longer than necessary. These will be gloriously high.

If you wish, place one or more of the remaining strawberries on each flat plate.

Apple-Cranberry Pudding

This is so easy there is nothing to it. The buttery part on the top is sweet and chewy and puddinglike. The cranberry part on the bottom is deliciously tart. If you like a tart flavor you will be wild about this—I do and I am. It is scrumptious served warm with vanilla ice cream.

Bottom Layer

Adjust a rack to the middle of the oven and preheat oven to 325°. Butter a shallow ovenproof baking dish with about a 2-quart capacity (11 x 8 x 1¾ or 2 inches). Set aside.

Place the berries in a bowl of cold water to wash, pick over them, and then drain on a towel. Let stand.

Peel, quarter, and core the apples. Cut each piece into ½-inch chunks.

In a bowl mix the cranberries with the apples, pecans, and sugar. Turn into the baking dish and smooth the top.

2 cups fresh cranberries
2 large, firm cooking apples (preferably Granny Smith or Jonathan)
½ cup pecans toasted (see To Toast Pecans, page 6), broken into medium-size pieces
½ cup granulated sugar

6 TO 8 PORTIONS

Top Layer

In the small bowl of an electric mixer beat the eggs to mix. Beat in the sugar, then add the flour and the melted butter at the same time and beat until smooth.

Pour the batter evenly over the bottom layer.

Bake for about 50 minutes until the top is golden and a toothpick inserted into the center comes out clean.

Serve hot, warm, or at room temperature, preferably with vanilla ice cream.

2 eggs
1 cup granulated sugar
1 cup unsifted all-purpose flour
6 ounces (1½ sticks) unsalted butter, melted

Grapefruit Ice

This is white and looks somewhat like vanilla ice cream; the flavor is tantalizing. I am crazy about it.

Sprinkle the gelatin over the water in a small cup and let stand. Meanwhile, mix the sugar and boiling water in a saucepan over high heat. Stir with a wooden spoon until the mixture comes to a boil. Boil without stirring for 2 minutes.

Remove from the heat, add the softened gelatin, and stir to dissolve. Add the salt. Stir the sugar mixture into the grapefruit juice. Cool to room temperature and then chill well before churning. (If you can arrange to freeze this a few hours before serving it is best.)

Freeze in an ice cream maker according to the manufacturer's directions.

½ envelope unflavored gelatin
⅛ cup cold water
1 cup granulated sugar
½ cup boiling water
Pinch of salt
2½ cups fresh grapefruit juice

1 QUART

Orange Ice

This is as cool and refreshing as a dip in a cool mountain lake. The flavor is mild; the color is pale, pale orange—only enough to give barely a hint of the flavor. But wait until you taste it. Delicious! Serve a scoop on a fruit salad. Or, for true luxury, serve a combination of this and Strawberry Sorbet (see page 242).

Sprinkle the gelatin over ⅛ cup of the water in a small cup and let stand. Combine the remaining 2 cups of water with the sugar in a saucepan. Stir over moderately high heat, bring to a boil, and let boil without stirring for 5 minutes. Remove from the heat, add the softened gelatin, and stir to dissolve.

Pour into a bowl or pitcher and let stand for about 5 minutes. Then add the orange juice, lemon juice, Cointreau, grated rinds, and salt. Stir to mix.

Let stand until cool, then strain through a fine strainer. Chill briefly in the freezer or refrigerate.

Freeze in an ice cream maker following the manufacturer's directions.

½ envelope unflavored gelatin
2⅛ cups water
1 cup granulated sugar
1 cup fresh orange juice (grate the rind to use below before squeezing the juice)
⅛ cup fresh lemon juice (grate the rind to use below before squeezing the juice)
⅛ cup Cointreau
Finely grated rind of ½ large orange
Finely grated rind of ½ large lemon
Pinch of salt

1 QUART

Lemon Ice

Extra sour, extra wonderful, extra special—and so easy I can't believe it.

As much as I love to use grated lemon rind, I do not use it for this recipe. It settles in lumps on the dasher, and even if you stir it around to mix it in after the ice is frozen, frozen grated lemon rind in this recipe is not so great.

C ombine the water and sugar in a saucepan over high heat. Stir with a wooden spoon until the sugar is dissolved and the mixture comes to a boil. Boil without stirring for 5 minutes.

2⅔ cups warm water
1⅓ cups granulated sugar
⅞ cup fresh lemon juice

1 QUART

Remove from the heat and let stand until completely cool. Stir in the lemon juice.

If you chill this well before freezing it, it will save churning time.

Freeze in an ice cream maker following the manufacturer's directions.

Don't be surprised when you remove the cover of the churn to see that this is white, not yellow.

Some people especially enjoy this with a splash of gin, vodka, crème de menthe, or rum poured on it.

NOTE: As soon as this is frozen, and for several hours after, it has a terrific texture— just firm enough but not too firm. After a day or two in the freezer it becomes too firm.

Strawberry Sorbet

This light sherbet is quite incredible. The strawberry flavor seems stronger and more intense than in strawberries alone. When I served this at a dinner party it caused a run on ice cream makers the following day; everyone wanted to make this.

Fresh raspberries can be used in place of the strawberries to make a raspberry sorbet, or you can use some of each for a combination that is wonderful.

lace the berries in a large bowl of cold water; quickly pick them out, remove the hulls, and drain on paper towels.

1⅓ 1-pint boxes (1⅓ pounds) fresh strawberries
1 cup granulated sugar
Pinch of salt
2 teaspoons fresh lemon juice
⅔ cup cold water

1 QUART

Slice the berries in half and place them in a roomy bowl. Add the sugar and salt and stir to mix. Let stand, stirring occasionally, for about 2 hours until the sugar is dissolved and the berries are soft.

Purée the mixture in a food processor or a blender.

Now, a question: To strain or not to strain? I do, but it is a job. You must use a rather fine-meshed strainer or the seeds will go through. Do not attempt to strain this in a narrow-diameter strainer; it must be a wide one or you will be at it for hours. If you examine the strained mixture, you will see that a few seeds have gone through anyhow—that can't be helped. And you will have quite a large number of the seeds in the strainer to be discarded.

Add the lemon juice and cold water.

Freeze in an ice cream maker according to the manufacturer's directions.

Plum Sorbet

For many years, when plums were in season (or using plums from Brazil when they were not in season here), I made honeyed plum sauce, especially to serve over sliced fresh or stewed peaches (a luscious combination), or over vanilla ice cream (exotic), or simply to eat with a spoon or drink from a glass. Once, when I had made a large amount of the sauce, we suddenly decided to close the house and go for a long trip. I put the sauce in the freezer, thinking that I would let it thaw when we returned. But I did not let it thaw; I ate it with a spoon and found that it was a wondrous sorbet. It is slightly tart; very, very good; unusual, and too easy to make.

Cut the plums into halves or large pieces and remove the pits. Place the plums, honey, and water in a heavy saucepan. Cover and cook over moderate-low heat, stirring occasionally, until the plums begin to soften. Then uncover and continue to cook, stirring occasionally, until the plums fall apart and are completely softened (it might take about 20 minutes).

Press the mixture through a strainer set over a bowl. At the end, work through as much of the thickened remains as you can (still, some will not go through and will have to be discarded).

Stir in the maraschino liqueur.

Place the mixture, uncovered, in a bowl or container in the freezer until it is firm. Then cover it with plastic wrap, placing the plastic directly on the top of the sorbet.

It might take 5 to 10 minutes to freeze solid, depending on the container and whether the mixture is shallow or deep.

Now, this frozen mixture must be beaten once sometime before serving. It may be done immediately before, or hours before. I love it immediately after it is beaten, but although it becomes firmer as it stands in the freezer, the texture remains nice for many hours. This beating may be done in a food professor fitted with a metal blade or in the large bowl of an electric mixer. Either way, chill the bowl and blade or beaters. In a mixer you can beat it all at once. In a processor do it in small batches, adding the frozen mixture by spoonfuls through the feed tube.

Process or beat until the mixture is slightly lighter in color, very smooth, and a little fluffy, but not until it melts or becomes runny.

Serve immediately or return to the freezer.

2 pounds red plums (about 12; I use President or Santa Rosa plums)
⅓ cup honey
¼ cup water
2 tablespoons maraschino liqueur (I have only used maraschino, but in place of it, I would think you can use any liqueur or brandy, such as kirsch)

1½ PINTS

Note: Always cover with plastic wrap directly touching the sorbet, otherwise ice will form in the space between the sorbet and the covering.

Sorbet Cassis

This is from my friend Betty Rossbottom, a wonderful cook and teacher (her school is La Belle Pomme in Columbus, Ohio). She served this when she invited us to her home for dinner. After the first bite, I asked, "Can I please have the recipe?" It is a sherbet made without an ice cream maker. It has a most delicious flavor and a sensational purple color. You need room in the freezer for a large bowl.

D rain the berries in a strainer set over a bowl and reserve the juice (you will need 1 cup of drained blackberry juice).

Purée the berries in a food processor fitted with the metal blade or in a blender. Strain through a large, rather coarse strainer to remove the seeds. Stir in the sugar, lemon juice, 1 cup of drained blackberry juice, water, and cassis. Beat the eggs to mix them well and stir them into the blackberry mixture. Mix thoroughly.

Now strain it all again either through the same strainer or preferably through one with slightly smaller openings.

Place the mixture in a large bowl (stainless steel works best because it gets very cold; the bowl should be large enough to give you plenty of room to stir vigorously), cover with plastic wrap or foil, and place in the freezer.

When it starts to harden (when about 1 inch is frozen around the edge), use a large, strong wooden spoon and stir the mixture vigorously. Refreeze and stir again when it gets to the 1-inch rim stage. Repeat the freezing and stirring at least four times—the more the better (it should be at about 45-minute intervals). Then cover airtight and return to the freezer for at least 6 hours or overnight.

Sometime before serving, which may be right before or up to 3 hours before, beat the sorbet either in an electric mixer or in a processor. The bowl and beaters or metal blade should be chilled first. If you use a processor, process in small batches, adding the frozen sorbet by spoonfuls through the feed tube. Beat or process only until the mixture becomes fluffy and slightly lighter in color, but not long enough for it to melt—it should remain firm enough to hold its shape.

Serve immediately or return to the freezer for up to 2 or 3 hours—the sorbet will remain soft-frozen for 2 or 3 hours. If this is frozen for several days, it should be beaten or processed again before serving.

It is nice to pass the bottle of cassis at the table to be poured over individual portions.

Betty often serves this piled high in large, scooped-out lemon shells (cut a thin slice off the bottom so it will stand straight) with a sprig of fresh mint in the top of each; it is a riot of colors—purple sorbet, yellow lemons, and green mint.

2 1-pound cans blackberries (Betty and I use Oregon brand), packed in syrup

1 cup granulated sugar

½ cup plus 2 tablespoons fresh lemon juice

½ cup water

½ cup cassis liqueur or crème de cassis (cassis is black currant)

4 eggs

3 PINTS

Frozen Grand Marnier Mousse

This is a dream recipe. It is easy to make; it does not call for an ice cream maker; it is elegant and delicious; it is prepared in individual soufflé dishes, custard cups, or coffee cups; it is served directly from the freezer with no last-minute attention; and it may be frozen for a month. It does not freeze hard; it is a light and creamy mousse, lighter than ice cream, sprinkled with a mixture of Grand Marnier and macaroon crumbs. Although this makes 12 portions you should plan on serving seconds.

Macaroon Mixture

The macaroons must be ground fine. To grind them in a food processor (fitted with the metal blade) or in a blender crumble them coarse and then process or blend to make fine crumbs. Without a processor or blender place the macaroons in a strong bag and pound them with a hammer or any heavy tool. You should have about 1¼ cups of crumbs.

In a small bowl mix the orange juice and Grand Marnier. Add the crumbs and mix thoroughly; it will be a crumbly mixture. Set aside.

6 ounces Amaretti or any dry almond macaroons (to make 1¼ cups crumbs)
2 tablespoons orange juice (grate the rind before squeezing the juice and reserve it for the mousse)
3 tablespoons Grand Marnier

Mousse

In the small bowl of an electric mixer beat the egg yolks with ½ cup (reserve the remaining 3 tablespoons) of sugar for several minutes until very pale and thick.

Mix the grated rind and the Grand Marnier. Remove the yolk mixture from the beater and stir in the grated rind mixture. Set aside.

In a chilled bowl with chilled beaters whip the cream until it holds a shape but not until it is really stiff. Set aside.

Add the salt to the whites and beat until the whites hold a soft shape. On low speed gradually add the reserved 3 tablespoons of sugar; then increase the speed and beat only until the whites hold a shape but not until they are stiff or dry. In a very large mixing bowl with a large rubber spatula fold together the egg yolk mixture, the whipped cream, and

5 eggs, separated
½ cup plus 3 tablespoons granulated sugar
Finely grated rind of 1 large, deep-colored orange (see ingredients for macaroon mixture above)
3 tablespoons Grand Marnier
2 cups heavy cream
Pinch of salt

12 PORTIONS

the beaten egg whites, folding all three mixtures together at once and handling lightly only until the mixtures are barely blended.

Line up 12 individual soufflé dishes, custard cups, or coffee cups, each with about a 6-ounce capacity.

Spoon half of the mixture into the cups, filling them only about halfway; do not smooth the tops. With your fingertips sprinkle about half of the prepared macaroon mixture over the mousses. Top with the remaining mousse mixture, do not smooth the tops, and sprinkle with the remaining macaroon mixture.

Place the mousses in the freezer for about an hour until they are firm enough to be covered. Then cover each one with a piece of plastic wrap large enough to fold under the bottom; do not pull it so tightly that it squashes the top.

Freeze for at least 3 or 4 hours or as long as 3 or 4 weeks. Serve directly from the freezer.

Joan's Frozen Lemon Mousse

This wonderful fix-ahead frozen dessert is a recipe from my friend Joan Borinstein. It resembles ice cream, prepared in a crumb crust. It is easy to slice, and is a deliciously light and refreshing dessert to serve after a dinner party. It must be prepared at least a day ahead; it can be prepared 2 weeks ahead. If you prepare it far ahead, wrap it airtight in plastic wrap to store in the freezer. You will need an 8 x 3-inch springform pan.

Crust

Butter the sides only of an 8 x 3-inch springform pan. (It is easier to transfer if the bottom is not buttered, or, if you are serving it on the bottom of the pan, it makes it easier to serve.) Make fine crumbs of the wafers, either in a food processor fitted with the metal blade, or in a blender, or by placing them in a strong bag and pounding firmly with a rolling pin.

Melt the butter and add it to the crumbs; mix thoroughly until completely blended.

Now, it is easier if you do not put all of the crumb mixture into the pan at once;

1 12-ounce box vanilla wafers (to make 3¼ cups crumbs)
4 ounces (1 stick) unsalted butter

work with about one-quarter of the mixture at a time. First press a firm layer on the sides of the pan, up to the top of the pan, and then on the bottom.

Filling

In the small bowl of an electric mixer beat the yolks until they are pale. Add ¼ cup, reserving remaining ¾ cup, of the sugar and beat at high speed for a minute or two. On low speed gradually add the lemon juice, scraping the bowl with a rubber spatula and beating only until smooth. Remove from the mixer and stir in the grated rind. Set aside.

In a small clean bowl with clean beaters beat the egg whites with the salt until they hold a soft shape. Reduce the speed to moderate and gradually add the reserved ¾ cup of sugar, adding only 1 or 2 tablespoons at a time. Increase the speed to high again and continue to beat until the whites and sugar become thick and marshmallowlike. Do not beat until stiff. Set aside.

In a chilled bowl with chilled beaters whip the cream until it holds a shape but not until it is stiff.

In several small additions fold the yolks into the whites. Then, in several additions, fold the yolks and whites into the whipped cream.

Turn into the crumb-lined pan and smooth the top. Freeze for a few hours until firm. Then cover airtight with plastic wrap or aluminum foil. Freeze overnight or up to 2 weeks.

To remove the side of the pan: Use a 5- or 6-inch firm-bladed (not flexible), sharp and heavy knife; cut around the sides between the crust and the pan, pressing the blade firmly against the pan. Release and remove the side.

Then, to remove the dessert from the bottom of the pan, cut between the bottom and the crust to release. With a wide metal spatula transfer the dessert to a large, flat serving plate.

This can be served immediately, or it can be replaced in the freezer.

Use the same firm-bladed knife to slice portions.

4 eggs, separated
1 cup granulated sugar
½ cup fresh lemon juice (grate the rind of 3 or 4 lemons before squeezing the juice to use below)
Finely grated rind of 3 or 4 lemons
Pinch of salt
1½ cups heavy cream

12 TO 16 PORTIONS

Optional Sauce

Thaw the fruit and purée it with its syrup in a blender or a processor. Strain it through a fine strainer to remove the seeds. Pass the sauce separately.

NOTE: The filling can also be prepared in individual glasses, without any crust.

1 10-ounce box frozen boysenberries, packed in syrup
1 10-ounce box frozen blackberries, packed in syrup
(or any other fruits or combination)

Frozen Lemon-Rum Soufflé

This is a powerful concoction—very rummy, very tart, and very sensational! It can be served 3 or 4 hours after it is made or it can wait in the freezer a day or two. You will need room in the freezer for a soufflé dish with a 3-inch collar.

Prepare a 1-quart soufflé dish as follows: Tear off a piece of foil long enough to wrap around the dish and overlap by at least a few inches. Fold it in half the long way; the fold will be the bottom. Very lightly spread a thin layer of tasteless vegetable oil over the upper (open) half of the length. Wrap the foil around the dish. Tie it securely with a piece of string. Place it on a plate and set aside (see Notes).

Sprinkle the gelatin over the cold water in a heatproof bowl or cup; let stand for about 5 minutes.

Meanwhile, in the large bowl of an electric mixer beat the lemon juice and egg yolks at high speed for 5 minutes. Add the sugar and rum and continue to beat at high speed for about 5 minutes more until the sugar is dissolved. Reduce the speed slightly if necessary to avoid splashing.

Meanwhile, place the cup of gelatin in a little hot water in a saucepan on low heat. Stir occasionally with a metal spoon until the gelatin is dissolved.

Reduce the mixer speed to low, add the gelatin, and

1 envelope plus 1½ teaspoons unflavored gelatin
½ cup cold tap water
1 cup fresh lemon juice (grate the rinds of 2 of the lemons before squeezing to use below)
8 egg yolks
2 cups granulated sugar
⅔ cup dark rum (I use Myers's rum)
Finely grated rind of 2 large lemons
2 cups heavy cream

6 TO 8 PORTIONS

beat until thoroughly mixed. Remove from the mixer and stir in the grated rind.

The mixture must now be chilled until it thickens slightly. It can either be done by placing the bowl in the freezer, or by placing the bowl in a larger bowl partly filled with ice and water. Either way, it should be stirred occasionally to be sure it thickens evenly.

Meanwhile, in a chilled bowl with chilled beaters whip the cream until it holds a shape but not until it is really stiff. Transfer the whipped cream to a larger mixing bowl.

When the gelatin mixture begins to thicken, gradually fold it, in several additions, into the whipped cream. It is best to fold with an extra-large rubber spatula. If the gelatin mixture seems to sink to the bottom, place the whole bowl in the freezer (or in a larger bowl of ice) briefly and fold occasionally until the gelatin no longer sinks. Then pour the mixture into the prepared soufflé dish.

Freeze for at least 3 hours until the soufflé is firm.

If the soufflé is going to stand and you want to cover the top, wait until the soufflé is completely frozen, then cover it with plastic wrap.

Immediately before serving, remove the foil collar. (It will be easy.) The top of the soufflé is about 2 inches above the top of the dish—beautiful.

This can be decorated any way you wish: rosettes of whipped cream, candied violet or rose petals, chopped unsalted green pistachio nuts, chocolate shavings, etc. But it is such a super dish that I think adding anything is unnecessary. However, it is nice with softly whipped cream flavored with sugar and vanilla. And, if you wish, pass a bowl of plain or brandied black Bing cherries (see Notes).

NOTES: Once when I made a cold soufflé for a party, I went to the kitchen just before dinner to remove the foil collar and decorate the soufflé. I had oiled the inside of the foil collar and I guess I had used too much oil. I took the dish out of the freezer, holding one hand on each side of it, and was shocked to see the whole thing, except the foil, slide gracefully out of my hands and land on the floor. Since then, I have always placed the soufflé dish on a plate for putting it into and taking it out of the freezer.

To make your own brandied cherries, drain canned pitted black Bing cherries. Add about ¼ cup each kirsch and cognac or brandy. Let stand, stirring occasionally, for a day or more in the refrigerator.

Sauces and Extras

Top Secret

While I was working on the recipe for Lemon Cream Cheese Pie (see page 74) I experimented with several different types of cottage cheese: large curd, small curd, huge fat, low fat—whatever. After the recipe was written I had several containers of cottage cheese that I had processed left over in the refrigerator. One day for lunch I put some fresh strawberries on a plate and spooned some of the processed cheese over the top. I swooned. I said that nobody would guess that it was cottage cheese. I tried it out on friends. They said sour cream, crème fraîche, yogurt, cream cheese and heavy cream, food of the gods, and whatnot. Nobody guessed cottage cheese, just plain cottage cheese. (Incidentally, ½ cup of cottage cheese has from 80 to 110 calories, depending on its fat content; ½ cup of sour cream has about 400 calories.)

I was in some new kind of heaven and vowed that I would eat nothing but strawberries and processed cottage cheese as long as berries were in season; then I would switch to some other fruit. I loved each bite of the pure, simple, natural, bland, maybe-a-bit-sour-but-not-really-sour flavor.

I also tried it with a bit of sweetening and flavoring. For each ½ cup of cheese I mixed in 1 teaspoon of granulated sugar—or 1 teaspoon of mild honey—and a few drops (very little) of vanilla extract. I can't tell you which is better, sweetened or not, because they are equally divine. (The small amount of sweetening really only cuts the slight sourness of the cheese; add more, if you wish.)

This may be served immediately after it is prepared, but if it is refrigerated for a few hours the mixture will thicken and become even better. Prepare as much or as little as you want. Plan on ½ to 1 cup per person if you are serving this with strawberries or sliced fresh peaches. If you serve it with apple pie or baked apples or with peach or blueberry cobbler or something filling like that, you might not need so much. But when someone knows what this is—how low in calories—they will eat twice as much.

Place the cottage cheese (see Note), 1 to 2 cups at a time, in the bowl of a food processor fitted with the metal chopping blade. Process for 1 full minute (no less) until as smooth as honey. You will think it is ready sooner, but please do process for the full minute, at least. Stop the machine once to scrape down the sides during processing. When you think it is done, process still a few seconds longer. The sugar or honey and vanilla may be added before, during, or after the processing.

Transfer to a covered container and refrigerate for several hours or longer.

This Top Secret or the following Ricotta Cream can be made in a blender. It is possible, but just barely. In my Waring blender I have to do it in many very small additions, stop and start the machine frequently, and use low speed at first for each addition. It is a hassle. It really is best to use a food processor.

NOTE: I like this best made with large-curd 4 percent milk fat cottage cheese (Seal-test). If you use 1 percent milk fat cottage cheese it will be a thinner, airier mixture without the depth and grandeur of the 4 percent milk fat cheese. (The 1 percent cheese has about 80 calories to a ½-cup portion, and the 4 percent cheese has 100 to 110 calories for the same amount. Not much difference in the numbers, but a big difference in the taste and texture.)

Ricotta Cream

This recipe is the same as the preceding Top Secret, but it is made with ricotta cheese instead of cottage cheese; this is a little blander and lighter—cottage cheese has more of a tart flavor and is denser after it is processed. I like both cheeses equally for these recipes. I use any all-natural whole-milk ricotta cheese. This totally bland flavor is sensational with tart foods.

Honey Ricotta Cream

This is a sweetened and flavored version of the preceding recipe. Serve it as a thick sauce with any fresh or cooked fruit (it is wonderful with raw pears) or with fruit cobbler, fruit pie, baked apples, et cetera.

Process the cheese in a food processor for 1 minute, scraping down the sides after about ½ minute. Then add the yogurt and honey and process again only to mix.

Refrigerate in a covered container for a few hours or overnight.

1 15- or 16-ounce container ricotta cheese
¼ cup unflavored yogurt
¼ cup honey

White Custard Cream

Serve this divine sauce with almost any fresh fruit; or serve it with bread pudding, baked apples, apple pie, et cetera. It is similar to a soft custard, but is lighter since it is made with egg whites only, no yolks. It is about as thick as soft whipped cream—almost the consistency of sour cream—extraordinary.

2 cups whipping cream
2 tablespoons granulated sugar
4 egg whites (to make ½ cup of whites; they may be whites that were frozen and then thawed)
1 teaspoon vanilla extract
Few drops almond extract

2½ CUPS

Place 1 cup of the cream (reserve the remaining 1 cup of cream) in the top of a large double boiler over hot water on moderate heat, uncovered, to scald. When you see a thin skin over the top or small bubbles around the edge, stir in the sugar and temporarily remove the top of the double boiler.

In the small bowl of an electric mixer beat the remaining cup of cream with the (unbeaten) egg whites for about a minute only to mix very well; the mixture will not increase or thicken.

Stir a little of the beaten mixture into the hot cream, stir in a little more, and then stir in all of it.

Replace the top of the double boiler over hot water on moderate heat. Cook, stirring and scraping the sides and bottom of the pan constantly for 5 or 6 minutes until the mixture registers 170° to 175° on a sugar or candy thermometer and thickens enough to coat a spoon. (This will thicken more as it chills; do not overcook now or the mixture will lose its smoothness.)

Remove the top of the double boiler and strain the sauce through a fine strainer set over a bowl. Stir frequently until completely cool. Then stir in the vanilla and almond extracts. (To add only a few drops of the almond extract it is best to pour a few drops slowly onto a spoon; pouring directly into the sauce is dangerous—use very very little.)

When cool, refrigerate. This may be refrigerated for a day or two. To cover for the refrigerator, first place a paper napkin or towel over the top of the bowl and then cover that with plastic wrap or foil. Otherwise, moisture forms on the underside of the plastic wrap or foil and drips back into the sauce, thinning it slightly.

Sweet Sour Cream

Serve this with cobblers, apple desserts, fresh pears, fresh figs, mangoes, melon, fresh berries; almost any time you would serve whipped cream or Crème Fraîche. There's nothing to it, everyone loves it, and it lasts for several days. For every cup of sour cream use ½ teaspoon of vanilla extract and 1½ teaspoons of granulated sugar. Place the cream in a bowl, whisk it until soft, whisk in the vanilla and sugar, and then either serve right away while it is a rather thin mixture, or refrigerate it until it thickens again, or longer. I like it thick, but for some desserts it might be better a bit thinner; just whisk it briskly to thin it.

Crème Fraîche

Only a few years ago this was practically unheard of in America. Now, many people make their own, or buy it in fancy food stores.

There is nothing to making your own, but it must be made ahead of time. It takes from 1 to 3 days; then it can be kept for about 4 weeks.

It is divine with fresh berries, fresh figs, baked apples, fresh peaches, fruit pie, fruit pudding, et cetera, et cetera.

When this is served with fruit as a dessert, it is best to plan on 1 cup of cream for every 3 portions. Multiply the recipe as you wish.

Pour the cream into a jar with a cover. Add the buttermilk and stir to mix. Cover the jar and let stand at room temperature for from 1 to 3 days, until it is as thick as commercial sour cream.

Refrigerate for at least 24 hours or up to 4 weeks, or for as long as it still tastes good. In the refrigerator, after a day or so, it will thicken quite a bit more and will become very firm. Use it as it is (I love it thick) or whisk it a bit to soften.

1 cup whipping cream
1 teaspoon buttermilk

3 PORTIONS

The Governor's Crème Fraîche

I have tried to sweeten and flavor crème fraîche before mixing the cream with the buttermilk and before letting it stand to thicken, but it does not work. The mixture never does thicken if it has sugar. So, this is made with prepared Crème Fraîche.

S tir the ingredients to mix. Taste for additional nutmeg; you should be able to taste the nutmeg but only faintly. When you mix the ingredients, the sugar will melt and cause the Crème Fraîche to become thinner. Refrigerate. After a few hours it will thicken to a nice consistency for a sauce. If it stands overnight, it will become almost as thick as it was before the sugar was added; delicious either way.

1 cup Crème Fraîche (see preceding recipe)
3 tablespoons light brown sugar, firmly packed
½ teaspoon vanilla extract
Pinch of nutmeg

3 PORTIONS

Gingered Crème Fraîche

M ix the ingredients. This is delicious with apple or pumpkin pie. Or with almost any fresh or stewed fruit or with baked apples. Or just with a spoon.

1 cup Crème Fraîche (see page 255)
2 tablespoons honey
2 to 4 tablespoons finely chopped candied or preserved ginger

3 PORTIONS

Brandied Butterscotch Sauce

Caramelized sugar, cream, butter, and cognac—heaven! With fruit and ice cream this should be enough sauce for 6 generous portions.

Recently I have been using a nonstick frying pan for caramelizing sugar, and it is great. The sugar seems to melt and brown better, and there is no hassle washing caramelized sugar off the pan—it just floats off. (Although the interior of the pan is dark, it does not interfere with judging the color of caramelized sugar.)

P lace the cream in a small saucepan, uncovered, over moderate heat and let it come to a low boil. Meanwhile, place the sugar in a frying pan that is about 11 inches wide and has about a 2-quart capacity (the pan may be nonstick or not). Place the frying pan over high heat and stir constantly with a long-handled wooden spoon until the sugar starts to melt and caramelize. At this point, while there are still some lumps of unmelted sugar, reduce the heat to moderate and let cook briefly until the sugar is smooth and is a rich mahogany color.

1 cup whipping cream
1 cup granulated sugar
3 tablespoons unsalted butter,
    cut into small pieces
1 teaspoon vanilla extract
3 tablespoons cognac

1½ CUPS

The cream should be very hot now; it should be ready to boil, if not actually boiling. Remove the frying pan from the heat; gradually add the hot cream, stirring constantly with the long-handled wooden spoon. (The mixture will bubble up furiously.)

When the cream is added to the sugar it will cause a few lumps to form in the mixture. Stir over moderate heat, again letting the mixture boil (adjust the heat as necessary to prevent boiling over), until all the lumps melt and the sauce is smooth.

Remove from the heat, stir in the butter, then the vanilla and cognac.

Carefully pour the mixture into a bowl and whisk it briskly with a wire whisk until the butter is incorporated and the sauce is as smooth as honey (although a bit thinner).

This can be served at any temperature, but I like it best very cold; the sauce thickens when it is refrigerated to a gorgeous consistency, thicker than honey.

Butterscotch Custard Sauce

Make this ahead of time and serve it very cold with any cobbler or pandowdy, bread pudding, et cetera.

Place the milk and cream in a heavy saucepan, uncovered, over moderate heat to scald, or until you see a slightly wrinkled skin on the top.

Meanwhile, in the top of a large double boiler, off the heat, whisk the yolks lightly just to mix. Gradually mix in the sugar and salt and whisk briskly for about a minute.

Slowly add the scalded milk and cream, whisking steadily.

Place over hot water on moderate heat. Scrape the bottom and sides constantly with a rubber spatula and cook until the mixture thickens slightly and will coat a metal spoon; it might take about 10 minutes. When it is ready it will register 180° on a sugar or candy thermometer.

Remove from the heat immediately and without waiting pour the sauce through a fine strainer set over a bowl. Stir in the vanilla.

Cool, uncovered, stirring frequently and gently. Then cover and refrigerate.

Serve very cold (you might place it in the freezer for about 15 minutes before serving). Stir briefly before serving.

This amount should serve 8 to 10 people.

1 cup milk
1 cup whipping cream
4 egg yolks
⅓ cup dark brown sugar, firmly packed
Pinch of salt
1 teaspoon vanilla extract

2⅓ CUPS

Raisin Blueberry Sauce

We had this in Maine, on pancakes. There it was made with small wild blueberries. Here I make it with large, silvery, commercial berries. It is terrific on vanilla ice cream, on cheesecake, bread pudding, sliced fresh peaches, or sliced oranges.

lace the raisins in a vegetable steamer or a strainer over shallow hot water on moderate heat. Cover, bring to a boil, and let simmer for 10 to 15 minutes. The raisins should be very soft and moist. Uncover and set aside.

In a 4- to 5-cup heavy saucepan mix the sugar, cornstarch, cinnamon, and salt; stir well. Add the water and lemon juice and continue to stir with a rubber spatula until the dry ingredients are thoroughly moistened and there are no lumps. Add the berries.

Place over moderate heat and stir occasionally until the mixture begins to simmer. Reduce the heat slightly and simmer gently for 2 minutes, stirring a bit with a rubber spatula. (Cornstarch thins out if it is overcooked or overbeaten.)

Some of the berries will be broken, some will remain whole; the liquid will be deep purple, slightly thickened—wonderful. Add the raisins. Remove from the heat.

Transfer to a wide bowl to cool. Then refrigerate.

Serve cold.

This should be enough for 4 portions.

¼ cup raisins
⅓ cup granulated sugar
1 tablespoon cornstarch
⅛ teaspoon cinnamon
Pinch of salt
2 tablespoons cold water
1½ teaspoons lemon juice
2 cups fresh blueberries or frozen (not thawed) dry-packed blueberries

1½ CUPS

Cranberry Topping

Cranberries have been on American menus since the Pilgrims' first Thanksgiving. The sauce is spectacular on vanilla ice cream or custard or bread pudding or anything bland and creamy (cheesecake) or on baked apples, apple pies, or on sliced bananas or sliced or sectioned oranges (the fruit may be drizzled with Grand Marnier first)—or just on a teaspoon. This may be made with fresh or frozen cranberries. It can be served at room temperature, or only slightly warm (when it is very cold the flavor seems weaker, and when it is very hot it is still delicious but thin). A jar of this makes a gorgeous Christmas present.

Just read the ingredients—what a combination!

f you use frozen berries do not thaw them first. Pour the berries into a large bowl of cold water and swoosh them around; loose stems will settle to the bottom, so, with your hands, lift the berries from the top and drain them in a strainer.

Place the butter and brown sugar in a covered saucepan with about a 2-quart capacity. Stir occasionally over moderate heat until the butter melts. Add the cranberries and Grand Marnier. Cover and cook until the mixture comes to a boil. Then adjust the heat so that the mixture simmers and cook, covered, until the berries pop and/or soften. You may press some of them against the side to mash them slightly. Do not cook too long; some berries should remain whole and the others should be coarse. Stir in the cream.

Remove from the heat and let cool.

Transfer to a covered container or two. Let stand or refrigerate.

To serve, this may be warmed slightly in a pan over low heat.

1 12-ounce package (3 cups) fresh or frozen cranberries
4 ounces (1 stick) unsalted butter
1 cup light brown sugar (see Note)
½ cup Grand Marnier
½ cup whipping cream

3 CUPS

NOTE: Although this tastes just as delicious with dark brown sugar the color will not be as bright and pretty.

Strawberry-Strawberry Sauce

This is a thin sauce with no thickening; it is light and fresh and has a delicate flavor. Perfect over vanilla ice cream and/or cooked or uncooked peaches, or seedless grapes, fresh pineapple, fresh raspberries, or fresh strawberries.

This amount will possibly be enough for 3 or 4 portions. The sauce may be refrigerated for several days.

Wash, hull, and drain the berries (see page 14) and set them aside on paper towels. Place the water, preserves, and sugar in a small saucepan over low heat. Stir occasionally and bring to a low boil.

Place the berries in a food processor bowl fitted with the metal chopping blade and process them to a smooth purée. (Or purée them in several batches in a blender.) Add the warm strawberry preserve mixture and process (or blend) again briefly.

Place a wide but fine strainer over a wide bowl. Pour

2 cups (generous ½ pound) fresh strawberries
3 tablespoons water
3 tablespoons strawberry preserves
2 tablespoons granulated sugar
½ teaspoon lemon juice
2 teaspoons kirsch

1¼ CUPS

the purée into the strainer. Press down on the purée with a ladle to push it through the strainer. Discard the seeds that remain in the strainer.

Stir the juice and kirsch into the sauce.

Transfer to a covered container and refrigerate.

Serve very cold.

California Cream

Here's a substitute for Crème Fraîche that can be made in a moment—it is thicker than the real thing.

Place all the ingredients in the bowl of a food processor fitted with the steel blade, or in the jar of a blender. Process or blend until perfectly smooth.

Ladle over berries or pass separately with fruit pies or tarts or with baked apples.

1 egg yolk
4 ounces Philadephia brand
    cream cheese, at room
    temperature
1 cup sour cream
1 cup heavy cream
Optional: 1 teaspoon honey
    or granulated sugar

2¼ CUPS

Fantastic Vanilla Ice Cream

Rich, luxurious, extravagant, delicious, de luxe, smo-o-oth; the best! This fabulous ice cream will not freeze too hard to serve easily—it will remain creamy and heavenly and perfect—even after days in the freezer.

Place 1 cup of the cream (reserve the remaining 1 cup) in the top of a double boiler over hot water on moderate heat. Let stand, uncovered, until a slightly wrinkled skin forms on the top of the cream.

Meanwhile, in the small bowl of an electric mixer, beat the yolks for a few minutes until they are pale and thick. On low speed gradually add the sugar. Then beat on high speed again for 2 or 3 minutes more.

2 cups heavy cream
4 egg yolks
½ cup granulated sugar
1 teaspoon vanilla extract

1½ PINTS

When the cream is scalded, on low speed, very gradually add about half of it to the beaten-yolks-and-sugar mixture. Scrape the bowl well with a rubber spatula. Then add the yolk mixture to the remaining cream. Mix well, and place over hot water again, on moderate heat.

Cook, scraping the bottom and sides frequently with a rubber spatula, until the mixture thickens to a soft custard consistency. It will register 178° to 180° on a candy thermometer. (When the mixture starts to thicken, scrape the bottom and sides constantly with the rubber spatula.)

Remove from the hot water, transfer to a larger bowl, stir occasionally until cool, and mix in the vanilla and the reserved 1 cup of heavy cream.

It is best to chill this mixture for an hour or more before freezing it. Freeze in an ice cream maker, following the manufacturer's directions.

Devil's Food Chocolate Sauce

Elegant, rich and buttery, dark and delicious chocolate. Serve warm or at room temperature; it may be reheated. Or serve it cold (it is great refrigerated—it becomes very thick when it is cold) over coffee ice cream.

This wants desperately to burn on the bottom of the pan while you are making it; use an enameled cast-iron pan (Le Creuset or any other equally heavy one).

In a 1- to 2-quart saucepan over low heat, melt the butter and chocolate, stirring occasionally. Add the sugar, cocoa, and cream. Stir with a wire whisk until thoroughly incorporated. Increase the heat a bit to medium-low. Stir with a wire whisk occasionally and also scrape the bottom with a rubber spatula occasionally, until the mixture comes to a low boil. (If you are impatient and if you use medium heat, scrape the bottom constantly with a rubber spatula.) Watch carefully for burning and adjust the heat as necessary.

When the mixture comes to a low boil, remove the pan from the heat and stir or whisk in the vanilla.

Serve hot or cooled. Reheat carefully to prevent burning (a double boiler is the safest way). Refrigerate up to 2 weeks, if you wish.

4 ounces (1 stick) unsalted butter
1 ounce unsweetened chocolate
⅔ cup granulated sugar
¼ cup unsweetened cocoa powder (preferably Dutch-process)
½ cup heavy cream
1 teaspoon vanilla extract

1⅔ CUPS

NOTE: I like to double the recipe and have an extra jar for our guests to take home.

Index

A

Almond paste
  patching pastry with, 21
Almond Roca, 54
Almond-Apple Pudding,
  174–75
Almonds
  blanching, 6
  slivered, 6
Aluminum foil frame, 21
Amaretti (Italian maca-
  roons), 54
Amaretti di Saronno
  (Lazzaroni &
  Company), 54
Apple and Orange Cobbler,
  138–40
Apple Bread Pudding,
  172–73
Apple Cream Cheese Pie,
  70–71
Apple desserts
  Almond-Apple Pudding,
    174–75
  American Baked Apples,
    168–69
  Apple Bread Pudding,
    172–73
  Brandied Apples, 169–70
  Connecticut Apple Betty,
    175–77
  Ginger Honey Baked
    Apples, 170–71
  Saidie Heatter's Apple
    Fritters, 165–66
  Vermont Baked Apples,
    167–68

Apple Pie U.S.A., 26–28
Apple pies
  Apple Cream Cheese Pie,
    70–71
  Apple Pie U.S.A., 26–28
  Colorado High Pie, 51–52
  Mom's Apple Pie, 24–26
  Tart Tatin (Upside-Down
    Apple Pie), 89–91
Apples
  choosing, 138, 155, 168,
    170
  Golden Delicious, 155
  Rome Beauty, 168
  Apricot Bread Pudding,
    221–22
Apricot Glaze, 95, 120
Apricot pies (and turnovers)
  Fresh Apricot Pie, 29–31
  Prune and Apricot
    Turnovers, 82–85
Apricot Sauce, 173
Apricot Tart, 91–95

B

Baked pie shell, 18–20
Banana Fritters, 166
Banana Pies
  Savannah Banana Pie,
    53–54
Banana Pudding, 228–29
Beating egg whites, 3–4
Bimini Chocolate Sauce, 69
Biscuit Topping, 139–40
Blackberry Pie, 35–36
Blanching almonds, 6

Blueberries
  washing, 14
Blueberries and Cream, 187
Blueberry and Peach Buckle,
  148–50
Blueberry Cream Cheese Pie,
  71–72
Blueberry Crumble, 150–51
Blueberry Custard Tart,
  105–7
Blueberry Pie #1, 32–33
Blueberry Pie #2, 33–35
Blueberry pies
  Blueberry Cream Cheese
    Pie, 71–72
  Blueberry Pie #1, 32–33
  Blueberry Pie #2, 33–35
Blueberry tarts
  Blueberry Custard Tart,
    105–7
  Strawberry and Blueberry
    Tart, 103–5
Borinstein, Joan, 246–48
Brandied Apples, 169–70
Brandied Fresh Peaches, 180
Brandied Prunes, 191–92
Brandied Strawberries with
  Cream, 160
Bread Pudding
  Apple Bread Pudding,
    172–73
  Apricot Bread Pudding,
    221–22
  Bread Pudding with
    Peaches, 224–25
  Fried Bread Pudding,
    223–24

Bread Pudding with Peaches,
 224–25
Broiled Grapefruit, 190
Broiled Peppered Pears,
 183–84
Bread crumbs
 homemade, 13–14
Bridge Kitchenware, 10
Brown & Haley, 54
Brown sugar, 6–7
 making your own, 6
 moistening hard sugar, 7
 storage, 7
Buckle
 Blueberry and Peach
  Buckle, 148–50
 origins of, 148
Buttermilk Biscuits, 133–35
Butterscotch pies
 Old-Fashioned
  Butterscotch Pie,
  55–56

C

California Fresh Figs, 192
California Lemon Pudding.
 231–32
Candy-jelly-frosting ther-
 mometer, 11
Casserole
 Down Home Apple
  Casserole, 136–38
Cassis Grapefruit, 181
Cassis Raspberries, 181
Chiffon pies
 Marbleized Chiffon Pie,
  61–62
 Strawberry Chiffon Pie,
  40–42
Chocolate Mousse Pie,
 65–66

Chocolate pies
 Chocolate Mousse Pie,
  65–66
 Marbleized Chiffon Pie,
  61–62
 Salted Almond Chocolate
  Pie, 63–64
Chocolate Topping, 66
Chocolate Wafer Crumb
 Crust, 60, 63
Clarified Butter, 224
Cobblers
 Apple and Orange
  Cobbler, 138–40
 Georgia Peach Cobbler,
  140–41
 New York State Apple
  Cobbler, 134–36
 origins of, 140
 Pennsylvania Dutch
  Peach Cobbler, 143–45
 Washington State Cherry
  Cobbler, 132–35
Coconut Cream Pie, 56–57
Coconut pies
 Coconut Cream Pie,
  56–57
 Creamy Coconut Cream
  Cheese Pie, 68–69
Coffee and Cognac Cream
 Pie, 57–59
Cold Orange Soufflé, 214–15
Colonial Blueberries, 151–52
Colorado High Pie, 51–52
Confectioners sugar
 and powered sugar, 7
 sprinkling, 7
 straining, 7
Connecticut Apple Betty,
 175–77
Cottage Cheese and Jelly
 Tart, 127–28
Cottage Cheese Filling, 128

Cream pies
 Coconut Cream Pie,
  56–57
 Coffee and Cognac
  Cream Pie, 57–59
 Chocolate Mousse Pie,
  65–66
 Old-Fashioned
  Butterscotch Pie,
  55–56
Cream Cheese Flan (Flan de
 Queso Crema), 229–31
Cream cheese pies
 Apple Cream Cheese Pie,
  70–71
 Blueberry Cream Cheese
  Pie, 71–72
 Creamy Coconut Cream
  Cheese Pie, 68–69
 Florida Cream Cheese
  Pie, 67–68
 Lemon Cream Cheese
  Pie, 74
 Peach Cream Cheese Pie,
  72–73
Creamy Coconut Cream
 Cheese Pie, 68–69
Crème Renversée, 201–2
Crisps
 Ginger-Pear Crisp,
  185–86
 Peach Crisp, 145–46
Crumb crust, 22
Crumb topping for
  Blackberry Pie, 36
Crumble
 Blueberry Crumble,
  150–51
 Rhubarb Crumble, 153
Crust
 aluminum foil frame, 21
 baked pie shell, 18–20
 Chocolate Wafer Crumb
  Crust, 60, 63

crumb crust, 22
extra deep pie shell, 20
Macaroon Crust, 53
pie pastry, 17–18
Crystal sugar, 7
sprinkling, 7
Custards
Blueberry Custard Tart,
105–7
Crème Renversée, 201–2
French Baked Custard,
198–99
French Custard, 201–2
Orange Custard, 200
Grape-Nut Custard, 199

D

Date Pecan Pie, 75
Dates
Jensen's, 76
Shields Date Garden, 76
Deep-dish pies
Individual Deep-Dish
Strawberry-Rhubarb
Pies, 38–40
Desserts, fruit. *See* Fruit
desserts
Double boilers
Revere Ware, 9
where to buy, 9
Down Home Apple
Casserole, 136–38

E

Egg Wash, 34, 84–85
Egg whites
beaten egg whites, left
standing, 12
beating, 3
folding, 12–13
leftover, 4

Eggs, 2–4
beating egg whites, 3–4
freezing whites or yolks, 4
to open, 2
to separate, 2–2
Electric mixers
adding dry ingredients
alternately with liquid,
12
importance of stand, 9
large and small bowls, 9
space to scrape, 9
Equipment, 9–11
double boilers, 9
electric mixers, 9
flan rings, 10
pastry bags, 9–10
quiche pans, 10
rolling pins, 10
spatulas, 10
thermometers, 11

F

Fig desserts
California Fresh Figs, 192
Fillings
Cottage Cheese Filling,
128
Orange Filling, 100
Flan
Cream Cheese Flan (Flan
de Queso Crema),
229–31
Flan pastry
Rich Flan Pastry (pâté
sablee), 92–95
Flan rings, 10
for dessert tarts, 10
using, 10
where to purchase, 10
Flaxenburg, Jean and Eric, 80
Florida Cookbook
(Nickerson), 67

Florida Cream Cheese Pie,
67–68
Flour
measuring, 13
sifting, 4
Flour sifter, washing, 4
Folding ingredients together,
12–13
beating air into them, 12
bowl space and size, 12
gelatin mixtures, 13
into warm mixture, 12
over beating, 12
spatulas, choice of, 12
spatulas, use of, 12–13
Food & Wine Magazine, 91
Food processor
ginger, grating in, 5
nuts, grinding in, 14
Freezer thermometer, 11
Freezing whites or yolks, 4
French Baked Custard,
198–99
French Custard, 201–2
Fresh Apricot Pie, 29–31
Fresh ginger. *See* Ginger
(fresh)
Fresh Strawberries in
Honeyed Raspberry
Sauce, 162
Fresh Strawberries with
Raspberry Sauce, 163–64
Fresh Strawberries with Sour
Cream, 158
Fried Bread Pudding, 223–24
Fritters
Banana Fritters, 166
Saidie Heatter's Apple
Fritters, 165–66
Frozen Grand Marnier
Mousse, 245–46
Frozen Key Lime Pie, 48
Frozen Lemon-Rum Soufflé,
248–49

Frozen Peanut Butter Pie, 60–61

Frozen Raspberries (sauce), 216

Fruit desserts, 158–96
  Almond-Apple Pudding, 174–75
  American Baked Apples, 168–69
  Apple Bread Pudding, 172–73
  Banana Fritters, 166
  Blueberries and Cream, 187
  Brandied Apples, 169–70
  Brandied Fresh Peaches, 180
  Brandied Prunes, 191–92
  Brandied Strawberries with Cream, 160
  Broiled Grapefruit, 190
  Broiled Peppered Pears, 183–84
  California Fresh Figs, 192
  Cassis Grapefruit, 181
  Cassis Raspberries, 181
  Connecticut Apple Betty, 175–77
  Fresh Strawberries in Honeyed Raspberry Sauce, 162
  Fresh Strawberries with Raspberry Sauce, 163–64
  Fresh Strawberries with Sour Cream, 158
  Ginger Honey Baked Apples, 170–71
  Ginger Pears, 184–85
  Ginger-Pear Crisp, 185–86
  Honeyed Grapes, 191
  Island Pineapple, 194–95

Mangoes, Key West Style, 193–94
  Oranges à la Grecque, 188
  Portuguese Pineapple, 195–96
  Raspberry Oranges, 189
  Raspberry Pears, 182–83
  Rhubarb Strawberries, 164
  Saidie Heatter's Apple Fritters, 165–66
  Southampton Strawberries, 161
  Stewed Apricots with Brandy, 180
  Stewed Peaches, 178–79
  Stewed Peaches with Brandy, 179
  Strawberries De Luxe, 159
  Sugarbush Mountain Peaches, 177–78
  Vermont Baked Apples, 167–68

Fruit Pies. *See* Apple pies; Apricot pies; Blackberry pie; Banana pies; Blueberry pies; Lemon pies; Lime pies; Orange pies; Peach pies; Rhubarb pies

G

Gelatin mixtures
  folding with others ingredients, 13
Georgia Peach Cobbler, 140–41
Ginger (fresh)
  cutting, 5
  buying, 4
  food processor, grating in, 5
  Hawaiian, 5
  peeling, 5
  storing, 4–5

Ginger Honey Baked Apples, 170–71
Ginger-Marmalade Yogurt, 219
Ginger-Pear Crisp, 185–86
Ginger Pears, 184–85
Grand Marnier Strawberry Soufflé, 237–38
Grandma's Molasses, 6
Grape Tart, 122–24
Grapes
  Honeyed Grapes, 191
Grapefruit desserts
  Broiled Grapefruit, 190
  Grapefruit Mousse, 208–9
Grapefruit Mousse, 208–9
Grapefruits
  peeling, 15
  preparing, 14–15
  rind, grinding, 14–15
  rind, preparing, 15
  to section, 15
Grape-Nut Custard, 199

H

Hershey company, 61
Honey Yam Pie, 79
Honeyed Grapes, 191
Hot Lemon Soufflé, 217–18

I

Ices
  Lemon Ice, 241–42
  Orange Ice, 240–41
  Grapefruit Ice, 240
  See also Sorbet
Indio Whipped Cream, 76
Individual Deep-Dish Strawberry-Rhubarb Pies, 38–40

Ingredients
    eggs, 2–4
    flour, 4
    ginger (fresh), 4–5
    nuts, 5–6
    sugar, 6–7
    strawberries, 7–8
    whipping cream, 8
Ingredients (techniques for)
    adding dry alternately
        with liquid, 12
    folding, 12–13
    measuring, 13
Inn at Saranac Lake (NYS),
    199

J

Jelly Roll Biscuits, 155
Jensen's, 76
Joan's Frozen Lemon Mousse,
    246–48

K

Key Lime Pie, 46–47
Kirsch Strawberry Pie, 37–38
Knopf, Mildred, 191
Kuchen
    origins of, 146
    Peach Kucken, 146–48

L

Lemon and Almond Tart,
    114–16
Lemon Cream Cheese Pie,
    74
Lemon Meringue Pie, 43–44
Lemon Mousse, 203–4

Lemon desserts
    California Lemon
        Pudding. 231–32
    Frozen Lemon-Rum
        Soufflé, 248–49
    Hot Lemon Soufflé,
        217–18
    Joan's Frozen Lemon
        Mousse, 246–48
    Lemon and Almond Tart,
        114–16
    Lemon Cream Cheese
        Pie, 74
    Lemon Meringue Pie,
        43–44
    Lemon Mousse, 203–4
    Lemon Tartlets, 117–18
Lemon pies
    Lemon Cream Cheese
        Pie, 74
    Lemon Meringue Pie,
        43–44
    Lemon Tartlets, 117–18
Lemon tarts
    Lemon and Almond Tart,
        114–16
    Lemon Tartlets, 117–18
    Rancho Santa Fe Lemon
        Tart, 119–21
Lemons
    peeling, 15
    preparing, 14–15
    rind, grinding, 14–15
    rind, preparing, 15
    to section, 15
Lime desserts
    Sour Lime Mousse with
        Strawberries, 209–10
Lime pies
    Frozen Key Lime Pie, 48
    Key Lime Pie, 46–47
    Mrs. Foster's Lime Pie,
        44–45

M

Macaroons
    Amaretti (Italian maca-
        roons), 54
    Macaroon Crust, 53
Mangoes, Key West Style,
    193–94
Marmalade
    Ginger-Marmalade
        Yogurt, 219
    Marmalade Sauce, 218
Mary Mac's Tearoom, 60
Marzipan
    patching pastry with, 21
McCully, Helen, 191
Measuring, 13
    glass or plastic cups, 13
    precision, 13
    standard measuring
        spoons, 13
Meringue pies
    Lemon Meringue Pie,
        43–44
    Orange Angel Pie, 48–50
Molasses
    Plantation Brand
        Barbados Unsulphured
        Molasses, 82
    Shoofly Pie, 80–82
    Turkey Table Syrup, 82
Mom's Apple Pie, 24–26
Mother's Spanish Cream,
    226–28
Mousses
    Chocolate Mousse Pie,
        65–66
    Frozen Grand Marnier
        Mousse, 245–46
    Grapefruit Mousse, 208–9
    Joan's Frozen Lemon
        Mousse, 246–48
    Lemon Mousse, 203–4

Orange Mousse with
  Blueberries, 206–7
Sour Lime Mousse with
  Strawberries, 209–10
Tangerine Mousse, 204–5
Mr. and Mrs. Foster's Place
  (NYC), 44
Mrs. Foster's Lime Pie, 44–45

N

New York State Apple
  Cobbler, 134–36
Nickerson, Jane, 67
Nuts, 5–6
  almonds, blanching,
    slivered, 6
  grinding in food processor,
    14
  pecans, toasting, 6
  pistachio nuts, 6
  storing, 5

O

Odence, 21
Old-Fashioned Lemon
  Sauce, 177
Orange Custard, 200
Orange Filling, 100
Orange Mousse with
  Blueberries, 206–7
Orange pies
  Orange Angel Pie, 48–50
Orange Tart, 99–100
Oranges
  peeling, 15
  preparing, 14–15
  rind, grinding, 14–15
  rind, preparing, 15
  to section, 15
Oranges à la Grecque, 188
Oven temperature, 11
Oven thermometer, 11

P

Pandowdy
  origins of, 142
  Peach Pandowdy, 142–43
Pastry
  patching, 20–21
Pastry bags, 9–10
  canvas with plastic
    coating, 9
  filling, 9–10
  washing, 9
Pastry brushes
  washing, 16
Patching pastry, 20–21
  with almond paste, 21
  with marzipan, 21
Peach and Almond Tart,
  111–12
Peach Cream Cheese Pie,
  72–73
Peach Crisp, 145–46
Peach desserts
  Brandied Fresh Peaches,
    180
  Stewed Peaches, 178–79
  Stewed Peaches with
    Brandy, 179
  Sugarbush Mountain
    Peaches, 177–78
Peach Pandowdy, 142–43
Peach pies
  Peach Cream Cheese Pie,
    72–73
Peach tarts
  Peach and Almond Tart,
    112–13
Peach Topping, 73
Peanut butter pie
  Frozen Peanut Butter Pie,
    60–61
Pear Desserts
  Broiled Peppered Pears,
    183–84

Ginger-Pear Crisp, 185–86
  Ginger Pears, 184–85
  Raspberry Pears, 182–83
Pear tarts
  Pear and Almond Tart,
    107–9
Pears, 106, 183
  choosing, 182, 184
Pecan pies
  Date Pecan Pie, 75
Pecan tarts
  Individual Maple Pecan
    Tarts, 124–26
Pecans
  toasting, 6
Pennsylvania Dutch Peach
  Cobbler, 143–45
Pepper
  grinding over strawberries,
    8, 162
Phoenix Restaurant
  (Warren, VT), 167
Pie Crust
  aluminum foil frame, 21
  baked pie shell, 18–20
  Chocolate Wafer Crumb
    Crust, 60, 63
  crumb crust, 22
  extra deep pie shell, 20
  Macaroon Crust, 53
  pie pastry, 17–18
Pies
  cutting, 16
  size of portion, 16
Pies (types of). *See* Apple
  pies; Apricot pies;
  Blackberry pie;
  Banana pies; Blueberry;
  Butterscotch pies; Chiffon
  pies; Cream Cheese pies;
  Chocolate pies; Coconut
  pies; Cream pies; Deep-
  Dish pies; Lemon pies;
  Lime pies; Meringue pies;
  Orange pies; Peach pies;

Peanut Butter pie; Pecan pies; Potato pies; Rhubarb pies; Shoofly pie; Yam pies
Pineapple desserts
  Island Pineapple, 194–95
  Portuguese Pineapple, 195–96
Pistachio nuts
  chopping, 6
Potato pies
  Honey Yam Pie, 79
Preserves, 171
Prune and Apricot Turnovers, 82–85
Puddings
  Almond-Apple Pudding, 174–75
  Apricot Bread Pudding, 221–22
  Banana Pudding, 228–29
  Bread Pudding with Peaches, 224–25
  California Lemon Pudding. 231–32
  Fried Bread Pudding, 223–24
  Raspberry Bavarian, 212–15
  Zabaglione Freddo, 211–12
Pumpkin Pie, 77–78

Q

Quaking Custard. *See* Mother's Spanish Cream
Quiche pans, 10
  for dessert tarts, 10
  using, 10
  where to purchase, 10

R

Rancho Santa Fe Lemon Tart, 118–20
Raspberry Bavarian, 212–15
Raspberry Pâté, 233—34
Raspberry vinegar
  using on strawberries, 8, 162
Refrigerator thermometer, 11
Rhubarb Crumble, 153
Rhubarb pies
  Individual Deep-Dish Strawberry-Rhubarb Pies, 38–40
Rhubarb Strawberries, 164
Rich Flan Pastry (pâte sablée), 92–95
Rolling pins, 10
  different sizes and shapes, 10
  substitutions, 10
Rossbottom, Berry, 244

S

Saidie Heatter's Apple Fritters, 165–66
Salted Almond Chocolate Pie, 63–64
Sauces
  Apricot Sauce, 173
  Bimini Chocolate Sauce, 69
  Caramel Sauce, 98
  Frozen Raspberries (sauce), 216
  Island Sauce, 195
  Marmalade Sauce, 218
  Old-Fashioned Lemon Sauce, 177
  Raspberry Sauce, 163
  Strawberry and Raspberry Sauce, 218
Savannah Banana Pie, 53–54
Savannah Sugar Refinery, 7
Shields Date Garden, 76
Shoofly Pie, 80–82
Shortcake
  Strawberry Shortcake, 130–31
  Sorbet Cassis, 244
  Strawberry Sorbet, 242
  See also Ices
Sorbet
  Sorbet Cassis, 244
  Plum Sorbet, 243
Soufflés
  Cold Orange Soufflé, 214–15
  Frozen Lemon-Rum Soufflé, 248–49
  Grand Marnier Strawberry Soufflé, 237–38
  Hot Lemon Soufflé, 217–18
Sour Cream Apple Tart, 96–98
Sour Lime Mousse with Strawberries, 209–10
Southampton Strawberries, 161
Spatulas, 10
  choice of, 12
  substitutions, 10
  use of, 12–13
Stewed Apricots with Brandy, 180
Stewed Peaches, 178–79
Stewed Peaches with Brandy, 179
Strawberries, 7–8
  buying, 7–8
  grinding pepper over, 8, 162
  using vinegar on, 8, 162
  washing, 14

Strawberries De Luxe, 159
Strawberry and Blueberry
　Tart, 103–5
Strawberry and Raspberry
　Sauce, 218
Strawberry Chiffon Pie,
　40–42
Strawberry desserts
　Brandied Strawberries
　　with Cream, 160
　Fresh Strawberries in
　　Honeyed Raspberry
　　Sauce, 162
　Fresh Strawberries with
　　Sour Cream, 158
　Grand Marnier
　　Strawberry Soufflé,
　　237–38
　Rhubarb Strawberries, 164
　Sour Lime Mousse with
　　Strawberries, 209–10
　Southampton
　　Strawberries, 161
　Strawberries De Luxe, 159
Strawberry pies
　Individual Deep-Dish
　　Strawberry-Rhubarb
　　Pies, 38–40
　Kirsch Strawberry Pie,
　　37–38
　Strawberry Chiffon Pie,
　　40–42
Strawberry Shortcake,
　130–31
Strawberry tarts
　Strawberry and Blueberry
　　Tart, 103–5
Strawberry Topping, 42
Strawberry Yogurt Cream,
　235–37
Sugar, 6–7
　brown sugar, 6–7
　confectioners sugar, 7
　crystal sugar, 7

measuring, 13
vanilla confectioners
　sugar, 7
Sugarbush Mountain
　Peaches, 177–78
Sun Inn (Bethlehem, PA),
　80
Sussman, Peter, 167
Swartz, Michelle, 80
Sweet Celebrations, 7

T

Tangerine Mousse, 204–5
Tarts
　cutting, 16
　size of portion, 16
Tarts (types of), 88–128
　Apricot Tart, 91–95
　Blueberry Custard Tart,
　　105–7
　Cottage Cheese and Jelly
　　Tart, 127–28
　French Tart Pastry, 88
　Grape Tart, 122–24
　Individual Maple Pecan
　　Tarts, 124–26
　Lemon and Almond Tart,
　　114–16
　Lemon Tartlets, 117–18
　Orange Tart, 99–100
　Peach and Almond Tart,
　　112–13
　Pear and Almond Tart,
　　107–9
　Purple Plum and Almond
　　Tart, 110–12
　Rancho Santa Fe Lemon
　　Tart, 119–21
　Sour Cream Apple Tart,
　　96–98
　Strawberry Tart, 101–2
　Strawberry and Blueberry
　　Tart, 103–4

Tart Tatin (Upside-Down
　Apple Pie), 89–91
Techniques, 12–16
　blueberries, washing, 14
　bread crumbs, homemade,
　　13–14
　ingredients, adding dry
　　alternately with liquid,
　　12
　ingredients, folding,
　　12–13
　measuring, 13
　oranges, grapefruits, and
　　lemons, preparing,
　　14–15
　pastry brush, washing, 16
　pies and tarts, cutting, 16
　strawberries, washing, 14
　vanilla extract, adding, 15
Thermometers, 11
　candy-jelly-frosting, 11
　freezer, 11
　oven, 11
　refrigerator, 11
Toppings
　Biscuit Topping, 139–40
　Chocolate Topping, 66
　Crumb Topping, 35–36
　Peach Topping, 73
　Sour Cream Topping, 98
　Strawberry Topping, 42
　See also Whipped Cream
　　Toppings
Turnovers
　Prune and Apricot
　　Turnovers, 82–85

U

Ultra-pasteurized (UHT), 8

V

Vanilla confectioners sugar
    how to make, 7
    sprinkling, 7
    straining, 7
Vanilla extract
    adding, 15
Vermont Baked Apples,
        167–68
Vinegar
    using on strawberries, 8,
        162

W

Washington State Cherry
        Cobbler, 132–35
Whipping Cream, 8, 202,
        227–28, 234
    folding, 12–13
    folding into warm mix-
        ture, 12
    Indio Whipped Cream, 76
    old-fashioned, 8
    ultra-pasteurized (UHT),
        8
    whipping, 8
Whipped Cream toppings
    for Chocolate Mousse Pie,
        66
    for Coconut Cream Pie,
        57
    for Coffee and Cognac
        Cream Pie, 57–59
    for Colorado High Pie, 52
    for Honey Yam Pie, 79
    for Key Lime Pie, 47
    for Kirsch Strawberry Pie,
        37–38
    for Marbleized Chiffon
        Pie, 62
    for Mrs. Foster's Lime Pie,
        45

    for Pumpkin Pie, 78
    for Savannah Banana Pie,
        54
    for Strawberry Chiffon
        Pie, 42
    for Strawberry Tart, 103
Whites (egg), freezing, 4
Williams-Sonoma, 10

Y

Yam pies
    Honey Yam Pie, 79
Yogurt
    Ginger-Marmalade
        Yogurt, 219
    Strawberry Yogurt Cream,
        235–37
    Yogurt Cheese, 220
Yogurt Cheese, 220
Yolks (egg), freezing, 4

Z

Zabaglione Freddo, 211–12

Metric Conversion Chart

Common Measurement Equivalents

1 teaspoon	=	5 ml				
1 tablespoon (tbsp)	=	3 teaspoons (tsp)	=	15 ml		
2 tbsp	=	⅛ cup	=	1 fluid ounce	=	30 ml
5 tbsp plus 1 tsp	=	⅓ cup	=	80 ml		
12 tbsp	=	¾ cup	=	180 ml		
1 cup	=	½ pint	=	8 fluid ounces (oz.)	=	240 ml
1 pint	=	2 cups	=	16 fluid ounces		
1 quart	=	4 cups	=	32 fluid ounces	=	950 ml

Conversions of Ounces to Grams*

OUNCES	GRAMS	OUNCES	GRAMS	OUNCES	GRAMS	OUNCES	GRAMS
1 oz	30 g	6 oz	180 g	11 oz	310 g	16 oz	450 g
2 oz	60 g	7 oz	200 g	12 oz	340 g	20 oz	570 g
3 oz	85 g	8 oz	225 g	13 oz	370 g	24 oz	680 g
4 oz	115 g	9 oz	255 g	14 oz	400 g	28 oz	790 g
5 oz	140 g	10 oz	285 g	15 oz	425 g	32 oz	910 g

Approximate. To convert ounces to grams, multiply number of ounces by 28.35.

Conversions of Pounds to Grams and Kilograms*

POUNDS	GRAMS/KILOGRAMS	POUNDS	GRAMS/KILOGRAMS
1 lb	450 g	5 lb	2¼ kg
1¼ lb	565 g	5½ lb	2½ kg
1½ lb	680 g	6 lb	2¾ kg
1¾ lb	800 g	6½ lb	3 kg
2 lb	910 g	7 lb	3¼ kg
2½ lb	1,135 g; 1⅛ kg	7½ lb	3½ kg
3 lb	1,350 g	8 lb	3¾ kg
3½ lb	1,600 g; 1½ kg	9 lb	4 kg
4 lb	1,800 g	10 lb	4½ kg
4½ lb	2 kg		

Approximate. To convert pounds into kilograms, multiply number of pounds by 453.6.

Conversions of Inches to Centimeters *

Inches	Centimeters	Inches	Centimeters	Inches	Centimeters	Inches	Centimeters
¹⁄₁₆ in	¼ cm	4½ in	11½ cm	10 in	25 cm	21 in	53½ cm
⅛ in	½ cm	5 in	13 cm	11 in	28 cm	22 in	56 cm
½ in	1¼ cm	5½ in	14 cm	12 in	30½ cm	23 in	58½ cm
¾ in	2 cm	6 in	15 cm	13 in	33 cm	24 in	61 cm
1 in	2½ cm	6½ in	16½ cm	14 in	35½ cm	25 in	63½ cm
1½ in	4 cm	7 in	18 cm	15 in	38 cm	30 in	76 cm
2 in	5 cm	7½ in	19 cm	16 in	40½ cm	35 in	89 cm
2½ in	6½ cm	8 in	20 cm	17 in	43 cm	40 in	102 cm
3 in	7¾ cm	8½ in	21½ cm	18 in	46 cm	45 in	114 cm
3½ in	9 cm	9 in	23 cm	19 in	48 cm	50 in	127 cm
4 in	10 cm	9½ in	24 cm	20 in	51 cm		

Approximate. To convert inches to centimeters, multiply number of inches by 2.54.

Conversions of Fahrenheit to Celsius *

Fahrenheit	Celsius	Fahrenheit	Celsius	Fahrenheit	Celsius
170°F	77°C	300°F	150°C	450°F	230°C
180°F	82°C	325°F	165°C	475°F	245°C
190°F	88°C	350°F	180°C	500°F	260°C
200°F	95°C	375°F	190°C	525°F	275°C
225°F	110°C	400°F	205°C	550°F	290°C
250°F	120°C	425°F	220°C		

Approximate. To convert Fahrenheit to Celsius, subtract 32, multiply by 5, then divide by 9.

Conversions of Quarts to Liters *

Quarts	Liters	Quarts	Liters
1 qt	1 L	5 qt	4¾ L
1½ qt	1½ L	6 qt	5¾ L
2 qt	2 L	7 qt	6½ L
2½ qt	2⅜ L	8 qt	7½ L
3 qt	2¾ L	9 qt	8½ L
4 qt	3¾ L	10 qt	9½ L

Approximate. To convert quarts to liters, multiply number of quarts by 0.95.